The Docks

The Docks

Bill Sharpsteen

UNIVERSITY OF CALIFORNIA PRESS

Berkeley   Los Angeles   London

*The publisher gratefully acknowledges the generous support of the
Lisa See Endowment Fund in Southern California History
of the University of California Press Foundation.*

University of California Press, one of the most distinguished university presses in the United
States, enriches lives around the world by advancing scholarship in the humanities, social
sciences, and natural sciences. Its activities are supported by the UC Press Foundation and
by philanthropic contributions from individuals and institutions. For more information, visit
www.ucpress.edu.

University of California Press
Berkeley and Los Angeles, California

University of California Press, Ltd.
London, England

Frontis: View of the Port of Los Angeles from the bridge of the *Wan Hai 312*.
Photo by Bill Sharpsteen.

Library of Congress Cataloging-in-Publication Data

Sharpsteen, Bill, 1954–.
    The docks / Bill Sharpsteen.
        p.   cm.
    Includes bibliographical references and index.
    ISBN 978-0-520-26193-8 (cloth : alk. paper)
    1. Harbors—California—Los Angeles.   2. Stevedores—California—Los Angeles.   I. Title.
    HE554.L7S53   2011
    387.109794'94—dc22   2010009706

Manufactured in the United States of America

20   19   18   17   16   15   14   13   12   11
10   9   8   7   6   5   4   3   2   1

This book is printed on Cascades Enviro 100, a 100% post consumer waste, recycled, de-inked
fiber. FSC recycled certified and processed chlorine free. It is acid free, Ecologo certified, and
manufactured by BioGas energy.

For Connie, who first introduced me to the docks

CONTENTS

ILLUSTRATIONS

All photographs are by the author unless otherwise noted in the accompanying captions.

PREFACE

The intention behind this book is to introduce readers to the world at the Port of Los Angeles through my eyes as much as possible, by planting myself in the middle of the maelstrom that is the docks and describing what I see. That kind of approach, I've always felt, gives me a unique objectivity. In theory, my point of view isn't cluttered either with prejudices that might filter out what I don't want people to know about or with efforts to promote a particular image. As a journalist, I'm simply there to piece together a story based on what I see and hear, recording little slices of life as they present themselves.

Trouble is, when it comes to a place as complex as the docks, simple observation doesn't get the complete story. I also needed the perspectives of people who have seen the same things for years and have a pretty good idea what it all means in larger—and smaller—contexts. Thus, as you can see by perusing the references listed at the end of the book, my research was heavily dependent on interviews and nearly devoid of scholarly texts, no matter how knowledgeable such texts may have been. I wanted to understand this world as the people who work, live, and do business there understand it.

As I suggest in the opening chapters of the book, this wasn't easy. The first time I called the port's public information office to set up an interview with the environmental management department concerning the air pollution coming from ships and trucks associated with the port, I left a message that wasn't returned. In fact, I called a total of ten times without a response. I finally decided I needed a little face-to-face chat about the situation and attended a meeting of the Board of Harbor Commissioners, where, during a break, I introduced myself to a port official and explained my needs and my frustration at the lack of cooperation. Turns out I stumbled onto a woman high up on the food chain, who explained that it wasn't the port's policy to stiff-arm reporters, and soon all the interviews I could possibly want suddenly came my way.

One of the best stories in the book, about port pilots, came about through the public information office. During my first interview with Dr. Geraldine Knatz, the port's executive director, she mentioned the six-figure salaries port pilots earn. This was the first time I had learned such a job existed. I arranged for a visit to the port pilot office and asked if it might be possible to ride along with one of the pilots. So long as I was willing to climb up a ship's hull on a wet, slippery rope ladder, then, yes, I could go. (Actually, they didn't make the access conditional on that, but they did imply I would have to demonstrate a sense of adventure in order to do the job.) Based on interviews and observation, the resulting story is primarily about one man, Captain Ron Rogers, which to my mind makes it far more interesting than if I had done most of my research from books and articles. (Well, come to think of it, there isn't too much material on port pilots out there.)

The International Longshore and Warehouse Union, the ILWU, was a harder nut to crack. In general, both union officials and the rank and file have a longstanding mistrust of reporters for exhibiting anti-labor biases, or at least what the union people believe are anti-labor biases. For years, the *Los Angeles Times,* for instance, was viewed with suspicion for its former business-friendly, union-busting slant. However, I figured I was only trying to tell a story devoid of my own opinions, but I never got to argue the point. Every time I was able to talk to a union person on the phone, I would inevitably be told the same thing: "I need to look at my calendar and get back to you." They didn't do as promised, and despite repeated calls to them afterward, I never spoke to them again. Again, it took actually asking for an interview in person—and when the guy dove for cover with the calendar excuse, I insisted that he check right then. Got the interview. So in the end, meeting the longshore workers and union officials profiled in the book involved more than cold calls. I had to first meet people who knew them and then be introduced. In one case, it took a year and a half to finally nail an interview appointment, but I never would have gotten it without the friend of a friend approach. So how did I meet the friends? Pure chance in some cases. Somehow, when you start exploring a particular world, eventually the encounters come to you. I can't explain it beyond that.

The ultimate result of this work is, of course, the book you're reading. I wanted to show a largely unexplored world from as human a level as possible and tell the stories of the people who inhabit it and make it run. Yes, there is a larger theme here as well—the port's ultimate importance to the nation's economy and how the people who work there are a part of that—but in the end, the research required a more personal approach, and that's why I tackled the topic the way I did. Not with previous tomes, but with handshakes, a digital recorder, a camera, and lots of curiosity.

Should you, the reader, have any questions or comments about anything in the book, feel free to contact me at thedocks@yahoo.com.

· · ·

In some ways, this book started in 1995, when I first met Connie Chaney, a longshoreman turned clerk. From her, I learned about a court order called the Golden Consent Decree, which she said was going to end three years from then without the longshore union and the employers meeting the legally mandated hiring goals for women. So my first thanks go to her for all the patient explanations she provided over the years about the complex, mysterious longshore world. But I should also backtrack a bit and acknowledge Howard Bennett for introducing Connie to me. Then again, there was Eileen Heyes, who introduced me to Howard. I probably could reach back even further to all the human connections and small events that invaded my life so I could meet Eileen, but you get the idea.

From there came Tom Politeo, a San Pedro resident and Sierra Club activist who gave me the names of all the people who could help get me even closer to the docks of the Port of Los Angeles. One person I met through him was Art Almeida, who spent several hours taking me back to what it was like to be a hold man in the 1950s.

Slowly, I sneaked further into the world of the docks, much of my entry assisted by Arley Baker, the port's senior communications director. Also giving me a hand were the Harry Bridges Institute, Gene Vrana of the ILWU Library, and George Love.

I'd also like to thank my patient editor, Jenny Wapner, for all her wonderful suggestions and support; my copyeditor, Mary Renaud; and Dore Brown, who guided the book through the production process.

Introduction

The Port of Los Angeles is bewildering in its size. And yet, because its function is so simple, so timeless, in a way—a place where cargo is moved from ship to shore or vice versa—few people notice the port or realize how important it is to the various markets it serves throughout the United States. I have to admit, after living in Los Angeles for more than ten years, the port was for me nothing more than a bit of economic DNA until 1998, when I sneaked onto a pier posing as a longshoreman wannabe (hey, the guard bought the story). I was writing a magazine article about women dockworkers, and I had asked my main subject, a clerk, if I could watch her do her job.

So after slipping through the gate—an act that now would be considered a serious violation of various security laws—I sat next to her in a golf cart that looked like it could have been crushed by a coffee can, let alone by the monstrous cargo containers ping-ponging just a few feet above us. I watched trucks with empty chassis that pumped like heartbeats from an unseen source briefly stop beside a ship the size of a horizontal skyscraper, where 40-foot containers delivered by an eight-story crane seemingly crashed onto the chassis. The continuous boom-boom thunder of metal against metal penetrated the docks, and pretty soon I felt as though the cacophony would take physical form and smash our little vehicle. There were moments when it seemed that this brutal place needed only eternal flames to complete its hellish chaos. If that sounds overstated, consider that hundreds in the longshore workforce would be injured that year, and even a few killed. If nothing else, I was glad to be a mere visitor.

I now realize that those first impressions didn't teach me the most important fact about the port—it's so big, so vital, that if it suddenly shut down, which has happened, our entire country would buckle at its knees, which has also happened. Those who run the port certainly understand this point, as they gaze on the imposing industrial land-scape with its spindly cranes and millions upon millions of cargo containers moving through the docks every year. While I saw a place barely holding together in its bedlam, they embrace the port with a kind of lust. The nearly continuous production means money for Los Angeles, which owns the port, as well as money for shippers, ship owners, and workers. And, by the way, that's a lot of money: in 2008, $243.7 billion in global trade came and went through the Port of Los Angeles.

Nearly three-quarters of all Asian imports are pumped into the United States through L.A. and the adjacent, slightly smaller Port of Long Beach. At one point, port analysts and others in the shipping industry happily predicted that cargo volume would triple by 2025 (with a cooler economy and greater competition from other ports, they've since backed off from that exuberance, projecting, maybe, a doubling of volume, which still makes one wonder how the port would manage to keep up). Not only are we dependent these days on the imports coming through Los Angeles—largely because we don't make the products ourselves anymore—but by extension we need the port to keep functioning at top speed. Incredibly, all it takes is an equipment breakdown at one dock, lasting a few hours, for the hiccup to vibrate east through other parts of the country, depriving stores or factories of the shipments they expect and need to continue business. No other port in the United States has that kind of influence on the nation's economy.

How the port got so big is relatively uncomplicated. Until the mid-

1700s, San Pedro Bay, where the Port of Los Angeles eventually located, featured nothing more than a sleepy mix of flatlands, shallow tidal lagoons, and a few friendly Gabrielino Indians. This lasted until Spanish missionaries landed and took one scornful look at the amiable Indians' soon-to-be-doomed way of life. In short order, the padres plopped two missions nearby, forced religious conversions throughout the region, and put the now-baptized locals to work tending livestock or housekeeping at the missions, among other unpaid tasks. This effort was sustained through biannual supply ships coming from Spain's House of Trade, a kind of government-run mafia that controlled commerce in the Spanish Empire. The ships anchored offshore in the bay, protected from any occasional storms by the Palos Verdes Peninsula to the west, and the crews off-loaded their freight into rowboats. Despite the calm waters, the relatively short excursion to land must have been a tedious trip for sailors used to open seas, given that they had to plod through thick marshes before landing on the shore. The padres met them with the local labor pool (well, Indian slaves), who had just hauled oxcart loads of hides and tallow to the shoreline, destined for Spain. This was the first case of San Pedro Bay being a place for both imports and exports. Indeed, the nascent port remained the most dependable place for shipping once Los Angeles, founded in 1781, started growing.

In 1871, Phineas Banning, a shipper and state senator, spurred the development of a channel 10 feet deep through the bay's tidal flats, a $200,000 federal project that allowed ocean vessels to come closer to shore, and built piers to meet them. He had already constructed his own wharf in nearby Wilmington as well as a ditchlike channel large enough for small barges to easily negotiate the marshes and run out to ships anchored offshore. To complete this maritime service, he also operated a stream of stagecoaches and wagons that carried passengers and cargo the 20 miles from Wilmington to Los Angeles. The next year, with Banning's push, the Southern Pacific Railroad extended a line to the newly completed Main Channel, which ended in San Pedro. This development eventually destroyed Banning's shipping empire by making his barge operation and coaches obsolete. For his sacrifice—whether short-sighted or civic-minded—he was dubbed the father of the port.

After the port's official birth on December 9, 1907, when the Los Angeles City Council created the Board of Harbor Commissioners (the Port of Long Beach was founded four years later), the facility went through a ragged, up-and-down period of development. It grew because of shipyards and canneries that no longer exist, and because of the need to transport oil, which had been pumped nearby, to other locations on the West Coast. For a good portion of the twentieth century, cargo primarily sailed up and down the West Coast, with relatively few goods coming from Asia. Instead, Europe supplied most of the imports. San Francisco was the coast's shipping hub and largest port.

But things changed. Southern California swelled into a huge market, with eighteen million consumers in 2009 and growing. Gradually, shippers and their import goods bypassed San Francisco for Los Angeles, where they could directly plug into this instant shopper bonanza. Plus, a well-developed rail line ran out from Los Angeles, across the Mojave Desert, and on to distribution hubs across the country, in particular Kansas City, Chicago, and, more recently, Dallas. Just as important, it was usually faster to off-load in Los Angeles and send the goods on a train than to sail east to other ports. Los Angeles and Long Beach both had another advantage: while other West Coast ports featured rail yards and other logistical attractions, overall they were limited by space concerns, which, until recently, have not been a problem for the Southern California port complex. All it took to create additional terminals in San Pedro Harbor was simply dumping rocks and dirt in the bay until there was enough fill to make an island.

With these factors in play, it's unlikely any facility will eclipse this monster. And that should also scare anyone who relies on imports—as most of us do, since they constitute a good portion of our economy, really—that are pumping through a single, vulnerable port.

ONE

Valet Parking

A SHIP ARRIVES

Most people board a cargo ship on a gangway, a safe, though perhaps steep, ramp that goes from dock to ship's deck with just enough metallic, rickety sounds to make it feel unique and even romantic in a nautical sort of way. Then there's how I'm about to board a ship with port pilot Captain Ron Rogers: we'll do it, like pirates, by climbing up a ship's hull on a wet rope ladder dangling above a sloshing ocean 2 miles from shore. And, oh, by the way, I'm told it's kind of dangerous.

This has me a little distracted when I walk into the port pilots dispatch office. As busy as the Port of Los Angeles is on paper, I'm a little surprised at the sleepy calm here. I had expected the chaotic charm of an air traffic controllers' tower—after all, the office oversees the six thousand ships that enter the port each year, sending out its cadre of fifteen captains to guide the vessels into their appointed berths. But on this day it might as well be a doctor's waiting room.

Dispatcher Beth Adamik, a tall, middle-aged woman with a friendly, grandmotherly voice, stands to shake my hand and then sinks back in her chair before a computer monitor that displays a jagged graphic of the California coast, the port, and a constant line of rectangular ship icons stuttering through a designated shipping lane. Instead of being made to feel like an intrusion, I'm told to relax, as if I'm a guest in Adamik's living room and we're here to hang out over coffee.

Sitting between two sets of living quarters for pilots, the two-story dispatch office looks through a wall of windows over the entrance to the port's Main Channel, a bright, glary view that's less informative than it first seems. Even on clear days such as this, the air has a translucent quality, so Adamik and the other dispatchers instead watch their monitors for the ships entering the harbor and look out only if they have a moment to check the weather while listening to the Sirius Radio Love Songs channel that plays off a television in a back corner.

The port requires all deep-draft vessels (any ship needing 55 feet of water to float) to be guided from open water to final docking by a port pilot. Nearly all ports in the world do this, and the reason is simple: for someone in a large ship accustomed to navigating the open seas, approaching the unfamiliar Port of Los Angeles is like driving a bus from an empty stadium parking lot into a narrow, dark alley full of unknown, hidden obstructions. Without a port pilot's local expertise to direct the ship through the harbor's unique currents and park it at the correct dock, the world's fleet would probably be dented and mangled (and the world's ports in far worse shape). For this expertise, port pilots are paid $150,000 to $300,000 a year.

Adamik points at the computer monitor and tells me that they've chosen the *Wan Hai 312* as the ship I'll be boarding. It's going to the back end of the port, she says, and that'll give me a long ride to soak up all the details I can. At the moment, the *Wan Hai 312* is easing down the California coast at 9.5 knots. We know this because information on each vessel is radioed from the ship via a mandatory Auto Identification System to the Marine Exchange, a nondescript building on a hill above the harbor, and then relayed to the dispatch office. On the computer monitor, each ship icon jerks in short steps down the grayed-out shipping lane, the traffic sometimes so heavy that vessel names overlay one another. Adamik can select any ship on the screen and with two mouse clicks determine its speed and distance from the port.

Just then, the captain of the *Wan Hai 312* radios to the dispatch office as required when the ship is 25 miles from the port entrance.

"Please prepare ladder on the starboard side," Adamik says crisply into a large microphone, referring to the Jacob's ladder constructed of rope and wooden rungs that Captain Rogers and I will use to board the ship. "Starboard side ladder one meter above the water, and call us again as soon as you enter the Precautionary Area." The captain repeats the instructions.

"Also, are your bow thrusters in good working condition?" Adamik asks. The *Wan Hai 312* is small enough that it will need only one tugboat to steer it through the port complex if the bow thrusters (water jets used for maneuvering) are operational.

"They're in good working condition, over."

"Thank you for that, captain."

I don't want to seem too concerned about this rope ladder business, so I ease into the subject as if I'm talking about the weather. Adamik plays along and implies that this is like a rite of passage for some at the port. Board a ship by scampering up its hull, and you've got the kind of minor bragging rights that impress just about everyone outside of the Coast Guard. That it has that kind of cachet has me a little worried.

I'm here for one main reason: I want to see what it's like for a ship to enter the Port of Los Angeles, slowly sailing past the dozens of piers and docked ships. I figure if I'm writing a book about the country's largest port, I need to know what a ship captain sees for the first time as he (not many women captains out there) leaves the comfortable open water off the California coast and snuggles into a berth for two days. The experience should give me a picture to paint that involves people and not just tons of steel.

Unfortunately, the carriers—the companies whose ships take cargo from point A to point B—weren't interested in letting me ride for awhile on one of their ships. Come to think of it, just about everybody in the ultra-competitive shipping industry, from the carriers to the shippers (those who hire the carriers to move their cargo) to the railroads who haul the cargo to the rest of the country, stiff-armed me every time I humbly asked for a little access. Seems they were worried I might inadvertently reveal to their competitors some profitable technique that had saved them a penny or two in costs per container. If that sounds like a flimsy excuse, they also threw out the security rationale, which these days seems to trump all else. While no one accused me of wanting to enter a restricted area (pretty much the entire port) with explosives strapped to my body, they politely treated the request for a visit as though as I were indeed a terrorist. In truth, most companies rarely give access to reporters unless there's a commercial or public relations angle, and apparently neither need jumped out at them when I called.

Finally, with help from the Port of Los Angeles communications department—which indeed saw a PR angle—I was able to arrange to ride with a port pilot and get the sailor's view of entering the world of the port. Attaching myself to Captain Rogers gave me an end-around on all the secrecy, and, for a few smug moments, I felt like I had sneaked past the gatekeepers.

As more ships enter Adamik's screen, she writes their names and estimated arrival times on a whiteboard behind her and then slides a magnetic name tag for one of the port pilots opposite each ship name. The list grows from five ships to a dozen, the last one arriving after dark. For the *Wan Hai 312,* Adamik fills out a green dispatch slip that goes to Captain Rogers, indicating where he's taking the ship—in this case, berth 139 in the West Basin, an odd-shaped parking lot for ships off the Main Channel.

Bringing in a cargo vessel is a complex, coordinated effort between the ship's agent and dozens of entities. Tugs are ordered. Longshore linesmen are scheduled; they tie up the ship to the dock. A longshore lashing crew, charged with unlocking the containers from the deck, as well as crane drivers and all the other workers required to unload and load a ship, are scheduled through the union's Local 13 dispatch hall. Clerks, who manage the paperwork and oversee the cargo operation, are brought in through the Local 63 dispatch hall. Chandlers, who supply ships with fresh food and other supplies, are told when to arrive at the docks. The U.S. Centers for Disease Control and Prevention (CDC) may be called if a crew member is sick. Captain Jim Morgan, manager of the Los Angeles Pilot Service, tells me later that he once counted all the steps involved in bringing in a ship and came up with two hundred phone calls.

Because time spent idling in port is costly, most ships try to arrive so that they're at the dock and ready for the longshoremen's 8:00 A.M., 6:00 P.M., or 3:00 A.M. shift start time. Getting in too early or too late can mean sitting for money-eating hours before the unloading and loading begin. As for the *Wan Hai 312*, it's headed for a 2:30 P.M. arrival, in time for the longshoremen's night shift, or so the captain hopes. The ship, capable of holding some thirteen hundred 40-foot containers, was built in early 2006 in Singapore's Jurong Shipyard for Wan Hai Lines. As it has done for most of the sixty-six ships in the Wan Hai fleet, the company gave it a prosaic name, *Wan Hai 312* (the one built before it was the *Wan Hai 311*). With a maximum 23-knot speed, the ship took eleven days to cross the Pacific Ocean from its last stop at Pusan, South Korea.

At about 1:45 P.M., Adamik calls Captain Rogers and tells him it's time for us to leave. He and I walk a short distance to a 52-foot boat with a two-man crew that will shuttle us 2 miles to the ship. As the boat approaches the *Wan Hai 312*, Rogers zips up his dark blue port pilot jacket and comes out from the cabin. He leans against the portside railing to get a better look, occasionally gripping it when the boat hits a chop, while the pilot boat circles from bow to stern.

Wearing slightly tinted aviator prescription glasses, he squints a bit on this bright, hazy day as he inspects the hull for any damage that could compromise his ability to pilot the ship into port. He also checks the depth markings on the hull to ascertain how low in the water the ship is riding. This isn't as important for a smaller ship such as the

Wan Hai 312, but the larger, heavily loaded vessels can come scrapingly close to the minimum 1.5-foot keel clearance the port requires between the ship's underside and the bottom of the Main Channel. (The Main Channel, which is the port's major arterial but isn't a natural body of water, was dredged with even sides and bottom to make it as simple as possible to navigate; pesky currents aren't a problem.)

Maybe it's because I'm not a mariner and don't know how to appreciate a ship's attributes, but the *Wan Hai 312* isn't much more to me than a big truck piled high with 40-foot containers. The red, green, and blue containers are crammed onto the deck as many as six high, looking like shoe boxes from a distance; and the ship itself, while as sleek as it needs to be to efficiently cut across the Pacific Ocean, looks so utilitarian that its only remarkable feature is its size. The *Wan Hai 312* is a monster, a metal mountain the length of two football fields that has no business floating. And yet, in today's shipping world, it's half the size of the current behemoths that are too large for some ports.

Rogers says little after he eyeballs the *Wan Hai 312.* He's a wiry sixty-six-year-old, and he comes across more like a grandpa hanging out with one of his grandkids than a man responsible for parking some of the world's biggest ships. He's almost serene in the wind and spray, a man so comfortable after fifty years on the water that he's like a veteran shortstop confidently strolling onto the ball field, ready to react to anything hit his way but also pleased just to be there. He casually mentions retirement as though it's something he should do eventually, like eating more vegetables, but he exudes such joy and energy for his job that I can't believe he's serious. Indeed, port pilots are known to work into their seventies or eighties. One octogenarian Japanese pilot is famous for being so frail he has to be carried up the gangway when he boards a ship.

Rogers started his maritime career in 1958, when he was sixteen, working on Island Boat Service passenger boats that made their summer runs to Catalina Island, a resort 22 miles off the coast from Long Beach. I'm tempted to romanticize this as some childhood passion to be a sailor, but Rogers doesn't get so carried away. It was just one of those happy accidents that plop into people's lives like a winning lottery ticket. Three years later, he more or less stumbled into tugboats after he checked into the longshoremen's hiring hall looking for work and saw a notice for a relief deckhand. He ended up working for Red Stack, which eventually became Crowley Tugs. "No one ever said, 'You're a permanent employee,'" he tells me. "I spent twenty-nine years, ten months there. They never told anyone they were permanent in those days."

In 1990, Rogers decided to leap from tugs to the maritime world's top spot, port pilot. That meant starting at the bottom and training for two years with established pilots, gradually going from smaller ships to bigger ones. Rogers, even with his experience, had to complete one thousand ship moves before he could graduate from trainee to port pilot II. Now a senior pilot, he's required to attend a training course every two years. He seems especially proud that he just came back from Port Revel, a tiny lake in the French Alps, and the location of perhaps the most elite course for port pilots, where captains drive 40-foot models designed to handle like real tankers and container ships.

The pilot boat continues around the *Wan Hai 312* to the starboard side. We approach this way so that any wake the speeding boat creates on the port side will be muffled by the ship's hull. Also, this is the lee side, where the day's gentle breeze is blocked by the ship, making the seas calmer than on the opposite weather side. The water needs to be as still as possible for one good reason—to keep Rogers alive. The only true danger in the job is boarding the ship, which requires that Rogers, then I, step from the (ideally) steady pilot boat to the ladder without falling into the cold ocean.

The boat slows to match the ship's 5-knot speed, and in the surreal moments when our relatively tiny vessel bangs up against the ship's massive hull, it seems as though we're not even moving. With two members of the ship's crew peering over the railing and the mate of the port pilot boat standing behind him, Rogers casually but quickly grabs onto the rope ladder, curls his fists around the rope, and then lightly steps off the boat. He has about 15 feet to climb. He's not wearing a flotation device, but no one seems to care; if he fell, he could be crushed between the two vessels before he had a chance to drown. In the past year, four pilots in other ports have died after slipping off the ladder.

The pilot boat continues to bump against the ship's hull while Rogers, wearing black, rubber-soled shoes, scampers up the ladder, his back slightly arched while he tries to keep his chest as close to the hull as possible. He hits each wooden rung with just his toes, and he struggles for a moment when he hits the top, where a chunk of deck railing has been removed to accommodate the ladder. He briefly straddles the top before saying hello to a crewman in dirty coveralls and a third mate sent to escort him to the bridge.

Now it's my turn. I stuff everything but my camera into the pockets of my fleece jacket, hang the camera around my neck, and step up to the ladder. The pilot boat's mate can't really do much to help me, and before I have a chance to get a close look at the ladder, he yells at me to grab it and climb without stopping. The rope is rough, almost too thick to grip tightly, and slickened with seawater. Immediately I feel the ladder pulling away from me. The rungs bang against the hull, and I wonder if I'd be able to grab the rope and stop myself from falling into the water should my foot slip from a rung. I pause about 5 feet up to make sure my fingers aren't sliding on the wet rope, and I can hear the mate screaming to keep moving. While Rogers scurried up the ladder with what I now understand to be as much survival instincts as seventeen years of practice, I deliberately, slowly haul my butt up, hyperaware of every slippery surface I'm touching, how my tennis shoes slide from side to side. I ease over the side onto the deck trying to look like that was no big deal, but the two crew members are barely paying attention.

The third mate escorts us up a steep, narrow, steel stairwell to an elevator not much bigger than a refrigerator box, which takes us to the ship's bridge. Captain Shen Kuo Chung greets Rogers with a broad,

Captain Ron Rogers scampers up the slippery Jacob's ladder and boards the ship.

stained-teeth smile and then amiably shakes my hand. Rogers routinely uses this moment to gauge a captain's comfort with a stranger coming on board to control his ship as it moves into the port. While Chung is still ultimately in command, he seems momentarily tense until Rogers, a gregarious fellow who's both professional and relaxed, engages him as if they're longtime associates, even though they haven't met before this moment. The captain answers Rogers's questions about his trip, whether he had any troubles along the way, and whether the bow thrusters are working properly. When I ask about his eleven-day trip across the Pacific Ocean, Chung shrugs, "Not so bad."

The captain's body language finally eases, and he glances at the port with its skyline of cranes, still a hazy 2 miles away, perhaps relieved he doesn't have to pilot the ship himself into the harbor. No taller than Rogers, Chung has a crew cut and a wispy tuft of gray hair below his lower lip. With wire-rim glasses and a khaki shirt and pants, Chung— who's Taiwanese—has the moody look of someone who enjoys giving orders. He's been a captain since 1998.

After Rogers looks over the bridge to see if there's anything he'd like to change—such as switching the radar from a 6-mile scale to his preferred 3-mile, for its greater detail—he goes to a starboard-side counter covered with navigational charts to pick up a laminated copy of the pilot card, which lists the ship's dimensions and engine stats. He studies it for a moment and then has Chung sign a contract agreeing to the port's tariff, the terms and conditions that go with entering the port and using the pilot services. This includes pilot fees based on the ship's length and gross tonnage. Wan Hai Lines will be charged $1,326 for the ship's length (213 meters, or almost 700 feet) and $95 for gross tonnage.

Once the paperwork is finished, Rogers gives his first command to the quartermaster, a tall Asian man wearing jeans, a gray hooded sweatshirt, and an orange Wan Hai coat that goes nearly to his knees. "Starboard twenty!" Rogers says with a mixture of soothing authority and geniality. He means turn to the right twenty degrees.

"Starboard twenty!" Captain Chung barks out.

On the ship's bridge, Rogers calls out commands to the quartermaster.

After a short delay, the quartermaster returns, "Starboard twenty, sir!"

"Thank you," Rogers says when he sees the ship change course. By international rule, ships must have one person on the bridge who speaks English. According to Rogers, Russian ships are the worst when it comes to language barriers. Ship owners, he says, have cut costs by hiring crew who can't always communicate in English. On the *Wan Hai 312*, it's not clear if the quartermaster actually understands anything but the commands Rogers gives him. However, Captain Chung speaks English smoothly, with only the occasional syntax error, and seems at ease with the language. Nevertheless, Rogers keeps his commands crisp and short and always double-checks to be sure they've been followed correctly.

PARALLEL PARKING 700 FEET OF SHIP

Captain Rogers has a problem. He first notices it when Captain Chung's otherwise stoic face tightens, looking like he has a bit of indigestion, though it's hardly the sort of grimace you see on a ship's bridge unless something really, really bad is about to happen. Rogers calmly asks if there's anything wrong, and the captain tells him the ship's engines have just died. His 698-foot container ship is technically adrift in the port's Main Channel, a 1,000-foot-wide lane lined with piers and docked ships; it's moving so slowly that even the rudders are useless. By the strange physics that govern these moments, the ship is heavier and harder to stop because it's in shallow water. If a strong wind slapped the ship's broad hull right now, Rogers would be fighting nearly 28,000 wayward tons with very little to keep the *Wan Hai 312* from plowing into a dock, a ship, or a crane.

The only way to steer is with two tugs and bow thrusters, and at the moment, there's just one tug at the ship's bow, starboard-side. In any case, neither the tug nor the thrusters can do much to move the ship forward. You need engines for that, and at the moment, the *Wan Hai 312* is bobbing about the Main Channel like the biggest piece of flotsam you'll ever see.

Rogers's usually jovial face contorts between concern and slight amusement, a practiced reaction, he told me earlier, that is mainly for the benefit of the ship's crew—a calm, nearly impassive demeanor demonstrating that he's so much in control, the worst that could happen won't. His eyes narrow, but a half smile puckers through as he starts to talk. He stands directly behind the bridge's broad window to watch for the second tug he's ordered on a cell phone he keeps with him but rarely uses (it messes with the ship's electronics). This doesn't mean he'll necessarily get a tug right away. Tugboats aren't always available on such short notice, given how many ships are sailing in and out of the port, and he may end up having to wrestle the ship down the Main Channel with just one tug and bow thrusters.

I glance at Chung, who looks like someone who can't find his car keys, pacing for a moment before standing at one instrument panel or another, almost embarrassed at what has happened. He should be worried. In 1996, a fully loaded Liberian bulk carrier, the *Bright Field*, temporarily lost power just like this while sailing down the Mississippi River near New Orleans. The ship struck a wharf where a shopping mall, a parking garage, and a hotel were located, causing sixty-two injuries and $20 million in damages.

A few minutes later, Rogers asks, "What caused the problem, captain?"

"The signal," Chung says tersely. A faulty sensor detected a phantom pressure drop somewhere in the engines and shut them down, using the kind of electronic logic with which the system was designed.

"We'll work it out," Rogers tells Chung reassuringly. Chung turns off the sensor, and Rogers proceeds by giving commands to the engine room "the old-fashioned way," as he puts it.

Unfortunately, you don't just crank up a 34,000-horsepower engine as if it were some Ford in the garage. Starting a diesel engine this size requires a strong shot of air to get the pistons turning, something like the starter in a car. Under the circumstances, this shouldn't be a problem, because a ship usually has enough compressed air stored in tanks for seven starts (the first try doesn't always work). Then again, that air is also used for other systems and could be depleted just when it's needed the most. In any event, this is going to take a few minutes. For the first time, Rogers seems a little tense as we enter the West Basin while passing another ship being piloted out.

I have to admit this makes the ride into the port a lot more exciting for me; while I stand beside Rogers taking notes, I'm already figuring out how I might write a lead for my chapter on port pilots. No, I'm not so shallow that I want this little mishap to lead to the *Wan Hai 312* taking out a pier; I want to tell a story, not witness destruction. But just the same, I feel a need to behave calmly and appear detached so Rogers doesn't think I'm actually enjoying this.

I join Rogers for a moment at the window, but the shipping containers block out most of what we can see from the bridge, including the tugboat on the starboard side, so we walk out to the bridge wing—a metal balcony jutting out on either side of the bridge—for a better view. On larger ships, the containers are often stacked so high that the port pilot has to lean out from the bridge wing just to see ahead. Above him, as a courtesy to the port, a U.S. flag flies, hung higher than the flag of Singapore, which flutters with a snapping sound from a separate pole. A steady hum surrounds us, the combination of ship sounds, water splashing against the hull, and the wind blowing in my ears. I can smell an oily, briny odor but only if I take a deep whiff, and even then it seems more like an olfactory illusion than anything real.

Rogers looks astern to a thin foamy line trailing behind the ship on either side, called the history, which is made from bubbles kicked up by the ship as it plows through the water. If he needs to, he can use this to visually confirm that the ship is headed in the direction he's commanded to the quartermaster. The history can also indicate if there's an unseen, rare current that pushes the foam to one side.

At the same time, an orange Coast Guard Dauphin helicopter buzzes quickly overhead. "They're checking us out to make sure we're okay," Rogers says. According to the Coast Guard, a quick swoop overhead hardly qualifies as an inspection; it's just a look, if that, to make sure everything appears normal, at least from some 500 feet above. Then again, the major preoccupation these days is port security, and no matter how flimsy a feeling it is, there's still something reassuring about the Coast Guard looking down on us, if indeed the crew bothered to give us more than a glance.

With the engines restarted, we slowly move toward our eventual berth, and I take in my first shipside view of the country's largest container port. The place seems nearly shut down. The eight-story cranes, big enough to reach across the world's largest ships and pluck off the containers one by one, stand like unused parking meters on a city street. The asphalt-covered terminals where ships dock—essentially huge waterfront parking lots for containers—have a few people standing about them, but no one acts as though they're busy.

After months of research and interviews, the Port of Los Angeles has been feeling to me like a place in constant turmoil. When seen under a microscope, conflict oozes and bubbles as if a flame burned underneath. The longshore union beefs about the employers—mainly the terminal operators and carriers—over everything from safety to benefits. The employers take carefully worded potshots at longshoremen for what they see as a lack of work ethic. Residents and environmentalists say the port is poisoning the local communities with air pollution. The entire nation, it would seem, frets about a terrorist attack on the port.

I know all this festers here, and yet, as we glide past the piers and ships, it seems as tranquil as an abandoned beach. In a way, I'm disappointed. I was hoping for a visual metaphor to show a ship entering the port from relatively calm waters into a scene of utter chaos that reflects not only how busy a place the Port of Los Angeles actually is but also how important it is. But this is what the world's sailors see—after all, that's ostensibly why I'm here, to get the mariner's view of the facility— and I wonder if, in their jadedness, the port looks just like any other or if the calm also strikes them as unusual.

This project began after I published a magazine piece about women longshoremen (their preference was to be called longshore*men*). The next day I got calls from two movie producers wanting to make films based on the article. While all the phone conversations and a lunch at a nice restaurant were lovely for my ego, when it came down to actually committing to anything, I swiftly realized that they were missing the necessary cash to do anything but talk and eat arugula salads. Nevertheless, the experience planted the idea that people might be interested in longshoremen and the port itself. So, finally, here I am aboard a ship—and all I see is a place on a coffee break.

As if he senses I need a little drama, Rogers begins telling me about the hazards he worries about. For starters, although the Main Channel is deep enough for a fully loaded container ship, there's a danger that if Rogers sails in too quickly, the ship could push aside water so fast that it creates an aquatic trough of sorts, which the surrounding water can't fill in quickly enough. The ship could literally sink low enough to scrape the bottom, a phenomenon called squat. Wind is another factor. With so much hull and so many stacked containers to whack against, strong winds push ships about in the water as though they still had sails. If you happen to be following a ship during such conditions, you'd see the stern swing from side to side as the port pilot fights for a straight path through the Main Channel. I realize how lucky we are today that the wind is calm. With a strong breeze and the engines dead, Rogers might have watched the vessel slam into a pier or another ship.

The Vincent Thomas Bridge, a 2.2-mile suspension span connecting San Pedro to the port's Terminal Island and beyond to Long Beach, is a rare obstacle. On August 27, 2006, an improperly stowed crane aboard the *Beautiful Queen,* a cargo ship, hit the bridge's scaffolding underneath the roadbed. The damage was minor, and the road opened later that night. When we pass the still-visible damage, Rogers is almost amused. I don't think he's indifferent, but he's relieved it didn't happen to him.

Finally, there are the collisions, usually between a ship and a dock. Just three days before Rogers boarded the *Wan Hai 312,* another pilot underestimated how far the bulb—a kielbasa-shaped protuberance at the ship's bow—stuck out; and as he maneuvered into a berth, the ship plowed into some ten pilings.

Not that Rogers hasn't suffered his own indignities. He once had a ship nearly run aground, but that didn't stop him from coolly shutting down the engines, dropping anchors as fast as possible, and using the tugs to halt the ship before—according to him—it nearly sliced in half the port pilots dispatch office, which is only a few feet from the Main Channel. Seems he told the quartermaster to turn starboard, but the quartermaster went the opposite direction, and before Rogers could correct the mistake, the ship "hit the mud" before taking out any structures.

Rogers goes back inside. The captain offers him a cup of coffee, which a third mate brings a few minutes later in a white china cup and saucer. Captain Chung appears restless, distracted, as if he doesn't know what to do with himself while Rogers is in control. He alternately sips his own coffee and watches the view with crossed arms. We talk about his ship for a moment, and, without prompting, he tells me, almost as if he's speaking about himself, that the *Wan Hai 312* is "small, very small." But not so small that it can't crush a small sailboat idling on the starboard side of the Main Channel.

"Captain. One long whistle, please," Rogers says when he sees the boat. The warning lasts six seconds, a deep, steamy honk that prompts the sailboat's captain to radio Rogers and acknowledge that he sees the ship.

After more than an hour of moving down the Main Channel and turning into the West Basin, a Y-shaped bay that Rogers says was once a marsh, the ship arrives at berth 139, which is tucked against a sharp, currently empty corner. Rogers walks out to the port bridge wing to see the dock better. With a portable control box, he adjusts the bow thrusters' power and direction, using a large dial to slowly ease the bow alongside the pier. He clutches a walkie-talkie and periodically directs the tugboat, which is unseen on the other side of the ship, pushing against the ship's stern in concert with the bow thrusters. Whenever Rogers gives a command to the tug, the boat's pilot acknowledges with a peanut whistle, a shrill beep that echoes like it's coming from a distant calliope.

At one point, Rogers leans forward over the railing for a better view and grimaces. Only about 20 feet of water separate the hull and the asphalt dock. He warily nudges the bow thruster control knob, continuously fiddling with it but making no broad moves. The ship creeps forward and closes the gap between hull and dock by a few more feet. Captain Chung walks out from the bridge and stands beside Rogers. Aware that the pilot is concentrating, he says nothing and just watches. As the bow inches alongside the pier, Rogers worries about the front bulb, which is used in the open seas to push aside water more efficiently but can't be seen because it's mostly submerged. If he misjudges how far the bulb sticks out from the bow, he could destroy the pier.

"Seventy-five feet to go, captain," he tells Chung. "That's the way to go," he coos, as if speaking to the ship. "Just like a little baby."

Waiting longshore linesmen walk to the pier's edge and watch for the ship's crew to throw them the narrow ropes called heaving lines, which are weighted at the end with so-called monkey's fists and tied to the much heavier hawser, a thick white rope for securing the ship.

"Finish engine," Rogers finally says after an agonizing half hour of maneuvering. The linesmen hook one of the heaving lines to a white Hummer H2 and pull it up until the hawser drags over the asphalt after being dunked in the water. It takes two men to wrap each of the four dripping hawser lines around a series of large, knee-high metal posts called mooring bollards. Rogers complains that the linesmen aren't taking out the slack enough, allowing the ship to move too freely, bobbing in and away from the dock. They finally tighten the lines and secure the ship.

Three U.S. Customs and Border Protection agents wearing dark blue uniforms, black boots, and small backpacks—two stern women and a younger man who looks amused, as though he's just heard a joke—watch the ship's crew struggle to pull the gangway out from the hull where it's secured and onto the terminal pavement. I can see a sidearm on one of the women. The three are here to check the crew's papers and other documents as well as to collect a tonnage tax, which the captain pays with a check. I'm not the sort to panic at the sight of authority figures, but in this case my stomach tightens. I had left my wallet in my car to leave room in my pockets for other things, and if they ask for identification, I'm screwed. After seeing their no-nonsense demeanor, I imagine strip searches, long interrogations, and finally getting home after a couple of months of detention at Guantanamo Bay.

Once the gangway comes down, the officers walk up and quietly pass Rogers and me. I later tell him I had no ID and wonder why they didn't bother to ask who I was. "It's because you were with me," he says matter-of-factly. So much for security. In a moment, Jessica Bautista from the dispatch office drives up in a van to take us back, a ten-minute ride. Just as the sun is setting, Rogers gets a call on his cell phone, and he leaves to pilot another ship, this time to guide it out of the port.

TWO

A Carpet of Containers

Riding a ship through the port's Main Channel is a lot like going down the central aisle in a huge shopping mall. The profusion of piers, ships, cranes, containers, and, if you look hard enough, people engulfs you. The rest of the world seems to disappear, and all that's left is an industrial bazaar with too much sensory input to adequately put any of it in perspective. I needed a way to view it all from a distance, to simplify the clutter that comes when you're in the middle of it, a way to let the parts blend together into a whole. Viewing the place from the air could give me a better appreciation of the port's enormous size.

I happened to mention to Arley Baker, the port's senior communications director, that I was looking for an aerial view of the docks—to soak up its enormity in one shot, if possible—and he told me he was about to go up in a helicopter to photograph a construction site and I was welcome to bum a ride.

A few days later, we drive to a parking lot below the Vincent Thomas Bridge, where we meet a bright red, four-seat copter that has landed in a fenced-in helipad. The pilot, Neil, takes off my door so I can get clear photographs of the view from 400 feet and then immediately hands us life vests (a somewhat disconcerting sequence of actions).

We start the flight by buzzing between a terminal run by Evergreen

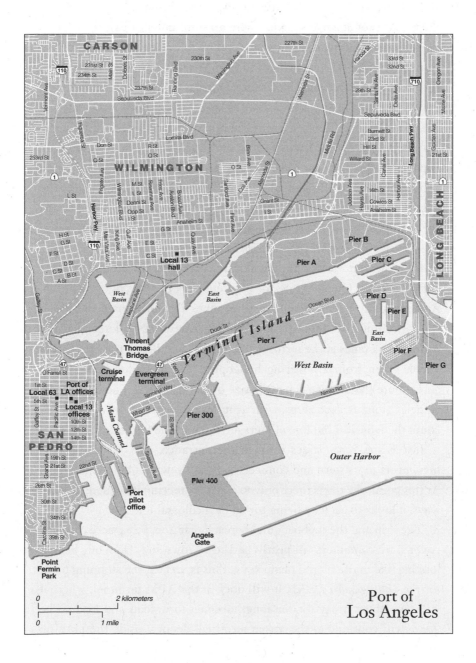

CARSON

231st St
234th St
237th St
Sepulveda Blvd
230th St
227th St

110

Vermont Ave
Dolores St
Main St
Harding Blvd
Wilmington Ave
Alameda St

33rd St
32nd St
Harbor St
28th St
Santa Fe Ave
Oregon Ave
Golden Ave
Maine Ave

710

Sepulveda Blvd
Burnett St
23rd St
Hill St
Canal Ave
Harbor Ave
21st St

Lomita Blvd
Don St
R St
Q St
253rd St
Eubank Ave

1

WILMINGTON

Blinn Ave
Bay View Ave
C St
Alameda St
O St
Willard St
16th St
Cowles St
Anaheim St
Judson Ave
Hayes Ave

1

M St
L St
Denni St
Opp St
I St
Reeves Ave
Fries Ave
Broad Ave
Avalon Blvd
Grant St
First Ave
I St

Anaheim St
G St
Wilmington Blvd
Mar Vista Ave
King Ave
Gulf Ave
Clay Ave
E St
C St

Local 13 hall

Pier B

LONG BEACH

Pier A
Pier C

H St
G St
F St
D St
C St
A St
B St

110

West Basin
Neptune Ave
East Basin
Pier D
Pier E

Gaffey St

Vincent Thomas Bridge
Ocean Blvd
East Basin
Pier F

Dock St
Terminal Island
Pier T
West Basin
Pier G

47

47
Cruise terminal
Evergreen terminal
Terminal Way
Nimitz Rd

O'Farrell St
1st St
Local 63
5th St
Port of LA offices
Local 13 offices
10th St
12th St
14th St
Pacific Ave
Main Channel
Wharf St
Earle St
Pier 300

SAN PEDRO
19th St
21st St
Grand Ave
26th St
30th St
34th St
39th St
Cabrillo Ave
22nd St
Seaside Ave

Outer Harbor

Port pilot office

Pier 400

Angels Gate

Point Fermin Park

0   2 kilometers

0   1 mile

Port of Los Angeles

Shipping Agency (America) Corporation and the terminal where cruise ships dock, the former busy, the latter empty. From there, we head to the breakwater at Angels Gate, where all ships enter or exit the port.

Without planning it this way, we end up following the path a typical container might take as it comes in from Asia. We see two cargo ships, the 905-foot *Japan,* owned by Orient Overseas Container Line, followed by the 964-foot Hapag-Lloyd *Ludwigshafen Express.* Both are headed to the port entrance from a seemingly empty sea. On this bright but hazy day, the vessels appear to emerge out of the glare as container-crammed apparitions floating over the dark blue water. The white and red *Japan* approaches the breakwater, a long, thin line of boulders that marks the harbor's outer boundary, ready to meet a tugboat stopped just inside the entrance, where a 1913 lighthouse sits on the western side. Another tugboat sits waiting for the *Ludwigshafen Express.*

If you were to follow the breakwater east, you would find another entrance called Queens Gate, for ships entering the Port of Long Beach. And from any perspective, except perhaps that of a map, there's no way of telling that this isn't just one gigantic port, so large that the eight-story cranes at the farthest end of the Long Beach port are barely visible, even from a hovering helicopter. The complex totals 10,700 acres, more than fifteen times the size of Central Park. The Port of Los Angeles alone is 7,500 acres, with 43 miles of waterfront if you were to count the labyrinthine line of piers jutting into the harbor.

Just as the *Japan* slides through the entrance, one of the tugboats maneuvers to its stern and connects to the ship with a long, thick rope. At this point, the tug is there only to assist in steering if needed; in some ways, it looks like a Jeep being towed by a colossal RV.

The ship and the tugboat quickly reach pier 400, a 484-acre complex covered by containers, all neatly parked in rows and, from our height, looking like multicolored piano keys. This is, in fact, the stopping point for the *Ludwigshafen Express.* It will dock at the APM terminal, where it will take about a day for the longshoremen to unload and load. (The *Japan* will continue to the Yusen terminal, deeper inside the port, on

An Orient Overseas Container Line ship enters the port through the Main Channel and passes pier 400, the world's largest container terminal.

Terminal Island.) Pier 400 has the look of a floating slab of concrete, shaped like a thick L. It was created out of 11 million tons of quarry stone, dumped into the harbor; the project began in 1994 and was finished eight years later.

We fly over to Terminal Island, a long, slightly curved artificial island, 2,854 acres in size, that was once a mudflat. The two ports each own part of the island, with Los Angeles getting the bigger share. I have to admit that for years I never understood what people were talking about when they referred to this island in the harbor. Some remembered the days when you took a ferry from San Pedro to get there, and the workers who commuted to the island had jobs in fish canneries or shipbuilding facilities. Now, three bridges lead to Terminal Island—

Containers fill the yard at the APM terminal, waiting to be picked up by a truck, sent east by train, or loaded onto the ship for transport. Most of the containers going on the ship are empties returning to Asia.

the most prominent being the green Vincent Thomas Bridge—and in heavy traffic, which means most of the time, you barely realize you've left the mainland.

Although the 2000 U.S. Census lists the island's population at 1,467, all one sees from the air is a carpet of containers, plus dozens of container stacks, some piled five high. The residents occupy a finger of land on the island's southwest point, where a low-security federal corrections facility is located, along with a Coast Guard base. On one corner of the base are several Spanish-style houses surrounded by grass and palm trees—not exactly a tropical getaway, but for a military base there's something slightly exotic about it. Before World War II, Terminal Island had for many years been home to a fishing village, where hundreds of Japanese Americans lived and worked. After Japan's attack on Pearl Harbor, these residents were forced off the island and into internment camps. The U.S. government razed their homes.

From the ground, it's easy to see just how close the towns of San Pedro and Wilmington are to the port, a physical proximity that isn't exactly prized by some of those who live there (see chapter 5 for more on that). From the air, the two entities appear smashed together, separated by mere streams of water. Homes cover the surrounding hills to the west, pouring down nearly all the way to the waterfront, and I wonder how anyone can coexist with a port banging away all day and night.

Our flight concludes by following the Alameda Corridor, a 20-mile string of rail lines flowing out of the port through a deep trench that keeps the container-laden trains separate from car traffic. Many of the thirty-six trains that run through the corridor on a daily basis go directly inland to Chicago, Dallas, or other hubs, from which the containers are distributed throughout the country. It's hard to resist the biological metaphor here: that the port is a massive heart, pumping what the country needs, or wants, through this major rail artery, which eventually separates out into thousands of smaller vessels and capillaries. And indeed, from the air, it has that appearance, an industrial vascular

Hundreds of Toyota vehicles cover the terminal where they've just been unloaded.

A K-Line ship is being unloaded and loaded. The on-dock rail line is behind it. The Port of Long Beach is visible in the background.

system whose disruption would cause an economic heart attack for the country.

On the ground, the various facilities that make up the port are gated off, sequestered from most of us for all sorts of reasons—security, safety, a little bit of secretiveness—as though the whole place had been grafted onto the once primitive shore and in some ways doesn't belong there. From the air, however, the port's true connection to the surrounding communities and, by extension, the rest of country becomes more apparent. The containers leaving the port seem less like invaders than they do from the street; instead, you might imagine them being absorbed into the consumer realm, dissolving into a million bits of products that will land on store shelves and factory floors. As you stare down, it's perhaps appropriate that behind all those docks is nothing but ocean, because, of course, it all starts there.

Moving Cans

Let's face it—there's nothing attractive about the *Xin Wei Hai*. Then again, how pretty does a ship need to be when its sole purpose is to haul some two thousand 40-foot containers stacked five high? As cargo ships go, it's medium in size, with the blunted lines of a skateboard. But the world's got enough sleek sailing vessels that can rip your heart out with their beauty. What we need now are big hulking tubs with one purpose—to lug all that stuff being made in Asia to our shores. About the only thing this ship's got going for it in the way of aesthetics is a fresh paint job—a dark green hull with bright red catwalks above the deck. Other than that, it's nothing more than a floating Peterbilt making a continuous circuit from Ningbo, China, to Los Angeles to Shanghai and then back to Ningbo. (In 2008, Shanghai was the world's third largest port in container traffic—Antwerp was on top—and Ningbo was number eight; Los Angeles by itself rated sixteenth in the world.)

For China Shipping Container Line, which owns the *Xin Wei Hai*, it's no doubt a handsome ship, one of 155 in its fleet (the name roughly translates to "new Weihai," referring to a port in northern China). Built in 2006 at China's Dalian New Shipbuilding Heavy Industry Co. Ltd.

shipyard, the vessel is nearly three football fields long with a 4,250 TEU capacity, representing more than $100 million of cargo in just one load. (A TEU, which stands for 20-foot equivalent unit, is one of the ways cargo is measured for determining shipping charges. Based on a standard 20-foot container, the more prevalent 40-foot containers are thus two TEUs.) As big as the *Xin Wei Hai* is, it's a dowdy barge compared to China Shipping's two biggest ships, the *Xin Shanghai* and the *Xin Los Angeles* (9,580 TEUs each), which rip across the seas at 25 knots, while the smaller and lighter *Xin Wei Hai* can't keep up, sailing 1 knot slower.

Still, the *Xin Wei Hai* has something most ships don't have: the ability to plug into shoreside electrical power. Most ships sit in port for an average of two days and run their diesel engines the entire time to generate electricity to keep their systems going. This produces tons of pollution, which rains down primarily on anyone who works or lives nearby, an invisible fog of particulate matter so fine that it enters the lungs and just keeps on going, passing right through cell walls. Given enough exposure, cancer sometimes results. When the port approved China Shipping's plans to build a terminal in 2001, the Natural Resources Defense Council and the Coalition for Clean Air sued, arguing that the diesel pollution would only get worse once the new facility went into operation and that the effect on the surrounding community had not been considered. (For more on this lawsuit, see chapter 5.) Nearly two years later, NRDC's argument prevailed, halting the work until the environmental impact could be assessed. As part of the settlement, a system that amounts to several giant electrical plugs was installed at the pier so the ships could turn off their engines and still have power.

This presented a novelty I thought I could exploit, an excuse to ease beyond the gates again, this time to see a ship unloaded at such close range that I would share the same filthy air the longshoremen breathed. China Shipping, which had announced the electrical system as if it had been the company's idea (and had in addition demanded $42 million in compensation from the port for the delay caused by the lawsuit, to which the port replied, "Forget it"), told me they didn't have time to show me the system. That's when Eric Caris, the port's assistant marketing director, stepped up and offered to give me a tour. With Caris acting as my escort, we drove onto the terminal with nothing more than a quick look at my ID by the guard. No secret handshake required.

After seeing the port from a relative distance on the *Wan Hai 312* (the ride described in chapter 1), I'm finally standing at pier 100, where the *Xin Wei Hai* is docked. Assaulted by the industrial din that's normal for a working dock these days, I feel like a molecule inside a loudly ticking watch. Noise pounds around me, sounding like a foundry. When Caris talks, I have to lean forward, nearly cheek to cheek with him so I can hear. Behind us, praying mantis cranes fling cargo containers the size of mobile homes overhead. Trucks with no speedometers pinball through the bedlam. From my perspective, the Port of Los Angeles is a noisy, smelly, smoke-choked, asphalt madhouse that shuts down (officially) only five days a year, and one of those holidays commemorates the deaths of several longshoremen who were murdered during the union's formation in the 1930s.

I turn away from Caris for a moment to watch several longshoremen hook up the ship to the Los Angeles electrical grid. It's not complicated. A small barge with a transformer the size of a large shed comes to the pier and is first plugged into a single "outlet" buried at the pier's edge. Once the workers connect the plug, which is about the size and shape of a gallon bleach bottle, a crane on board the barge hoists nine cables, three at a time, from the transformer to the ship's stern, where the crew connects them to an array of other outlets. After forty-five minutes of work, 6,600 volts are chugging through the transformer and are then stepped down to meet the ship's 440-volt electrical system needs. With that, the polluting engines kick off. (By 2009, the transformer was no longer needed; now the ships plug directly into a dockside "outlet" instead.)

I try to divide my attention between this little bit of environmental progress and simply watching the work of unloading a ship. There's something slightly sterile about the operation. The only items of cargo

I see are the containers, the metal boxes that hold most of the goods that come and go about the world. They might be visually uninteresting, but they represent shipping's biggest advance in the twentieth century.

Given that innovation isn't necessarily a quality often seen in the shipping industry, it's not surprising that these so-called cans were first launched not by a ship owner but by a New Jersey trucker named Malcolm McLean. He claimed that while he was waiting for cotton bales to be loaded onto his truck, a fairly elegant and more efficient way to handle cargo came to him. At the time, cargo was handled largely by hand, moved by longshoremen from the ship's cargo hold to large boards that were pulled up by winches and landed on the dock. McLean figured if someone were to modify truck trailers by removing the wheels so they could be stacked on a ship, transported by sea, and then at the next port returned to trucks, it would reduce how much the contents were handled, thus speeding up the loading/unloading operation and saving an immense amount of labor.

Not one to simply muse about a good idea, McLean later founded Sea-Land Service, after buying a small tanker company named Pan Atlantic. On April 26, 1956, he sent the first of two container ships from Port Newark, New Jersey, to Houston, Texas, with fifty-eight truck trailers strapped to its decks.

That's not to say McLean was the first to containerize. The U.S. military, when pressed for a quicker way to move cargo during World War II, loaded supplies onto pallets and then locked the material away in large boxes that were dropped into ships' holds.

West Coast shipping lines didn't embrace the container idea immediately because nothing had been negotiated with longshoremen concerning work rules and other matters pertaining to who would handle the containers. But, perhaps more to the point, no one wanted to spend the huge amount of capital required to purchase or retrofit ships, buy containers and cranes, and build all the necessary infrastructure without knowing the economic benefit, which at that point was only theoretical.

Just the same, by 1959, union president Harry Bridges and others in the International Longshoremen's and Warehousemen's Union knew that the efficiency of containerization would eventually trump the ship owners' reluctance to invest millions up front. And thus the union agreed to the 1960 Mechanization and Modernization Agreement. Hated by much of the rank and file at the time and for years afterward, the M&M stipulated that longshoremen wouldn't fuss over the implementation of containerization so long as they exclusively did all the work associated with it within the docks and employers opened their wallets a little wider for pay and pensions, among other things. Nevertheless, it took a decade or more before containers became the standard for sending cargo about the globe.

From a distance, most of what one sees of the port are those ubiquitous containers, along with the huge cranes and ships required to move them. But as I stand at the *Xin Wei Hai*'s stern, an inch or two from the dark, uninviting water that undulates like cold gelatin, I'm able to suck in many more details. Feeling like a voyeur, I self-consciously gaze at the longshoremen as they arrive at the dock, and some look back at me as though they recognize a stranger.

The *Xin Wei Hai* represents for the longshoremen at least two days of work to unload and load the cargo. The work starts with the lashing gang, a dozen or so sullen men and women who trudge in a tight, slow line up a steep 30-foot metal gangway angled alongside the ship's hull, protected from a dunk in the harbor by a loose net draped underneath. Some wear working-class formal wear, the orange coverall with reflective stripes, but most dress as anyone about to tackle a dirty job would: they sport jeans and t-shirts. All wear yellow or white hard hats and black boots; and, like gladiators, each carries an orange pole with double hooks on the end, one hook pointed up, one down.

They are perhaps the most cheerless workers I've seen at the docks. I'm not implying they'd be happier with a college degree and a desk job (and, to be sure, some of them have had both before coming here). They're dour for other reasons. Lashing is no fun. It's dangerous and physical. Lashers prepare the containers for unloading by climbing the narrow catwalks and then releasing 16-foot lashing bars that weigh 63 pounds (some are lighter and shorter, depending on function) and criss-cross the container stack to secure the cans to each other or the deck. (There's a false sense of security in all this rigging. While the ship can tip as much as 40 degrees without the containers spilling into the ocean, about ten thousand containers topple off each year as a result of storms or accidents.) With their hooks, the lashers pop open the automatic locks on each container corner that further connect the stack during transit. As simple as that sounds, plenty of lashers suffer back injuries or broken bones from falls, among other traumas. It's the most dangerous job at the docks, other than driving a utility tractor rig (UTR).

This task hardly appeals to most longshoremen, but they do have a choice about whether or not to take the job. By contract, the majority of longshoremen get their daily jobs through the ILWU dispatch hall in Wilmington, where the stevedoring companies or steamship lines—referred to by the union in a faceless sort of way as "the employers"—order up workers almost like someone calling a restaurant for take-out. Through a decades-old system designed to rotate jobs—and equalize hours—among all union members willing to work, longshore positions are assigned, in theory, indiscriminately. Therefore, you could find yourself driving Toyotas off a ship one day and lashing the next. (However, those in skilled positions such as crane drivers are often sent only to jobs that require their particular expertise.) When the lashing jobs are doled out, longshoremen will occasionally refuse them, a decision called flopping, and wait their turn for another, easier position.

While the lashers are busy, the crane drivers position the terminal's four Super Post-Panamax cranes, better known as hammerheads, that can reach over any ship's girth and, with a 1,000-ton capacity, snatch the containers one by one. The eight-story cranes creep almost silently along rails that are buried in the asphalt dock and covered by a thick rubber strip that ripples off to the side as the wheels push through it. While the cranes slowly move, they announce themselves with a siren-like whoop-whoop that echoes against the ship's hull and produces

A lasher at the bottom of a container stack releases a lashing bar in preparation for cargo discharge.

A straddle crane, known as a "strad," pulls a container off a stack.

Cranes reach over a fully loaded ship at the Maersk terminal.

enough decibels that anyone can hear the warning above the usual cacophony.

Finally, more longshoremen arrive alongside the pier's edge driving UTRs, which are small truck cabs (strangely missing speedometers) that pull an empty chassis, ready to go "under the hook" and take each can as it's unloaded from the ship—or, later, bring often empty containers for loading. Lowered onto the chassis by the crane driver, the container locks into place on four pins and can be taken away later by (usually) nonunion truck drivers for delivery to warehouses in Southern California. Other UTRs bring in so-called bomb carts, which cradle the cans so they can be easily lifted out and stacked elsewhere in the yard or go onto a train car, which might be headed for Dallas, Kansas City, or Chicago, where the cargo is further dispersed throughout the United States or Canada, either by rail or, more often, by truck.

I watch a 40-foot container, silent in the steel mill–like din, plunge on marionette cables and, improbably, stop precisely a foot above a chassis. The driver, a relaxed twenty-five-year-old woman in a white t-shirt, studies a side-view mirror the size of a skateboard. The signalman motions the crane driver sitting 118 feet above to lower the can. The front end tips forward and catches two pins on the chassis. Metal scrapes metal. The driver jostles in her seat as if she had just been rear-ended. The rest of the can drops onto the chassis. A violent shudder rocks the truck, and the woman's long, black hair flies about her shoulders.

GAMBLING WITH STEEL

Watching this makes me think about Connie Chaney. (The story of how she came to work on the docks is told in chapter 12.) She was once a UTR driver, enjoying the job's relative simplicity and autonomy, seemingly safe in her truck. At the same time, she was always aware of the occasional chaos that surrounded her and how worse things could happen to her than simply being tossed about her seat for a moment. She saw people mangled or killed in accidents often so predictable that they didn't have to happen. Other drivers sped about the yard on that slab of asphalt as if they were racing cars at the Bonneville salt flats. They crashed into one another or, occasionally, into unfortunate pedestrians. There were even hapless drivers who actually drove off the pier into the water. All it took, she thought, for this mayhem to stop was following the safety manual. After all, those rules were based on years of experience, a compendium of security, a written shelter against the mindless accidents that would otherwise result.

But in 1986, the rules failed to protect her. During the ordinary routine one day, she was assigned a truck and told to pick up a chassis and container parked in the yard. She took the container to a spot below the crane, known as "under the hook," where the can would be picked up and loaded on the ship.

According to the routine, the next step was for the swingmen to check to make sure the locks holding the container to the chassis were open, allowing the container to be lifted. The crane's spreader bar, a device that latches onto the top of a container, would then come down, grab the can, and start to lift it.

In an example of physics at work—one action causes an equal and opposite reaction—there were times when a can would start swaying as it was being lifted, as though flicked off its natural, vertical course by nothing more than a minute misstep by the crane driver or perhaps a shot of wind at the wrong time. While the thought of several tons wobbling over their heads should have made people scatter, those under the hook usually stared upward, barely concerned. Some crane drivers would stop the swinging by lowering the container until it bumped the chassis, a somewhat indelicate maneuver that nonetheless usually worked. In such cases, if Chaney was at all unsure about what would happen next, she would bail from the cab and wait for all the shaking to stop. She warned other drivers, particularly women who were new to the docks, to do the same. "You can't gamble with steel," she told them.

So, with a little caution, swinging containers shouldn't have been much of a danger. However, there was one problem: there are only so many UTRs and chassis, and occasionally a driver draws the broken equipment that should have been fixed but instead stayed in service. It is an accident waiting to happen. And, as I'm told by different longshoremen with a typical combination of bravado, hyperbole, and truth, there isn't too much on the docks that isn't busted in one way or another. Equipment maintenance is sadly, dangerously inadequate, they say.

Chaney had known about the chassis with the bent front pin. Everyone did. They also knew how to get around the problem and figured they could live with it. The maneuver was simple: drive the container under the hook, where the crane driver could latch onto the can and lift it up about 4 inches, with the bent pin at the chassis corner still holding onto the container. Then the driver would inch forward until the container popped loose. Not terribly worried, Chaney had hitched up to the damaged chassis and brought the can atop it under the crane. The swingmen twisted open the locks that held the container to the chassis at each corner with the usual bored looks of people who have been doing the same thing for hours and who figure, despite the tons of steel all around them, this is as casual as it gets.

The spreader bar dropped down on cables and grabbed the can. Chaney's boss signaled the crane driver, who started to lift up the container. Chaney watched her side-view mirror, and when the boss motioned her to move forward, she did so cautiously. The can shuddered as it popped loose and started swinging. All that steel swayed uncontrollably just a few feet above her truck, and still no one panicked. Chaney calmly watched all this through her mirror and waited for the crane driver to immediately set the container back down on the chassis to steady it. She braced herself for the shock of 18 shuddering tons landing behind her. Yes, it did cross her mind that she should probably follow her own advice and leave the cab until the situation was resolved. After all, she never knew what might happen with an out-of-control container. *Never gamble with steel,* she thought.

Instead, she waited, watching for the driver to set down the container. But he did nothing. She *wanted* him to steady the container—take care of the problem as fast as possible. Do what was *safe*. Instead, he pulled up on the container—a wobbling can of steel rising in the air and out of her mirror's view. Connie put the UTR into gear, ready to drive away, when the container suddenly fell back down on the chassis, as if the driver had panicked at the sight of all those tons still swaying underneath him. The can slammed down on the chassis' pins, which punched holes in the steel. The crane driver's alarm worsened, and he quickly reversed and pulled up the container again. But it was stuck on the chassis.

The entire truck lifted, jackknifed some 15 feet in the air, and then dropped when the can snapped loose. All Chaney could remember a few moments later was her hand on the gear shift, her foot about to move from clutch to gas, when in an instant she tipped forward, staring at asphalt. A second later, she dropped with her hand still braced on the gear shift. Her arm took so much force from the fall that her shoulder was dislocated.

A half-dozen operations followed. Four years altogether off the job. She now "wears steel"—her third artificial shoulder since the accident. The same stuff that nearly killed her is now holding her twisted joints together. "It takes a split second to get hurt," she told me years later with such insouciance you'd think this was a bee sting. At the same time, she doesn't miss the irony that she has always been the one to come down on safety violations, but she's the one who got clobbered.

The Pacific Maritime Association, which represents the employers in all things labor, tucks away in its annual reports—unlisted on the contents page—a breakdown of injuries, showing which occupations are the most dangerous (UTR driver, lasher, and mechanic, totaling 819 injuries between them in 2008) and the causes of the injuries sustained (strains, slips, "struck by" or "struck against" are the most common; one item down the list, "penetrating object," with 71 incidences, sounds like something out of a slasher movie). The most prevalent injuries are sprains, contusions, and cuts. The PMA even details the body parts most likely to get whacked (back, knee, shoulder, finger, and neck, in that order). In all, for the entire West Coast in 2008, the "Accident Top

Tens," as the report calls them, total 1,503 injuries among the different job categories.

Considering that the total registered union workforce (longshore, clerks, and foremen) for that year was 14,604, this makes the chances of someone getting hurt about one in ten. To be fair, this is considerably less than it was fifteen years before, when the odds were more than double that. However, it doesn't include the thousands of casuals also on the docks—nonunion temporary workers—hundreds of whom do their own share of hurting but sometimes don't report their injuries for fear they'll be blacklisted as unreliable. All this mayhem, from a longshoreman's point of view, makes the docks as dangerous as a war zone.

Marc MacDonald, the PMA's vice president of accident prevention, acknowledges that people are getting hurt out there, but when I ask him to explain all the apparent bloodshed and body mangling, he suggests it's not as bad as it first seems. "The severe accidents are a relatively low percent," he asserts. That is, the Occupational Safety and Health Administration (OSHA) wants just about every nick and scrape documented, so even minor accidents go in the record, somewhat distorting the true nature of dock dangers.

Having said that, however, how many workplaces involve the occasional death? Over the first half of the decade beginning in 2000, longshoremen were killed on the job at a rate of 17.3 per 100,000. (To put this in perspective, workers in the most dangerous occupation, commercial fishing, died at a rate of 112 per 100,000 in 2007, while police officers died at a rate of 21.4 per 100,000.) Strangely, deaths are one statistic missing from the PMA's annual report. For that, you have to be a regular reader of the union's monthly newspaper, the *Dispatcher*. For late 2007 through 2008, it listed three fatalities on the job:

Edward Hall, Local 10, struck and crushed by a yard hustler
Carlos Rivera, Local 13, hit by a forklift carrying rolls of sheet metal
Delmont Blakeney, Local 91, struck by a container and thrown into
    the bay at the Port of Oakland, where—with no emergency lad-

der available to reach him—he spent more than thirty minutes in the cold water and eventually lost consciousness; he was pronounced dead once he was pulled out and taken to a hospital

So I ask MacDonald why such an important statistic as deaths doesn't go in the PMA's record. "That's a fair question," he says. "When I do my speech at the annual awards dinner, I definitely mention the deaths. I definitely mention the person's name. I definitely have a moment of silence for those people. But, quite frankly, before you asked that question, I never considered putting it in the annual report. You follow a pro forma format year to year, and that's never been in there, quite frankly."

Longshoreman John Castanho isn't thrilled with that answer. He has an earnest, forceful way of discussing the dangers of the docks without sounding as rabid as some other union members. "My biggest beef is the lack of safety training," he tells me mildly. "Safety training is something we are so far behind the eight ball on for an industry that is as dangerous as ours. It's really pathetic." That's about as angry as he gets during our talk.

Castanho does have credentials for criticizing the industry. He's the former chairman of the ILWU Coast Safety Committee, and while he saves most of his shots for the employers, he isn't above gently lambasting his fellow workers for what he calls their "ignorance." He tempers this by explaining that they aren't stupid—they just don't realize the hazards of driving too fast or running around with an iPod stuck to their ears (both safety violations). Nevertheless, he mostly snipes at the employers for not, according to him, making safety a priority and providing more training. That still doesn't explain the basic reason why the waterfront is so dangerous, and for that, he has no clear answer.

"There really are a lot of factors that go into it," he says. "I've had a chance to look at it from different angles: the economic angle, there's the personal angle, there's the working angle, there's the ignorant thing going on about it." Once he's exhausted all the possibilities, he adds, as if drained, "If you come up with an answer, you can call me any time."

THE SHIP CHANDLER

While I'm there at China Shipping's facility, the chaos produces nothing that will make the Accident Top Ten. In a way, there are two scenes here. The buzzing UTRs and flying containers—which from a short distance seem to simply yo-yo about the pier's edge but never go anywhere—are one-half of the crazed, accident-prone action; and then there's the ship itself, so tightly moored to the dock that it barely moves, a seemingly safe mountain of steel. The *Xin Wei Hai* appears self-contained, independent of the nearby city, needing nothing more from the port than to load and unload cargo. The dozen or so crew members stay on board, a few leaning against the railing that surrounds the main deck, watching for a moment before leaving; they've seen the dockside operation enough times that brushing their teeth is probably more exciting. However, this separation between hectic action and apparent rest is another one of the port's illusions. While the longshoremen buzz about the ship, the ship's crew is busy preparing for the next leg of its Pacific Ocean milk run. They can't do that without the ship chandler.

Jeff Crouthamel, ship chandler and president of Harbor Ship Supply, likes to think of his job as shipping's "second oldest profession," the oldest being prostitutes who, until port security got too tight, frequented the porous terminals for lonely sailors or cash-laden longshoremen. Based in San Pedro with two warehouses just a few blocks from the port, Crouthamel supplies ships with fresh food, mattresses, cigarettes, liquor, brooms, detergent, ball bearings, coveralls, and just about any other consumable a ship needs to sail across the Pacific Ocean or wherever it might be headed next (items such as engine parts usually come from other sources). "Our job is to be experts at nothing, but know where to get everything," Crouthamel says.

When I press him for the more exotic items he's had to procure over the years, nothing pops into his head. "Think about it," he says. "It's consumables. It's gloves. It's duct tape. It's winter coats. It's hand tools they may need to replace. It's lightbulbs. It's slings. It's all the stuff that you'd use in daily use. They need pens. They need stationery. Anything you can think of. . . . 'We need a TV. We need a video. We need phone cards. We need a wrench.' Anything you can possibly think of has been supplied."

The fifty-four-year-old Crouthamel, the third generation in his family to run the business—his twenty-six-year-old son Brett is poised to take over in a few years—is a relaxed, young-looking man, slender with short, sandy hair. He's satisfied that his competitors are almost all gone while his company has survived. He puts his feet up on his desk and says in a deadpan tone, "There's only basically three [chandlers] on the whole West Coast. And of those three, we're the only one that's financially viable." (According to the 2009 *Port of Los Angeles Handbook,* there are a total of seven companies offering ship chandler services.) He's got operations in Oakland, Portland, and Seattle, all profitable enough that he can pay his bills on time, which, according to him, makes Harbor Ship Supply unique. His nearly eighty-year-old company runs so smoothly that he feels less and less inclined to visit his satellite offices.

He's found his niche in the shipping industry—in the world as well—and seems like a man with few if any career regrets. True, this is a job with no time off. After all, a ship is in port for at most two days. If a delivery has to be made on a Sunday afternoon or a holiday, then someone from Harbor Ship Supply has to work that day. The window narrows even further when you consider that a ship's crew is given only an hour to load the supplies from Crouthamel's truck, usually hauling them off the dock with a small winch, the products piled on a palletlike board. If it takes longer than a hour, longshoremen get involved, an extra expense to the ship. (By contract, the union handles all work at the dock; the hour given to the chandler to deliver supplies is about the only time the union allows others to work in its territory.) Being on call twenty-four hours is one of Crouthamel's only gripes about the job. He grumbles that some ships call late at night for four quarts of milk, but doesn't say this happens all that often.

Just the same, the job isn't as tough as it used to be. His grandfather, Charles Crouthamel, a navy boatswain who came from Pennsylvania and settled in San Pedro, started the company in 1932, when anyone with access to fresh produce and coal figured he could be a ship chandler. Also, there were the ethnic specialists who assumed that because they were, say, Greek, they would have an instant rapport with the Greek captains and score business through that relationship. Whenever a ship docked, chandlers of all kinds looking for a sale descended on the captain, who usually had a stash of money set aside for supplies.

"My grandfather would take captains home, take them to various places, buy flowers for the wives. Whatever he had to do to secure the business," Jeff Crouthamel says. Charles Crouthamel also occasionally delivered live cows or chickens for ships' crews who preferred fresher meat while at sea and didn't mind slaughtering the animals themselves. And, like other chandlers, he found himself paying kickbacks to captains in exchange for their business.

Unfortunately, that was a lot of work, and Crouthamel admits he might not have taken over the company from his father if the pace hadn't eased up a bit. Now, shipping companies or their representatives contact him for supplies, securing them either through a long-term contract or a ship-by-ship bid. Either way, the competition is far less—and with e-mail, he has the order in front of him before the ship arrives, not while it's at the dock as in the past, which gives him more time to put together the needed items. His former competition, he says, went out of business by getting too far in debt, an easy thing to do given that invoices are paid many months after the delivery.

"You don't know when you're getting paid," he says. "Ninety days is like cash to a Greek company.... I got a bid in here yesterday. They want terms. What terms you want? 'We want a ten percent discount if we pay you in a hundred twenty days.'"

Fortunately for him, ships will always need a chandler, and he figures no one will try to take the business from him because the margins are as low as 10 percent and the work still fairly hard for the small return.

"That's the one thing we know," he says confidently. "No one will get in the business."

Chandlers might be disappointed by their earnings, but for long-shoremen, a ship represents a fair stack of cash—labor costs are usually paid by the stevedoring company that runs the terminal and then charged to the steamship line along with other fees. Following the ILWU's 2008 contract with the PMA, basic wages for longshoremen run anywhere from about $31 an hour to more than $41 an hour (the union is always quick to claim that labor costs come to no more than 5 percent of an employer's total expenses, and the employers aren't especially loud in disputing that number). According to the PMA, full-time longshoremen can earn more than $114,000 a year and clerks more than $137,000 (overtime contributes to the high paychecks). They also receive a number of benefits, including full health coverage (with relatively minor co-pays and deductibles) and a pension that, as of 2008, can run as much as $66,600 per year.

The city of Los Angeles also profits from a vessel the size of the *Xin Wei Hai* spending time at its docks. The tab starts with the port pilot service, which charges about $3,100 based on the ship's length and gross tonnage. China Shipping is further dinged about $5,000 per twenty-four hours for time spent at the dock. However, the biggest cost goes to wharfage rates—the port's charge for using the docks, which is based on the cargo and its weight or measurement. This means the *Xin Wei Hai* might be roughly worth $500,000 to $600,000 to the port's coffers. It's no wonder that the Port of Los Angeles is self-sustaining, with total operating revenues of $417.2 million in fiscal 2007, and requires no tax dollars to operate.

None of this really comes up while Eric Caris, my guide, happily talks about China Shipping's shore power electrification, otherwise known as cold ironing, and how eventually this will be commonplace throughout the port as a means of cutting the diesel particulates (more on that later). I listen to his patter while trying to watch the operation at the same time, thinking I may never get the chance again. The multitasking isn't really necessary. The business-as-usual façade that still keeps me at a distance is about to disappear, and I'll soon be back, neck deep in the irresistible conflicts that make writers happy and drain them at the same time.

FOUR

The Landlord

Geraldine Knatz's fifth-floor office has the kind of boffo vista of San Pedro Harbor that you would expect for the executive director of the Port of Los Angeles. Nearly 50 feet of window space point east toward the port's 7,500 acres. In the sort of image that's starting to nag me, all one can see of this place is calm, like an industrial garden of metal petunias glittering in the sun, when—just as I felt standing on the bridge of the *Wan Hai 312*—the port's conflicted soul seethes somewhere below. It seems to me that in place of this tidy panorama Knatz should have some kind of special portal into the monster she runs from her cluttered desk—a window so close to the action you can hear the longshoremen curse.

Instead, the peaceful view features two green cranes that hover over the Main Channel's calm water, as though the Evergreen America terminal, where they sit at pier 232, hasn't seen work in weeks; from a distance, the container stacks appear rusted. The cruise ship terminal, where Carnival Cruise Lines and Royal Caribbean, among others, dock, sometimes three ships at a time, sits across the channel from Evergreen America, currently empty. Palm trees dot the area, looking more like weeds than deliberate landscaping. Hazy blue air blankets the silent scene. There's a metaphor in there: Los Angeles, let alone the rest of the country, hardly knows the port is profitably pumping cargo into every state. They see it from a distance, and everything looks quiet, even tranquil.

As if recognizing my thoughts, Knatz gazes from across a small conference table and wonders out loud, as though she's nothing more than Oz behind a curtain, *Does anybody know we exist?* She sits there in her large office, tightly coiled with her arms crossed and a little tense. At first glance, with her slender build, short, practical haircut, conservative business suit, and narrow, cat-eye glasses, she could be a librarian. But look a little closer. That suit jacket is bright red. Her glasses sport a leopard print. And she rapidly answers questions as if the caffeine in her morning Big Gulp Diet Coke was already speeding through her veins. Even her handshake earlier was a little jittery; she pumped my arm like it was a flyswatter.

Although Knatz's official title is executive director, she might be known more accurately as the Landlord because each company operating out there is merely leasing its patch of pier from her. Well, okay, Los Angeles owns the place, but she's in charge. And her more than sixty tenants are doing rather well for themselves. After all, in October 2006 (a few months before our first interview), the port notched a record 800,000 cargo containers going through in one month. No port in the country had even hit 700,000. From the distance of, say, your local Walmart, it would seem that operations are going smoothly and there's no need to worry about the place.

"I consider us the nation's port," Knatz tells me. (Indeed, the phrase "America's Port," borrowed from the title of a National Geographic documentary about the port, is now its registered trademark.) "Regardless of where you live in the United States, I would imagine a lot of the stuff that people have has come through L.A. and Long Beach, because half our cargo goes east of the Rocky Mountains."

More specifically, at the time of our first interview, the Los Angeles and Long Beach ports combined were responsible for 40 percent of all waterborne cargo entering the United States, with 65 percent of those containers continuing to the Midwest and the East Coast. This volume also makes the two facilities the world's fifth busiest port complex. They move nearly three times as much cargo as the nation's next busiest ports, New York/New Jersey. Finally, if jobs are the bottom-line indicator of prominence, 500,000 people work at the two ports, representing a $22 billion payroll, and more than 3.3 million other jobs nationwide have some connection to this economic behemoth. "If you bought it, we brought it," Knatz adds earnestly as if trying to sell a product, which I suppose she is.

Just the same, she recognizes that the see-how-big-we-are numbers don't mean a lot to most people, and so she's armed herself with the kinds of specific statistics politicians, in particular, can appreciate—for instance, what goods come through the port and land in their congressional districts. "If I happen to meet with a legislator from some place in Minnesota, you know, I can say, 'Oh, well, the three biggest importers or the three biggest exporters in your congressional district bring goods through L.A./Long Beach.'" She sounds delighted with the example. Suddenly her hands burst out, her perfectly plucked eyebrows pop up and down, and her words whip about the office as if she's pleading with me to understand her point.

"And it's turned out to be invaluable information!" she says. "A lightbulb goes on when you can say that to them. Because all across middle America you've got elected officials that don't think a whole lot about port stuff until you happen to mention to them that, hey, these are three big businesses in your district that do business through us." She explains that pols perk up at this sort of information because the businesses could be ones that contribute to their campaigns. Plus, when it comes to appropriation bills that bring money to port projects, such as added security measures, the lobbying information can have a way of winning votes from members of Congress. And as it turns out, Knatz says, every congressional district in the country has some commercial connection to the port of Los Angeles or Long Beach.

Big deal, the country seems to be saying. No matter how huge a

Dr. Geraldine Knatz, executive director of the Port of Los Angeles.

place it is, the port is more like the electric company—that is, rarely considered in daily life. There's nothing special about flipping on a light switch, and there's certainly nothing remarkable these days about imports or the semi-exotic shipping industry that brings imported products here across an ocean that no longer seems all that huge. Those wonderful walnut picture frames sold at the local discount big-box store may come from China, but they don't even look "imported." Strictly speaking, the culture-neutral frames may not be a completely Chinese product, given that the walnut might have been shipped to China from the United States, manufactured into frames, and then sent back.

If nothing else, the only way most people recognize an import is by the impossibly low price (so low that you'd rather not know how much they paid the person who made it). Just keep shoveling those imports our way, we seem to collectively say, and the cheap product addicts that we are will continue ignoring the labels or anything else about how they got here.

That is, unless something comes along to plug the flow. In mid- 2004, a labor shortage and an inadequate number of rail cars created a cargo backlog, and ships sat in a queue outside San Pedro Harbor for days waiting to be unloaded or loaded. This made for a lot of drama. While the ILWU and the Pacific Maritime Association haggled for weeks over boosting the workforce, as many as ninety-four ships idled, cargoes of fresh vegetables and fruit rotting on some. Earlier, during ten days in October 2002, the employers shut down the entire West Coast in reaction to longshoremen deliberately slowing their work pace to protest stalled contract negotiations. The lockout cost the economy an estimated $1 billion to $1.5 billion a day in lost productivity and finally had to be resolved through federal intervention. In the meantime, more rotting food.

For those brief moments, the country gets a hazy view of what life is like without the Port of Los Angeles. Knatz was the planning director for the Port of Long Beach during that time. "Some of us sort of thought about, oh, if that ten-day lockout had lasted just a little bit longer, people would have been squeezed a little bit more, and then they really would have gotten it."

It's not as though Knatz decided as a young woman that she wanted to run a major port facility. (Come to think of it, who does?) A budding marine biologist, she originally left her New Jersey home for Los Angeles in the early 1970s after graduating from Rutgers University with a BS in zoology, inspired by stories she had heard about diving in the clear waters off Catalina Island while studying the marine wildlife. She enrolled at the University of Southern California and earned an internship studying the effects of cannery discharges on San Pedro Harbor. The internship led to a job at the environmental office of the Port of Los Angeles. After four years spent monitoring the harbor's then sorry water quality and earning her PhD in biological sciences, she demonstrated an ambitious streak and took a job heading up the environmental office at the Port of Long Beach. "It was, like, a promotional opportunity," she says.

Trouble was, in order to advance at the port, she had to step out of her scientist sneakers and into an exec's high heels, hiring on first as the planning director and then as managing director, the port's number two position. "I worked there for twenty-four years," she tells me. "I loved it. The port gets in your blood. It's such a dynamic place. Things are always changing."

Unfortunately, she had little chance of climbing to the next logical position—as the port's executive director—because the existing Long Beach chief was younger than she was and behaved as though he liked the job. However, at age fifty-four, she had no desire to move from her Long Beach home to head a port outside the area, so when the call went out in 2005 for candidates to fill the top spot at the rival Port of Los Angeles, she applied, hoping to avoid uprooting her young sons.

She was a long shot, particularly to the local pundits who didn't even bother listing her among the top choices. "I was, like, behind the scenes," she says with equal amounts of pride and vindication. Indeed, after the first round of preliminary interviews, the recruiters shot back a rejection letter, coldly informing her that she hadn't even made the first cut. She had been given the heave-ho as though her experience meant nothing. She felt rightfully indignant but fatalistically accepted the decision as beyond her power to change.

"It has to be a mistake," her husband, John Mulvey, insisted. Most people would have meant that as a pointless cheerleading chant, but he was serious. Take it as irony or not, he worked for the California lottery, a perfect job for the optimist that he was, and he couldn't accept his wife's apparent misfortune. With a little convincing, Knatz called the company hired to shop through the candidates and suggested that perhaps she should have gotten a more positive response. Well, yeah, they said, digging through the files. You got the wrong letter. After more interviews, the politically appointed Board of Harbor Commissioners—

along with Los Angeles mayor Antonio Villaraigosa—chose her for the position, the first woman to run the Port of Los Angeles.

Knatz says that after a year on the job, with sixteen-hour days and a surrounding community that occasionally vilifies the port—and, indirectly, her—she has the same energy she did on her first day. "Even though I work the long hours," she tells me, "I've never been tired once. I'm just on an adrenaline high. Getting this job has been so exciting. It's been the most exciting year of my life, really."

"The Geraldine machine is hard at work," says David Freeman, chairman of the Board of Harbor Commissioners. "She is a very aggressive, successful manager that is driving the staff as it's never been driven before. . . . She gets up very early in the morning and works all day long. And sends out e-mails on Saturday and Sunday. She's just a very, very effective hard worker. Some people that work hard are not very effective. She's both."

Then again, her zeal is continually tested by the one issue that until recently the port hadn't shown much interest in solving: its role as the region's largest air polluter. According to San Pedro locals and environmentalists, her predecessors had done little to curb the diesel particulates and other pollutants from ships, cargo handling equipment, and trucks that spew emissions daily into the air and residents' lungs. Knatz has made the issue a priority, helping to push through the Clean Air Action Plan in late 2006, a joint project of the ports of Los Angeles and Long Beach, which cuts back on the pollution by forcing all those involved to either retrofit their equipment to run cleaner or scrap the oldest, dirtiest trucks altogether. (Like so much at the port, this relatively simple start toward solving the problem got complicated fast, and the issue pervaded many aspects of my story, as subsequent chapters explain.)

Trouble is, Knatz says, with the kind of frankness I find startling, the pollution is a distraction from the port's real job, which is moving cargo. "Sometimes I feel like I've gone a whole week and have not focused on the needs of my customers at all," she says softly. "I'm drawn into . . .

this issue and that issue, and some environmental stuff. And I'm not focusing on the business aspect. And that bothers me sometimes." She carefully adds that this doesn't mean the pollution issue isn't important; it's just that she would like to get it behind her. The ports' plan calls for doing that—or at least achieving a 47 percent reduction in port-related diesel particulates—by 2012.

I glance out the window to that peaceful scene. The green cranes as tall as the building we're in are now silently plucking containers off a ship. Again, I think of that lurking metaphor—how the view from her window represents the country's collective ignorance of the port, when in reality turmoil and resentment are just as normal as the briny smell that occasionally gets past the diesel fumes. Yes, from a distance, everything indeed looks fine. But after I finish the interview, the apparent tranquility quietly gasps and chokes the minute I go outside and talk to someone who believes the port has destroyed life in San Pedro.

FIVE

The Diesel Death Zone

THE ACTIVIST

As I approach San Pedro, driving south on the 110 freeway, the West Basin of the Port of Los Angeles seems to suddenly spring up in my windshield like a page from a pop-up book. It's not the cargo ships that first hit me but the cranes clustered around the water, so massive they actually blot out the Vincent Thomas Bridge, which was once the area's most prominent landmark. In fact, from just about everywhere in San Pedro that sports a harbor view, the 350-foot erector-set cranes scratch at the sky with such visual intensity that the stacks of containers, some five high, shrink into boxy blisters on the asphalt.

The first time I saw this, the little boy usually tucked away inside me gasped for a moment, with a feeling of wonderment over how people can build things so gigantic and powerful. But over time, the scene took on a grungy quality. From a distance, the jagged cranes were—for lack of a less fastidious term—untidy, messy, in a way, as if they had been tossed into a junkyard. As the economy grew worse in 2008 and 2009, more and more of the cranes were idle, with their giant arms, long enough to reach over the largest cargo ship, locked in a vertical position.

This made the rigs even taller and so obtrusive that they looked like a forest of radio towers.

Just the same, this is a working port, as anyone with a job there will tell you; you can't expect a pretty scene and maritime commerce at the same time. With no stake in the matter either way, I accept that explanation. Plus, for an outsider, at least, there's no denying the rough beauty the port exudes in all its gritty, complicated glory.

Nevertheless, a number of local homeowners bemoan their compromised views of the harbor and the Pacific Ocean beyond. Some of them have lived in San Pedro long enough to remember what they call blue water views, although today they're looking at the country's biggest port chugging away at all hours. They have pushed the port to prune back the conspicuous cranes and to instead adopt not-so-tall metal creatures still capable of plucking containers off the world's largest ships. The port studied the matter for more than three years and concluded in early 2006 that the so-called low-profile cranes were too expensive and not up to the practical task of safely moving cans at a productive pace (that is, as fast as possible).

To make this official, the findings of the study went to the Board of Harbor Commissioners for predicted approval at a public meeting on February 15. The vote, however, was preceded by public comments, a democratic custom that everyone in the room knew wouldn't influence the outcome.

Longshoremen first lined up at the microphone to slap down the notion that cranes should be anything less than the monsters they are. They felt safe with the current machinery, they said, because these cranes can hoist cargo without tipping over, which they claimed was a possible problem with the smaller, less unsightly rigs. As Dave Arian, a longshoreman since the late 1960s, put it, "The problem we have is somebody who stands in the way of the growth of the port not for environmental reasons [but] because they just may think [the port] is going to become Marina del Rey someday. It's not going to be. We are what we are. We don't want to be anything else." His fellow union members applauded his message: let's embrace our working-class port and the paychecks it provides and leave the posh harbors to the rich folks playing on their yachts.

Then a thin man named Noel Park stepped up to the podium and faced the board. He was dressed in a dark blue polo shirt and jeans; his tousled hair, gray around the ears, was pushed forward as if a breeze had just hit him from behind. His tired face revealed calm, authority, and a slight sense of disgust all at the same time. After introducing himself as the president of the San Pedro and Peninsula Homeowner's Coalition, he began his allotted three minutes by quickly reciting his reasons for disliking the cranes. Then, instead of emotionally pleading for relief from the visual affront, he went for the legal jugular, reminding everyone of a 1970 law called the California Environmental Quality Act (CEQA), a regulatory document that covers environmental issues so thoroughly it could be renamed the Eco Ten Commandments.

He argued that if the port wanted to expand and put up more cranes, which was its plan at the time, CEQA would require an evaluation of all impacts on the community, including aesthetics—that is, just how ugly a project can be before it's offensive to the senses. However, the port had yet to agree that the cranes had blighted the view of the harbor. "This is the genesis of this whole controversy," he said, looking down at the floor in front of him, occasionally glancing up to the board. "Because the port in its entire history of twenty-plus years of environmental impact reports has never found any significant impact upon aesthetics from its expansion and growth.... I've got copies from the pier 300, pier 400, a couple of other EIRs that will clearly show you they offer learned expositions into the values of scenic views and so on, and then they find no impact. We find that to be completely untruthful."

Once Park finished, board president David Freeman, who looked slightly bemused by Park's presentation, said, "You have always tried to be helpful to us," referring to Park's dozens of appearances before the board, the majority of them filled with biting criticism. Freeman then argued that any discussion of aesthetics was going to be "vague and uncertain." "Perhaps the community as a whole likes the looks of the port the way it is," he added. "That it's not a significant impact. I'm just asking."

Park sharply answered, "A thousand acres of blue water, Mr. Freeman, turned into industrial operations? There is clearly an aesthetic impact from that."

Park is just as much a lit fuse when we meet several weeks later for an interview. He hands me the latest issue of *San Pedro Magazine*, dated April 2006. His picture appears above the transcript of an interview with him covering the ills he believes the Port of Los Angeles has brought to San Pedro. He stares out of the photograph with a pained, murderous-looking scowl. His down-turned mouth is closed, his eyes are narrowed menacingly. His already thin face seems even more gaunt.

"People tell me that's a bad picture," Park says in a tired voice. The eight years he's spent railing at the port have finally worn him out. "I like it. It shows I'm not taking any crap."

Nor has he given up, despite his obvious fatigue. Park spends hours every week at public meetings, speaking to anyone who will listen to his obsession, or at least pretend to listen. A few days before we met, he was one of a long list of people giving oral testimony at an April 2006 California Air Resources Board meeting concerning air pollution produced during the movement of goods.

Unlike some lapel-grabbing zealots who torture you with their rambling screeds, Park speaks at these hearings in an engaging, intelligent manner that combines mouthfuls of statistics (most of which turn out to be accurate—not always the case on either side of an issue) and brief sarcastic rants that make him unintentionally entertaining at times. Just the same, it's the sort of effort to influence the decision makers that rarely yields any immediate results. His words go into the public record, and he can only hope that those in charge perceive the cumulative effect as sound advice from a reasonably articulate guy.

Also on his calendar have been meetings of the Tier II Community Advisory Committee related to the expansion of Interstate 710 (a major arterial for trucks moving containers to and from the port) and the Mayor's No Net Increase Task Force, which the year before had presented a plan—commissioned by Los Angeles mayor James Hahn—for reducing air pollution at the port to 2001 levels. And a few days after our interview, there will be a meeting of the San Pedro Coordinated Plan Subcommittee, a port-related group, where Park will lambaste a major international art show planned by the port for not addressing what he sees as the community's true need for open park space.

Park's office, which overlooks the Corvette repair shop he owns, is like a cave covered in stalagmites of stacked material related to the cause, instead of, say, shop manuals. Much of this material backs up his main beef over the negative impacts of port expansion, which many see as necessary to keep up with the seemingly ever-expanding volume of imports coming through Los Angeles. He doggedly questions the port's commitment to CEQA, which, among other things, mandates mitigation, the principle of balancing the negative environmental impact of, say, a project to increase a terminal's capacity (with the added air pollution and truck traffic it would bring) with another project that improves the environment, such as a park or wetlands restoration.

The port, he says, has resisted creating mitigation projects by angling the environmental impact reports (which are required before work can begin) so it appears on paper that the expansion of one terminal will do little harm. Park and others have picked apart the EIRs to find what they call misrepresentations of fact regarding the impact of several projects. "If you can't do a project without damaging your neighbors," Park concludes, "you shouldn't be doing it."

(To be fair, the port has since developed what it calls an aesthetics mitigation program, which includes a YMCA aquatics center in Wilmington, a lighthouse restoration project, and a park in San Pedro, among thirteen projects costing a total of $30.8 million. However, it should also be noted that these projects are the result of a 2004 court order stemming from the China Shipping lawsuit, described later in this chapter and in chapter 3.)

Given his consistently dour appraisal of the port's performance to date, I'm surprised to hear that Park was once much more optimistic, even conciliatory. Janet Gunter, who has been a port critic since the mid-1990s, tells me about one of the first public hearings Park attended with her: "When Noel first came into this thing, I had been in it for awhile. And I got up and testified, and he patted me on the back. [He said,] 'I know you've really been through the gamut, but I'm going to try and be a little bit more diplomatic.'"

That mood has clearly passed. When we meet, he isn't afraid to characterize the port administration as a den of liars. Despite that kind of passion, I quickly realize that he doesn't really want to do this, that the stress is chewing at his insides so voraciously that he won't be able to continue much longer. Like many activists, he'll say all he wants is justice, but this is also personal. Oh, sure, he's after a broader good, not glory for himself, but just the same, the kind of umbrage he feels—the kind of anger that fuels a protester of any stripe—started because of something that first happened to *him*. He's just one of those rare people who figures that if others have suffered the same offense, it must be stopped; and he's brave enough, energetic enough, perhaps foolish enough to stick himself out in front of that crowd as its leader. Trouble is, however righteous the cause, these things take a long, long time; and the exhausted Park looks to me as though he'd rather pull apart a greasy Corvette engine than berate another public official or, for that matter, sit for one more interview.

This makes me feel a little intrusive. After all, this guy isn't getting paid to do this, and because I haven't gotten to know him yet, the interview starts out merely as a routine counterpoint to the yeah-things-were-bad-but-it's-getting-better PR coming from the port. Perhaps to dilute the guilt that I might be just using him, I give him my best this-is-incredibly-fascinating demeanor. But soon I realize it's no longer a façade. Despite all his strident cynicism, I'm beginning to like him, and I almost want to take his side.

Park has lived in San Pedro since 1965, when he rented a studio apartment with a view of the ocean for $85. Now, he and his wife, Diana, a nurse, own a home in the hills above the town. "Many times I cursed the day I bought my house on Walker, because I had a chance to buy one on Patton where we had this beautiful view—you could see down the coast," he says. "Today, I'm happy I can't see the port because I don't want to see that son of a bitch. It's an insult to me."

Is it the cranes? I ask. "You know what it is?" he says. "It's the lies. That's the insult."

This is the central theme for Park and his fellow activists, who liberally sprinkle mentions of malfeasance throughout their discussions of the port, each brief example, they say, proving their elephantine neighbor can't be trusted.

Their recitations typically begin with Leland Wong, a member of the Board of Harbor Commissioners during the mid-1990s. Wong was sentenced to five years in prison in late 2008 for, among other things, taking payments totaling $100,000 from Evergreen Marine Corporation, which needed insider access and support to win more space at the port. Granted, he took the money a few years after he left the board, claiming that the payments from Evergreen were consulting fees, but I'm told that such larceny implies an all-too-cozy relationship between the port's tenants and port officials.

If that's a little too much innuendo, then the critics will scoot ahead to Larry Keller, who became the port's executive director in 1997, after working twenty years for shipping giant Maersk. While this might sound like nothing more than a slight shift in careers, it seems that Keller convinced his former employer in 1999 to leave the Port of Long Beach and take up a twenty-five-year lease with the Port of Los Angeles starting in 2002 at the newly built pier 400. This pier, which sits at the port's outer fringes, covers 484 acres, making it the world's largest container terminal. The pier and the Maersk deal wiped out much of the blue water view from Gunter's backyard—"That meant a lot to a lot of people. And so now that's gone," she says.

The Maersk deal had wider implications, too. The port had originally

The Exxon/Mobil oil liquid bulk terminal sits across the Main Channel from homes and businesses. Many San Pedro residents believe that such hazardous materials should be stored much farther from shore in case of an explosion or other accident.

promised to make pier 400 a so-called energy island, where terminals for oil, jet fuel, and other hazardous materials that were dangerously—and explosively—close to residents would be relocated. The port's 1980 Master Plan had allocated half of pier 400 for hazardous liquid cargo facilities. In 2001, Keller promised that he would find a safe place for these terminals in the next five years. Instead, Maersk got all but 15 acres of pier 400, and Gunter says the hazardous materials facilities have yet to be relocated.

If that wasn't fishy enough, she adds, Keller was still financially involved with Maersk, which had loaned him money to buy a house in Long Beach when he worked for the company. Then, according to public records, the loan was turned into a "gift" in 1999 when he was the port's executive director. (The port denied that anything about this was improper and stated that Keller had in fact replaced Maersk with another lender; it wasn't explained, however, how the word "gift" got on the deed.)

Keller was generally acknowledged as the person responsible for turning the Port of Los Angeles into the country's largest container facility, eclipsing Long Beach—not necessarily a laudable accomplishment in the eyes of local activists. Nevertheless, he resigned in 2004 under pressure from the Hahn administration. It was said that city officials were unhappy that Keller had pushed for a larger port without considering its impact on the surrounding communities.

As an interesting coda to all this, a few months later the Board of Harbor Commissioners exhibited short-term memory loss and awarded the sullied Keller a $540,000 consulting contract, which the Los Angeles City Council quickly canceled.

Just the same, the Wong and Keller tales aren't necessarily examples of the port's alleged institutional disregard for the community. For that, Park, Gunter, and others remind me of what can be considered the defining issue for all involved: the 2001 China Shipping lawsuit. In their view, it probably wouldn't have mattered who was in charge of the port at the time. The port's stated goal was to keep up with the growing cargo volume by expanding its facilities, and so when China Shipping Holding Company wanted to build a 174-acre terminal—as close as 500 feet from San Pedro residents—CEQA's requirement that the port first evaluate how this might affect those residents was ignored. In other words, construction began before a single consultant was hired to look at the plans or, for that matter, write up an EIR, a violation of state law.

The San Pedro and Peninsula Homeowner's Coalition, with Park as its president, hadn't yet realized that the port was attempting this end-run around CEQA, but the coalition members were upset over the plans to build the China Shipping terminal, with its attendant increased pollution and perceived blight on the landscape. Realizing that their angry, sometimes clever speeches before the Board of Harbor Commissioners were doing no good, they decided to bring in attorneys and fight. Unfortunately, as Gunter learned, legal firepower isn't easy to come by. She called nine lawyers who turned her down before she finally reached the Natural Resources Defense Council, a nonprofit organization with a staff of eco-attorneys, who took on the case, along with the Coalition for Clean Air, and quickly learned that construction had already started on the terminal.

Nearly two years later, a three-judge appellate court stopped that work and ordered the port to first prepare a proper EIR. Subsequent settlements mandated a fund for mitigation projects paid for by the port and a requirement that the majority of ships docking at the China Shipping facility hook into shoreside electrical power instead of continuously running their polluting diesel engines. (This method of powering the docked ships, known as cold ironing, is explained in more detail in chapter 3.)

The China Shipping lawsuit was pivotal. As Adrian Martinez, project attorney for NRDC puts it, the port is now under much greater scrutiny and is more likely to behave itself as a result. "I think it's a lot easier for agencies and other folks to come in and be really aggressive after you've had someone kind of stick their necks out," he says. "And that's what the community groups did. They stuck their necks out."

Park is far less sanguine. "The NRDC forced them to do that cold ironing at China Shipping," he says. "[The port] never would have done it otherwise. They fought tooth and nail not to do it for about two years until they finally saw the handwriting on the wall—they never were going to be able to open the terminal until they did it. Now China Shipping says it's a wonderful PR tool. They're known all over the world as this environmentally progressive group, after saying for two years, 'There's no way we're going to do it and you can't make us.'"

While the broader effect of the China Shipping lawsuit was that EIRs for port projects are now more complete than before—indeed, these paperwork behemoths totaling thousands of pages dwarf the previous pamphlet versions—Gunter believes the port is still brushing aside the aesthetics issue. It's actually easy to do, she says, because the port is allowed to hire the consultants who write each report, and then the port reviews the finished EIR and approves it.

"Who else in the world does that?" she asks. "Do you know any builders that can do that on a project? And not have to submit it to the city for approval? They're doing the whole show! It's the fox guarding the henhouse."

I ask someone I know who once worked for an environmental consulting firm if EIRs are manipulated for the clients' benefit. She tells me that, while it's unspoken, the consultants know in advance how the clients want the conclusions angled, and they do everything they can to accommodate that.

Indeed, the port's Community Advisory Committee in 2004 commissioned a $25,000 study (paid for by the port) of previous EIRs and found "that many of the documents examined fail to fulfill the purpose of the California Environmental Quality Act." For example, the overall expansion of the Evergreen America facility was broken up into three EIRs, each one for an individual, smaller parcel under construction, thus masking the overall impact of the entire project, a violation of CEQA guidelines. But the port's response to the study was to criticize its author, Sandra Genis, for not including the latest, more complete EIRs. In essence, the study went into a filing cabinet where prying reporters couldn't get at it. (Okay, I managed to get a copy, but from an outside source.)

If you listen to Gunter, nothing much has changed. In the case of a 2008 EIR prepared by the port's Environmental Management Division to address the China Shipping terminal project (phase one was completed in mid-2004; the 2008 EIR addressed additional construction), the report devotes little space to aesthetics but does make it clear that cranes are a visual problem: "In views from Channel Street and other nearby hillside residential areas, review of the simulation indicate [*sic*] that the presence of the 10 cranes in proximity to the [Vincent Thomas Bridge] would compete visually with the bridge and would diminish the role of the bridge as the focal point of the view." And even with mitigation measures, the report concludes, the impact "would remain significant and unavoidable."

CHOKING ON THE PORT

While the aesthetics debate tends to devolve into one person's idea of beautiful versus another's, a much less subjective debate, involving far more definable standards, concerns the diesel particulates spewing from the ships and trucks at the port. It's so bad that San Pedro and neighboring Wilmington are known as the "Diesel Death Zone." According to Park, that doomsday appellation came from Dr. John Miller, whom Park met shortly after the South Coast Air Quality Management District released a report in 2000 titled the *Multiple Air Toxics Exposure Study (MATES-II)*, detailing Southern California's air pollution. The report didn't just indicate where one could find the thickest, foulest air; it also quantified the awful prospect of possible cancer cases due to the pollution.

MATES-II included a map titled "Model Estimated Risk for the Basin," and smack over San Pedro and nearby Wilmington hung a blotchy, pixilated dark blob where the air pegged the meter on the chart's carcinogenic risk scale at 1,200 in a million. In cold, statistician vernacular, this means that if someone lived in San Pedro or Wilmington for 70 years, he or she would have a 1,200 in one million chance of contracting cancer, most likely due to air pollution. A few miles inland, the risk went down to 900. As a point of comparison, the next page in the report calculated the cancer risk residents would face if by some miracle the diesel barrage were to suddenly disappear. On that map, the two cities had comparatively clear, cancer-free skies.

Park handed out hundreds of the maps, which he downloaded from the Internet—"to the detriment of my bank account," he says—as though he could stir a revolution with just this one damning document. And, as he tells it, when he gave one to Dr. Miller at a community meeting, in a moment that can only be described as pure inspiration, the emergency room doctor gasped, "My God. We're at ground zero of the diesel death zone." If you want to get people's attention, use alliteration. Thus San Pedro/Wilmington—and, by extension, the port—had a new, not-so-great-for-public-image nickname. (While Miller confirms he's the author of that line, he says he actually first uttered it to a reporter who had called him for comment on the port pollution.)

Either way, this was all just branding for the cause. It's the statistics that have a way of really curling your toes. One ship, burning the dirtiest but cheapest diesel, a tarry substance known as bunker fuel (the most common ship diesel used worldwide, containing up to three thousand times more sulfur than the diesel fuel modern trucks run on), puts out as much exhaust as 12,000 cars. The Los Angeles/Long Beach port complex saw about 5,800 ships in 2005—my calculator tells me that's the equivalent of 190,684 cars a day adding to the area's already persistent pollution. To put this in perspective, during the same year an average of some 310,000 cars a day rumbled over the nearby Interstate 405 freeway, one of the two busiest roadways in America.

The ships, once docked, continue to run their engines to power the on-board electrical systems. According to the Port of Los Angeles, ships account for 59 percent of all pollution coming from the port. In 2009, the California Air Resources Board required ships to switch to cleaner fuel within 24 miles of the state's coast, which the ARB estimates will reduce diesel particulates by 75 percent. However, about 40 percent of ship captains sneak around the regulation by sailing outside the usual shipping lanes and beyond the 24-mile zone. Not only do the ships operate longer on bunker fuel before heading into port, but they've created new, impromptu shipping lanes that run through restricted military waters. At a February 2010 meeting of the Port of Los Angeles Community Advisory Committee (PCAC), Ralph Appy, the port's director of environmental management, allowed this might be a good thing because the ships were also staying clear of blue whales who congregate near the Channel Islands, close to the shipping lanes.

Some have suggested that the U.S. Environmental Protection Agency should create a 200-mile cleaner diesel fuel zone along the coast, which would prevent the ships from bypassing the pollution controls. But the international carriers argue that the EPA doesn't have the authority to regulate emissions so far out to sea.

Alongside ships are the trucks, cargo handling equipment, and rail locomotives that bring to the skies both diesel exhaust and nitrogen oxide (NOx), the stuff that helps create smog. These vehicles contribute 51 percent of the noxious overhead brew, while ships put out 36 percent.

Diesel particulates are the main concern because they're considered the most lethal form of air pollution, contributing to heart attacks, lung cancer, brain cancer, and asthma, among other ailments. Measured on a scale that categorizes the sizes of particles, some of the smallest are particulate matter 1, or PM_1, which is a micrometer or less in size, smaller than $\frac{1}{28}$ the size of a human hair. These are called "fine particles." In addition to these bits of black carbon are even tinier specks, the "ultrafine" particles, which are so tiny they don't just get in your lungs, they continue into the bloodstream, wreaking havoc on other body parts, especially the heart. They can penetrate cell walls and cross the blood/brain barrier, getting into places where they clearly don't belong.

"What they're finding is it's probably the really fine stuff [the ultrafine particles] that might be causing a lot of the problems because it gets into your blood system," Appy says. "And that can be coming from all combustion. [It might not just be diesel.] It could be coming from gasoline [vehicles] and all those things. There's a lot of research going on. We're just learning."

One of those doing that research is Arthur Winer, professor of environmental health sciences at the University of California, Los Angeles. In the interest of full disclosure, Winer is also a friend, but I really couldn't find anyone more immersed, more knowledgeable in the sometimes depressing field of air pollution than he is, a man with nearly two hundred peer-reviewed journal articles to his credit and almost forty years of experience. Talk to him for a few minutes about air pollution, and you'll want to move out of the city to a remote cabin in Arizona.

"People there [living in the nearby communities as well as longshoremen working in the ports] are undergoing just a tremendous impact from heavy-duty diesel trucks," he says, after telling me that he believes the trucks hauling containers in and out of the port are an even greater source of diesel particulate matter than ships, "plus the yard equipment, plus the locomotives, plus the ship emissions.... There's something like sixteen thousand trucks operating in the port, and they're dirty, almost all of them are very dirty." Perhaps more ominous, he adds, the ships are docked far enough away from the communities that the diesel particulates don't always reach residents' lungs, but the truck traffic is bringing the pollution right to people's doorsteps.

As part of a study sponsored by the University of California Transportation Center, Winer and his graduate students spent a summer in 2006 videotaping key intersections and arterials as the trucks passed through the cities on their way from the port to inland warehouses via the 110 and 710 freeways. When he tells me that at one intersection, Santa Fe Avenue and Pacific Coast Highway, they counted six hundred trucks an hour at morning and afternoon peaks, I make him repeat the details just to make sure he doesn't mean six hundred per day. He indeed meant *per hour.*

With that, Winer abandons his usual academic tone and actually sounds a little angry. "Here you have six hundred an hour at the peak, which is just outrageous. We're on the sidewalk doing this for twelve hours a day. We're coated in diesel soot. You can taste it and feel it. And here's these mothers with infants, these children, the workers, the people that live there, on the sidewalks right next to this.... You know, to be honest, it's not something my students or I could have ever imagined until we went down there. It's like something out of *Blade Runner*."

It gets worse. As one might expect, the concentration of ultrafine particles peaks at the roadway, but these particles also linger in the air in a 984-foot swath along the roadside before sticking to other ultrafine particles in the air and becoming heavy enough to settle to the ground.

That's during the day. Winer and his students crammed various measuring instruments into an electric Toyota Rav4 and drove around different Los Angeles locations collecting data on particulate levels. They were also studying what he calls micro-meteorology, that is, a specific location's weather conditions, to see if that had any effect on the air pollution. One of the most disturbing things they discovered is that in the pre-dawn hours, when air turbulence is often lowest, the ultrafine particles travel even farther from their roadway source—more than 6,500 feet—than they do during the day. "It has major implications, as you can imagine," Winer says, "because not only did we find that the radius of impact is ten times greater, but, believe it or not, the concentrations are higher in the pre-sunrise hour."

And it's not only the air that is polluted. Once the particulates and emission-related metals fall out of the sky, they can be washed off the streets, eventually making their way to the ocean through storm drains. This so-called dry deposition can bring to the marine environment chromium, copper, nickel, lead, and zinc with their attendant harm to wildlife.

With dozens of studies in the United States and internationally to back him up, Winer says, "People who are living and working and recreating in that envelope [downwind of diesel trucks] are going to have much higher morbidity and mortality compared to people who live outside that envelope."

Even if death isn't the end result, the air pollution along roadways can have a significant impact on children's lungs, which are still developing until they're about seventeen years old. One 2004 University of Southern California study, cited in area newspapers, reported that the proportion of children with low lung function was 4.9 times greater when they lived in an area with high levels of fine particulates, as opposed to children who lived where the levels were lowest. Three years later, the same researchers further confirmed that children living within 1,500 feet of a freeway in a polluted city had the greatest reduction in lung function, compared to those who lived in a low pollution area.

During our interview, Noel Park outlines a lot of the same material. He has no hesitation about directing his recriminations squarely at the port. Clearly incensed, Park concludes: "For a government agency like the Port of Los Angeles, with the full knowledge of all these things, to stall and obfuscate and delay and do nothing of any kind of proportionality to the problem, it's not only unconscionable, it's unbelievable. What are these people thinking? Do their God-almighty careers and their promotions and their retirements trump the public health? I don't get it. I don't get it."

THE NEW REGIME

Dr. Geraldine Knatz, the port's executive director, clearly thinks her people are far more upstanding than that and attributes any hard feelings as having begun with past, more lackadaisical administrations. When asked, she spreads her thoughts out away from any specific activists such as Park to a kind of "I feel their pain" general comment on decades of strained relations between the port and the surrounding community. (A former harbor commissioner once called the continuous conflict the "hundred-year war.")

"We've been here for a year," Knatz says in late 2006 of herself and the newest Board of Harbor Commissioners, "and we're yakking. We haven't done anything. And so we really have to deliver. It's been all talk. And so people are skeptical because they've heard the talk before. . . . But it's going to happen, because it's why I'm here—why I was brought here to do these things. I'm going to do those things. I'm driven to do those things. And I will deliver."

At the twice-monthly public meetings of the Board of Harbor Commissioners, local residents sometimes question that promise of what the port has come to call "green growth." Here, they're given a public comment session to criticize or, more rarely, praise the port on any relevant topic. On one particular night in late 2006, most speakers are furious about a BNSF Railway Company proposal to build a container transfer facility about 5 miles from the port.

The railroad company thinks this is a great idea because its existing yard, 20 miles away near downtown Los Angeles, is already the busiest rail yard in the country and is reaching its capacity of 3 million TEUs (measures of cargo based on the standard 20-foot container). With the newly proposed facility, BNSF could take containers out of the port and send them east by rail more efficiently, doubling the number of containers it moves. Trucks would bring the cargo the 5 miles from the ship to the transfer yard, reducing the truck traffic now moving containers 20 miles to the downtown location. The transfer facility would use electric cranes and yard equipment powered by liquified natural gas. Those living in the Diesel Death Zone, however, figure it's another way to increase air pollution, noise, and local road congestion, and some have come to the commission meeting to express their outrage.

Chairman David Freeman calls each speaker's name, and the individuals make their way through the stadium seating, down the aisle stairs to a long table facing the commissioners, who sit behind a long desk above on a stage. The speakers usually grip the sides of a dais located near the end of the table for apparent comfort and cautiously approach the microphone as if it's barbed.

The public comments this night start off with incredible vitriol. One person asks, "At what point will human life enter into your equation?" while another calls the rail yard "premeditated murder." Freeman answers for the five commissioners with a refrain he's been using for months now: he's "extremely concerned," but "we inherited the problems," meaning they've been at the job a little more than a year and are stuck cleaning up a mess that had been allowed to fester for decades. "Give us a break here," he tells one presenter, somehow managing not to whine.

Then the meeting takes on a poignant, even more depressing tone.

One woman holds up an 11×14 photo of her granddaughter and announces that the five-year-old suffers from such severe asthma that she needs medical machinery to sleep at night. Another woman in her seventies slowly stumbles to the microphone, breathing from an oxygen bottle. The entire audience shifts in their seats in what seems to be a collective sadness for how grueling the short walk is for her. She finally stands at the podium and says in gasps, "I wanted you to know [air pollution] affects the elderly, too."

Knatz sits to the side, wearing a red suit jacket, showing no reaction. From the press seats in a balcony area, I can see only the back of her head, but she appears to be staring at the floor, stiff and unmoving, her shoulders obviously slumped.

She says nothing at the time, but in our interviews she has endorsed both on-dock rail, where containers are loaded directly from the ship to the train, and BNSF's near-dock transfer facility. The reason for both is simple: the railroad wants to fill an 8,000-foot train with 240 to 280 containers, but not all containers coming off a ship are destined for the same inland location; so the company wants to transfer some of them to the near-dock facility and collect them there until enough arrive to fill a train. The same principle applies to exports: cargo would come off incoming trains at the near-dock yard and be separated into batches for different ships. Currently, the BNSF near-dock rail yard is scheduled to begin construction between 2013 and 2015.

"Some people don't get it," Knatz tells me later as we discuss her initiatives to address the Diesel Death Zone. "There's some people I'm never going to satisfy. They just don't want us to move cargo. And I can't focus on those. But there's a whole slew who recognize that we're trying to do things differently."

"People come to these meetings because they're angry," Freeman tells me. "You don't get very many people coming down and saying, 'I think you're doing a good job.' . . . I think the ones complaining about the pollution are reflecting a widespread public opinion. But I don't need them to tell me that."

Freeman seems incapable at times of dodging any question asked of him. At the age of eighty, with a career full of public service milestones—for example, he ran the Tennessee Valley Authority under President Jimmy Carter—he doesn't worry about PR. "I've not tried to absolve myself of responsibility," he says. " . . . I recognize that folks are angry. All I'm saying is, we did inherit this mess and we're trying to clean it up. But I understand that people are skeptical about whether or not we're all talk or we're going to make it happen. It remains to be seen."

In fact, Freeman and his cohorts have made significant progress by striking a deal with the Port of Long Beach called the Clean Air Action Plan (CAAP), which jointly holds the ports' tenants accountable for the lethal diesel particulates coming from ships and terminal facilities. The plan intends to eliminate more than 47 percent of diesel particulate matter coming from the ports by 2012, as well as more than 45 percent of smog-forming nitrogen oxide emissions.

CAAP was necessarily a two-port pact not only because the two entities are dealing with areawide air pollution; it was also true that if one port had implemented strict controls without the other, customers could have jumped to the less restrictive facility, a situation both ports, which are fiercely competitive, feared. In fact, there's so much competition between the two that when the respective harbor commissions convened to finalize the plan in 2006, it was the first time the two bodies had met since 1929.

CAAP is largely a knock-off of the recommendations developed by the 2005 No Net Increase Task Force. As Adrian Martinez from NRDC puts it, "I think that the No Net Increase Task Force, which was a lot of work, a lot of effort, a lot of time spent, and ultimately a really great product, a groundbreaking product—I think the Clean Air Action Plan was the port saying, hey, if we don't do this, someone else is going to prescribe something that we may not like as much."

I talked with Knatz just after CAAP was approved, and she was obviously proud of the document. "I want to get things happening on our own," she said of CAAP, "doing the right thing because it's the right thing, not because someone is pushing us to do it."

There's one catch to all these good intentions: most of the changes needed to reduce the air pollution must be made by the port's tenants, primarily steamship or stevedoring companies who usually have long-term leases that specified the port's operating standards at the time the contracts were signed. In theory, a tenant doesn't have to conform to the more stringent air quality control rules until the lease expires, when the new measures can then be written into the next lease (for example, Evergreen Marine Corporation's current lease runs until 2028). As a legal matter, the port can't unilaterally revise a lease before it ends.

However, as cargo volume in general increases, the tenants usually want to upgrade their facilities to meet the extra demand; to do so, they have to reopen the lease for negotiation. At that time, the port can add the pollution control standards into the lease. In addition, the required EIR for a project might recommend mitigation measures. The upshot is, the port may want to reduce the pollution sooner, but it isn't that easy.

Knatz tells me she's ready for any face-off that might occur in those negotiations, but so far, she says, it hasn't happened. The tenants recognize the port's clout—they can't up and leave without abandoning the huge Los Angeles market and the rail system that takes cargo to the east. "We have the leverage [on] our side," she states. "You hate to say that to your customers: 'I'm doing this because I have leverage over you.' But it's true. We can sort of drive the industry by doing things here that kind of ripple through."

The port wasn't always so self-assured. The minutes of an October 2004 No Net Increase Task Force meeting show Appy telling the committee that "the ability of the port to impose control measures on existing long-term leases might be problematic." Noel Park and others point to moments such as this as examples of how the port has resisted taking action until forced to do so.

Among the means for cutting back ship-created pollution that Knatz has in mind is cold ironing, shutting off the diesel engines while a ship is in port and connecting up to shoreside electrical power to run the ship's systems. The port expects to have ships at fifteen piers running on electricity by 2012. In 2009, only one terminal, run by China Shipping, had the ability to electrify a ship. Of the nineteen ships that docked at the terminal's pier 100 that year, fourteen were capable of hooking up to electricity.

Eric Caris, assistant director of marketing for the port, who had taken me to watch one of these ships plug in, admitted that the generating plants run by the Los Angeles Department of Water and Power were polluting as well, which meant this wasn't entirely a green solution. But he argued that it was easier to control emissions at a single plant than to control them on all the ships coming to the port. "It's a revolutionary technology for the container industry," he asserted. "And we're really proud of it. There are few ports, actually, that could have taken this on and made it happen."

While Park publicly told the Board of Harbor Commissioners he tacitly approved of its air pollution plan when it was being worked on—after all, he indirectly helped shape CAAP through his time on the No Net Increase Task Force—he's still skeptical of its overall impact, especially because he's been told that cargo volume is expected to increase. A 2009 forecast commissioned by the ports of Los Angeles and Long Beach predicted that container traffic would more than double by 2030. To him, more cargo means more pollution, wiping out any gains made by the current plan.

Freeman isn't convinced there's a contradiction. "If we could double the volume here and slash the total pollution, . . . in the course of that we'd be getting off petroleum and on to renewable energy, which is what everyone needs to do," he says. "So we would be setting an example of what society as a whole must accomplish if we're going to deal with the three poisons—global warming, oil dependency, and nuclear proliferation."

Setting an example is also important for other ports in the world, some much larger than Los Angeles, with similar pollution problems. (In 2004, the NRDC rated U.S. ports for how they're dealing with pollution and gave Los Angeles a C− grade; the Port of Charleston received a D+, Houston an F, and Seattle a C+.) In late 2006, Knatz used her port's clout as a major cargo destination to bring together a meet-and-greet among twenty-five Pacific Rim ports as an opening discussion on pollution issues. The reason was simple: if carriers face controls not only at Los Angeles and Long Beach but at other ports as well, they'll be less likely to fight the program.

With all the talk about San Pedro residents suffering from the pollution, it sometimes seems as though the people standing right under the rain of diesel particles—the longshoremen—aren't mentioned that often. That's no doubt because for years the ILWU stayed quiet about pollution, except for a few instances when, according to Park and Dr. John Miller, it protested demonstrations by environmentalists; the longshoremen argued that the high cost of forced pollution reductions would take away jobs. However, starting with the 2002 contract talks between the ILWU and the Pacific Maritime Association, the union has taken this up as a major labor issue, especially because, as cargo planner Gretchen Williams, an ILWU member, puts it, "people at the local are dropping like flies." That's an exaggeration, but it would seem that most longshoremen do know of others who've been diagnosed with cancer that they relate directly to diesel particulates (with or without proof that is more than circumstantial).

So in 2006 the ILWU proposed its own initiative, "Saving Lives," which called for, among other things, an 80 percent reduction in diesel emissions from cargo handling equipment by 2010 and a 95 percent reduction in locomotive-related diesel by the same date. "With the new effective technologies now available," then ILWU international president Jim Spinosa said when the program was announced, "there is no excuse for shipping lines to continue making record profits at the expense of lives of workers and communities in the ports."

TOURING THE DAMAGE

San Pedro can roughly seduce you with its grubby charm, or it can repel you with what Park refers to as blight. It's the kind of place that screams "Potential!" without yet delivering on the promise. The two main streets, Gaffey and Pacific, both running north and south, take one through a scrappy but characterless collection of small stores and a few fast-food restaurants. Gaffey, at least, deposits the patient traveler up on the Point Fermin bluffs, where there are not only several well-kept parks overlooking the Pacific Ocean but also an eclectic neighborhood of often beautiful, mostly modest homes.

This is where Noel Park lives, on Walker Street, which steeply angles up the hillside. From his three-level house, painted a nondescript gray, he can glimpse the Pacific but not the port to the east, which is blocked by other houses and geography. It's the closest to peace he seems able to find, and even that is interrupted by screeching wild peacocks that roam the hilly neighborhood.

To show what he means by blight, Park takes me on a jaundiced tour in June 2006 through San Pedro's wilted attempts at urban rejuvenation as well as areas where he believes the port's negative impact on the town is evident. We first drive down the hill from his home, past smaller and smaller houses, and then to Twenty-second Street, where an abandoned lot surrounded by a chain-link fence pokes us in the eye. Perhaps it's the overcast day, but the dried grass dotting the hard dirt looks as though it could be coated in toxic chemicals.

"This is the Unocal site," he says with bleak resignation, surveying the 18-acre site where petroleum products were stored in above-ground tanks. "And this has been empty like this for somewhere between fifteen and twenty years, looking just like that." (Actually, the oil company left in September 1994 when its lease expired.)

Our tour rolls down the street to Cabrillo Landing, a dilapidated marina that literally looks like it could sink into the oily water any minute, surrounded by Depression-era warehouses. "Well, you know, look at this. It's a post-industrial wasteland," Park says. "That's what it is. I mean, third world countries have more attractive waterfronts than this."

When we pass the Westways tank farm, Park seems to be running out of emotion. He tepidly complains that the port and Westways have been haggling for years over how to remove the facility, which he claims is "full of hazardous chemicals, so obsolete it could not be permitted today, for fire reasons." According to the port, the tank farm contained "some solvents and exotic oils (peanut, canola, etc.)" during its last decade of operation. The problem is that the lease doesn't run out until 2025, but at the time of our conversation, neither party was willing to pick up the tab for cleaning up the site. Park is worried about explosions, leaks, or any other manner of industrial accident that could befall the facility and affect nearby homes.

As if to make sure I don't interpret this as overheated or baseless speculation, he tells me about the *S.S. Sansinena,* an 810-foot cargo ship that exploded on December 17, 1976, with such force that people felt a rumble 25 miles away. Closer to pier 46, where the ship was discharging its load of crude oil at the Union Oil terminal, the concussion broke windows at least 3 miles away. Shattered glass littered the streets. The ship itself split in two and sank; the surrounding buildings were obliterated. Five crewmen, two ship's officers, and a security guard were killed in the explosion, which was caused when a hydrocarbon vapor cloud near the rear of the ship ignited.

As Park told *Random Lengths,* a San Pedro newspaper, "I saw a big yellow ball of light and watched for the blast. My neighbor's family was eating dinner in front of their dining room window. I reeled around afraid that the window would blast glass shards onto the family, but miraculously, the glass broke outward."

While focusing on air pollution is perhaps the most emotional and surest way to lambaste the port, Park's heart—and ire—is clearly more concerned with how much more livable San Pedro could be if the Port of Los Angeles, with its enormous influence, would take more responsibility for its impact on the town. This is, according to Park, the issue that got him started as an activist. He had been living in San Pedro for more than twenty years, and, with the exception of joining a group opposed to offshore oil drilling in San Pedro Bay in the early 1970s, he had never been inclined to pick a fight with anybody. Then he attended a 1997 public meeting put on by the Los Angeles Community Redevelopment Agency, which was preparing for a second shot at transforming San Pedro into a place people might actually want to visit or even live in. The CRA's head planner, Rafique Kahn, who presented the proposal, is one of the few people Park seems to truly admire.

"[Kahn] rented a helicopter, and he flew over San Pedro, took a bunch of pictures, and he glued them all together in a big mosaic of the waterfront, right?" Park recalls. "And he said, 'Here's your problem. You're cut off from the waterfront.'" The moment still resonates for Park, a grand, inspiring instant when he realized that San Pedro's dreary wasteland days could be ended by transforming the town's greatest asset, the waterfront, from industrial blight to gathering place and then reconnecting it to the rest of the town. You couldn't have one without the other, Kahn said. The theory made so much sense.

The CRA proposed a joint project with the port, but "the port said no," Park says, describing the port bureaucrats' response to the CRA proposal: "'We're not going to do that. We're in charge of this. We're not giving [you] any say over our property. We can do it better ourselves. Have a nice day.' That was 1999. Well, you can see what they've done so far." (This isn't entirely true, but it's close. The port did agree to be involved but later declined to participate because, as Knatz told me, they were worried about losing control over the project.)

At the time of our tour through San Pedro, the port had just proposed a massive 8-mile-long commercial development called the Promenade without much in the way of open space or parks.

"[To the port,] it's got to be huge or it doesn't count," Park grumbles. "Many in the community want something that's more in scale with the community. East San Pedro is devoid of parks, for example, public space. And we're thinking, well, here's all this dead space along the waterfront. The port has had this massive impact on our community. Give a little something back, create a little green space. Oh, well, 'How are we going to make any money doing that?'"

But isn't that the point? ask the local Promenade boosters who, from all appearances, despise Park's redevelopment notions. "A vocal minority have [*sic*] slowed down the process of waterfront development," wrote John Mavar, a member of the Northwest San Pedro Neighborhood Council and former honorary San Pedro mayor (the town is annexed to Los Angeles). "It's astonishing that there are subcommittees after subcommittees meeting with these individuals and dictating to the Port of LA on what they want. These minority views want more open space, like parks. However, open space is dead space and as [Promenade proponent] John Papadakis said, 'We need shoppers, not floppers.'"

"That's the level of discourse in our community," Park sighs. "And if anybody thinks subcommittees are dictating to the port what they want, that's because they never show up and they don't know what's going on. The port doesn't give a goddamn what subcommittees say. It does what it wants."

After finishing the San Pedro tour, Park slouches in my car while we talk, parked across the street from his house. "I'm approaching total burnout, quite frankly," he says. He feels like he's powerless and believes that the port has a staff with nothing better to do than work against him. I'm distracted for a moment when he gestures, and I can see cuts on his fingers and hands. I know they're from working on Corvettes during the day, but I imagine them as defensive wounds, physical metaphors for his years fighting the port.

"I don't have the energy to do this another ten years," he admits softly. "It makes me want to cry to think of it, but it's true. I've got to make some choices in my life. Which is unfortunate, because that's how it works. It's the passive-aggressive bureaucracy. They're there. They're funded. They're getting paid. It's what they do all day. Every day, people like me are sacrificing their family life, their business—I mean, I should be at work right now. And they wear you out."

I tell him about an activist I know who took on a cause so huge, so impossible, the stress eventually took him down with a heart attack. Park's face momentarily freezes, his eyes widen for a moment as though he realizes that could be him if he continues his angry fight. Sure, his wife the nurse has told him the same thing—that he could keel over if he doesn't slow down or stop. Perhaps my friend's example is more concrete than a wife's speculation, or Park just needed that one last reason to seriously, conclusively question his fervor. So I ask if he could quit and still live in San Pedro. No, he says sadly. He'd have to move.

In late 2006, a For Sale sign appeared in front of his house. By spring, Park and his wife had left the Diesel Death Zone. Noel Park had quit.

HIGH EXPECTATIONS

When I meet with Janet Gunter in mid-2010, she hasn't spoken to Park in a few weeks. As we talk, she concedes she's approaching burnout herself. "I'm totally worn out," she says. "I'm no longer a member of the Port Community Advisory Committee. I just went off the board of the San Pedro [and Peninsula] Homeowner's Coalition. I had to, because you just get to the point where you can't do it anymore."

Nevertheless, the passion—or perhaps bitterness—is still there. When I first see her hillside view of the port and much of San Pedro, I'm thrown into immediate envy. Her reaction is to point out that the huge pier 400, which fills up the harbor, didn't exist when she moved here and that the number of cranes—mere specks at this distance—have multiplied without end. "If I could move, I would move," she sighs. She and her husband have lived here since 1983.

Gunter is an open, friendly woman without Park's predilection for flamethrower critiques, and yet in her own way she's just as quick to toss daggers at the port—and her former friend Geraldine Knatz. She tells me a somewhat rambling story of having lunch with Knatz before the latter became the port's executive director. They sat at a restaurant on San Pedro's Fifth Street with a view of the port.

"She knew I was fighting the issue," Gunter says. "And she goes, 'Well, you don't like cranes, but, you know'—and she admitted they really should mitigate—'I don't why they don't, but they don't.' And then she goes, 'To me, Janet, I think cranes are beautiful. I get off looking at all these cranes and containers. I think that's great.' Excuse me, I'd have a skewed perspective, too, if I were you. But I'm not you. I'm just a regular Joe, and you know what? I'd rather look at the beach than look at a crane or a container."

Long before I met Gunter, Knatz essentially admitted to me her affection for the port and how it looks. In retrospect, she could have been thinking about Gunter. "There will always be the view of the harbor—some people don't—a few people don't like the view of the cranes, or don't like the harbor view," Knatz said. "They don't like the view of ships. And I'm, like, that's not going to change. This is a harbor, you know."

Still, it seems as though the port has—as Knatz once promised to me in 2006—worked hard to regain the community's trust. I mention this to Gunter, and she smiles at me as if I've been hoodwinked.

"Nothing has really changed," she says. "You've got them camouflaged in green, [but] it ain't there at the port. It's the wolf in sheep's clothing. I can't imagine it's going to change. I don't know what it's going to take [for them] to change. But I really believe if there is not somebody or a group that is vigilante about watching what is going on in this community, they're going right back to where they were before."

This is supposed to make me feel a little naïve about the port's good intentions, but instead it tells me that Gunter and others are so worn out from years of fighting the port that they can barely open their eyes to see what they've achieved—more stringent EIRs, mitigation, an air quality program, to name only a few improvements.

"The advocacy community tends to have a very high standard for what they're supposed to accomplish," NRDC's Martinez says when I ask him about activists dropping out. "I think sometimes there's a feeling that if you don't get perfection, you haven't accomplished what you set out to do. I think the community is accomplishing a lot, and some people want to give the big environmental groups [such as NRDC] undue credit for what a lot of community folks have done. And they really are shining a spotlight on this big source of pollution, this big source of impact."

NRDC—though willing to sue entities such as the port—is in a strange way the middle ground between the pitchfork-carrying activists and the supposed evil empire the port represents. In that role, Martinez makes it clear that the port has done a lot. Perhaps most important, port officials followed CAAP with a Clean Truck program, which started in late 2008; in just one year, it had reduced diesel truck emissions 70 percent by removing a large number of so-called dirty trucks from the road. The program's goal is 80 percent by 2012. (Chapter 10 talks more about this.)

CAAP's overall impact has also been significant. In an April 2010 press release filled with triumphant overtones, the port announced that the concentrations of elemental carbon, that is, diesel particulates, had dropped by 34 percent in San Pedro and 45 percent in Wilmington during 2009 as compared to 2006 levels. And for the first time since air quality measurements began in the port area, the concentrations of $PM_{2.5}$ particulates met federal and state standards.

Just the same, when I discuss this with John Miller, a man who first describes himself to me as a "humble emergency room doctor" but who has also been fighting the port for twelve years, he brushes off the numbers as nothing more than a reflection of the port's 21 percent drop in cargo volume since its peak in 2006. There are simply fewer trucks on the road and fewer ships coming into the port, he argues. This leads him to the sort of cynicism—justified or not—that I had heard from Park and Gunter: the port has ballyhooed the drop in air pollution as a significant accomplishment, but according to Miller, "They're not doing this out of the goodness of their heart. It's because we have utterly raised hell with them. And the reason we have any leverage is because we're telling the truth."

An example of this is the follow-up of CAAP's apparent success. In

2010, the Los Angeles and Long Beach ports ratcheted up their air pollution goals, promising to reduce port-related emissions by 72 percent for diesel particulates, among other pollutants, by 2014. According to an April 2010 fact sheet that accompanied their press release, the ports also proposed a "'health-risk reduction standard,' that will aim by 2020 to lower the potential cancer risk due to diesel particulates by 85 percent in the port region and in the communities adjacent to the ports."

However, the targeted air emissions reductions are based on a 2005 baseline, when pollution around the port was peaking, arguably making the goals easier to achieve and not putting as great a dent in the problem as it would at first seem.

"Shouldn't 1999 be used as a baseline?" Miller wrote in a critique he sent to the port, acting as chairman of the air quality subcommittee of the port's Community Advisory Committee. "After all, it was determined in the [South Coast Air Quality Management District's] *MATES II* study that by 1999 the air quality near the Ports was extremely unhealthful. Between 1999 and 2005 TEU volume at [the Port of Los Angeles] jumped from 3.8 million TEU to 7.5 million TEU, a 97% increase. Given that TEU volume is the main driver of Port related air emissions the situation in 2005 was far worse than in 1999." (The original CAAP had promised to bring emissions down to 2001 levels.)

As for the blight that was partially responsible for Park fleeing San Pedro, there has also been progress. At the Unocal site, once a weed-infested wound on Twenty-second Street, the port has converted the lot to open space with five hundred trees, seventeen hundred shrubs, and 4.5 acres of sod, all maintained with recycled water. In addition, the nearby marina was being renovated under a $125 million contract begun in 2009.

I last saw the abandoned Westways storage tank facility in 2009 while riding with the port police marine unit, and it looked pretty much the same as it did when Park first introduced the site to me in 2006. Not so obvious, however, is that a few months after Park's tour, Westways agreed to vacate the site by 2009, with the port paying for the estimated three-year clean-up. The port maintains this will all be demolished and has proposed that a "world class marine institute" be built there.

As for the issue of the port's past noninvolvement with the Community Redevelopment Agency, in April 2010, the Board of Harbor Commissioners reversed this prior position and voted to include the port in the CRA's plans.

Last, the port scaled back its ambitious plans for the Promenade and replaced it with a $1.2 billion collection of waterfront sidewalks, stores, hotels, and restaurants spanning 400 acres. By September 2009, the project had advanced beyond the noodling stage to breaking ground, when the Board of Harbor Commissioners certified the environmental impact report. According to some, the plan doesn't adequately tie the waterfront to the rest of San Pedro, as the CRA had recommended, but in general the public has lauded the project's design.

In a phone interview, Geraldine Knatz points to these areas of progress as reasons why the local activists shouldn't feel so abused anymore. The activists, on the other hand, accuse of her of being disingenuous. "I think she thinks she's doing a great job," Miller says, echoing a derisive tone of voice I heard many times from Park. "And I think maybe that's part of the ego that is required to do that job at all. She thinks she doesn't need the [Port Community Advisory Committee] air quality committee. It's a know-it-all attitude. 'We're the pros from Dover. We know what we're doing. Go away.'"

Martinez is far more diplomatic, slowly choosing his words when I ask him to assess the port's performance to date. "I think Geraldine is good," he says. "I think she's pretty responsive to the community. . . . With that said, I think people like Dr. Miller, Janet [Gunter], Andy Mardesich [of the San Pedro and Peninsula Homeowner's Coalition], NRDC, Coalition for Clean Air are integral because it's very easy to erode the progress we've made, and it's very easy for the port to— through press releases and things like that—hide from the fact that, hey, guys, you guys were really bad to start off with. You're getting much better, but we've still got a lot of work to do."

SIX

The Union

As I met more and more longshoremen, I couldn't believe my white-collar ears: "We run the place," they boasted, in one way or another. Even some of the people I met in the Port of Los Angeles administration implied that the union was in charge—you want to get access to the docks, they'd tell me, ask the ILWU local. As a guy who comes from a world where the term "employee" is synonymous with "powerless peon," I found this flip-flop in hierarchy at first nearly impossible to believe.

Granted, this power inversion is more a state of mind than actuality, but it's based on an often unspoken concern—felt by just about everyone with a stake in moving cargo—that the union could shut down all or part of the port. Although the contract between the International Longshore and Warehouse Union and the Pacific Maritime Association prohibits actual strikes during the duration of a contract—such a walkout is legal only if the contract has expired and negotiations to renew it have failed—the threat still hovers that longshoremen might use their united power to reduce the pace of production by, for example, simply moving a little slower or coming to work late en masse in order to protest something that management is doing or not doing. The most difficult labor tactic for employers to react to is what's known as "work-

ing to rule," the somewhat passive-aggressive act of taking extra time
to follow every last regulation to the letter, even ones that are usually
ignored for the sake of efficiency. There's an almost illogical virtue to
this that makes it hard for management to complain when the workers
claim—wink, wink—that they are "merely following the rules." And if
they are moving, say, only fifteen containers an hour per crane when the
average is closer to twenty-five, well, hey, too bad. *And by the way, now
maybe you'll listen to our grievances.*

These disputes may involve some arcane passage in the contract that
longshoremen say the employers are violating (and, make no mistake,
both sides are brilliant about picking apart the contract language and
applying it to life at the docks). Other times, the alleged violations
involve the contract's most important mandate—that the ILWU is the
sole source of labor at all the West Coast ports—and the claim that the
employers are trying to insert lower-paid, nonunion labor into the mix.
Over the years, that one rule has given longshoremen the notion that
they're pretty much in charge. The employers may sign the paychecks,
but that doesn't matter; longshoremen are "lords of the docks," as they
like to call themselves.

Nonetheless, there is a fear in the union's collective memory that this
dominance could end and that, however improbably, working conditions
could revert to those of the early twentieth century, when longshoremen
were treated as not much more than beasts of burden and the employers
were a largely abusive bunch with little concern for the workers under
their thumb. The union's history thus becomes an explanation for not
only the existing institutions at the docks but also the culture itself and
how the workforce operates and thinks.

As I dug into the seemingly constant raw feelings between labor and
management, I wanted to ask the union leadership at both the local and
international levels about this, but they evaded my interview requests.
The longshoremen most eager to talk were the old-timers, who didn't
view me with suspicion but rather saw my interest as encouragement
enough to tell their stories. So, drawing from interviews with union

pensioners as well as published oral histories of now deceased men who worked during the pre-ILWU days, I immersed myself in the union's history, imagining what it must have been like to be a "wharf rat" in the 1930s. What follows is that story.

FINK HALL

On San Pedro's Seventh Street, just blocks from the port, the "fink hall" was a place of chaos and little promise. Longshoremen crowded into the employer-run hiring hall each day, their shoulders bumping up against each other, like a jostling, desperate pack of hungry dogs, so close to despair that it seemed possible they would one day fold into a single organism and spontaneously riot. Instead, on the other end of the dignity scale, men shouted through the din to the ship bosses looking for workers, "Don't forget me!" in pleading voices they hadn't heard come from their throats since they were twelve. Sometimes they got a job, sometimes they didn't. And it probably didn't matter how pathetic they sounded as they begged for one of the few jobs available, hoping to avoid the frustration and shame of going home empty-handed.

This went on every morning, sometimes before dawn. Let's call it October 1933, a time when the daily struggle inside the fink hall—officially known as the Marine Service Bureau—was stirring the men's resentment to the boiling point. It had been four years since the stock market crash in 1929, and while the horrible economy contributed to the situation, the fink hall was as much a reflection of the employers' disdain for the workers as an example of the country's high unemployment.

The smaller steamship lines such as Pan Pacific, Nelson Line, and Alexander hired only through the hall, where ship bosses picked out of the crowd of hundreds a few dozen men for the day's work. Other lines, like Crescent, Matson, Metropolitan, and Banning, kept crews of steadies and rarely, if ever, hired from the hall. A crew of steadies had two advantages for the companies: the same experienced longshoremen came to work each day and knew the employer's system; and, because the men didn't have to grovel for work, they were far less likely to be interested in the current talk of joining a union. In fact, if a man ever dared to wear a union badge from the International Longshoremen's Association (ILA) on his cap, he would have been fired from a steady crew.

As for those who didn't have steady work, once it was clear there were no more jobs at the fink hall on any given day, many of the men walked down to the finger piers spread along the San Pedro Harbor waterfront to look for work. They called it prospecting, and, again, it wasn't the most dignified thing a man could do. If ship bosses needed an extra man or two because a worker had gotten hurt or they were short-handed after changing operations, they would suddenly appear from somewhere on the wharf and pick the men they needed from the crowd. Some sadistic bosses tossed two or three cards in the air, and whoever caught one got the job. Occasionally, it worked to slip a boss a buck or two for a job instead of going through all this humiliation for 75 cents an hour.

Then again, the work didn't always add up to a full day. Men grabbed at two-hour shifts simply because it meant working, even if they earned less than $2.00. Other times, a boss might hire a group of men at 8:00 A.M., but they'd have to sit for hours waiting until the ship was ready—earning nothing for that down time. Also, without much logic, a gang moving cargo off the dock after it had been discharged from the ship might make 50 cents an hour, a quarter less than those on the ship and about the same as a truck driver at the time. Or the boss might dock a man a dime an hour for daring to complain about any of the above.

For years, the bosses had essentially controlled every aspect of life and work on the docks. Through the fink hall, they had the power to blacklist workers not only from employment at a particular steamship line but from ever getting another job at any dock. Some longshoremen changed their names just to get around their supposed reputation as troublemakers, which could have been based on anything from uttering the word "union" to simply griping about getting no coffee break after working six hours.

When longshoremen did get jobs, the physical labor was grueling. In the early days, everything was hauled by hand. A ramp was installed between the dock and the ship's side port, and men pushed two-wheelers filled with heavy cargo down the ramp. By 1933, most vessels used winches to help move loads of cargo between the dock and the ship's hold (the area below deck where the cargo was stowed). To unload a ship, a gang of "hold men," usually about four men working below deck, stacked the heavy cargo onto reinforced pallets called lift boards or loaded it into large nets known as slings, which were then raised out of the hold and onto the dock using winches. The pace could be brutal: breaks were few. At best, a ship provided water in the hold, usually in a milk can, with the boss tossing down a cup for each man. Other ships didn't bother with cups, and the men all drank from the can, one by one.

Shifts sometimes lasted from 8:00 A.M. to midnight. But if that was not enough to get a ship out on time, the boss would instigate a speed-up, pressing the workers to move the cargo faster and faster. The men in the hold would hurriedly grab at the heavy boxes, barrels, and goods with their hooks (they used hooks of various shapes to more easily grasp certain cargo), rushing to load the lift board or the sling. The boss might also push them to try to haul more cargo per load than a winch was capable of lifting. Lines might snap, boxes and sacks would tumble, men could be hurt or killed.

Sitting at a computer reading through the old-timers' stories, I try to understand why the longshoremen endured this kind of treatment, from the fink hall to the speed-up. Certainly, the bottom line for most was the income, however sporadic; those without steady positions worked a total of perhaps six months out of the year. Few of them mentioned this as a motivation except in the context of feeding a family, and even then the financial reasons were pretty much brushed aside, as though they were saying, *Isn't it obvious I did this for the money?* They were, after all, in the midst of the Great Depression. In some cases, too, their fathers were longshoremen who expected their sons to grab a hook when they were old enough.

Still, despite the complaints contained within these reminiscences, one hears a passion for the job: physical labor can break a person into bits, but it can also feel satisfying in an exhausting kind of way. There was also a sense of accomplishment in being the linchpin of the shipping industry: the movement of cargo revolved around longshoremen and, in particular, the hold men. (Chapter 11 focuses on the hold men, through the eyes of two individuals who have done this work for many years.)

It wasn't all physical, either; there was a craft to what they did. Once one gang made some room in the hold from discharging cargo, another gang would start loading the outgoing goods—perhaps tins of tuna from the local canneries—that would be taken to the next port. The process of stowing cargo for the voyage was like working a jigsaw puzzle: it took skill to create a "tight stow"—loading a hold so that every inch was filled, with no gaps or wasted space, wedging the cargo in there with such precision that even the rats on board couldn't squeeze between the boxes. The main advantage of a tight stow wasn't necessarily economy of space, however; it was to prevent the cargo from shifting during the voyage, which could potentially tip a ship. You have to wonder if the hold men at the next port paused for a moment to admire the craftsmanship of the longshoremen from the previous port.

Just the same, whatever satisfactions the job might have offered were not compensation for the humiliating rituals that forced the men to grovel for work, for the sometimes abusive treatment by the bosses, and for a workplace filled with dangerous cargo and frequent accidents. The working conditions left many of the workers so discontent, so filled with frustration and anger, that an upheaval was almost inevitable.

In the alley outside the fink hall, men started to talk about a *real* union, one that would fight for them. In 1933, Congress had just passed the National Industrial Recovery Act. This legislation was mostly designed to stimulate the economy, but it also contained new guarantees for trade union rights. Now, by law, workers were allowed to organize and vote in a union to represent them. With that impetus, the ILA was organizing all along the West Coast, trying to establish its own locals with the ability to collectively bargain for higher wages and for work rules that protected the men from the bosses' capricious behavior.

The upheaval was coming. But that kind of overhaul—so extreme the companies fought it as though it threatened their lives—required a leader. And for that, the San Pedro dockworkers would have to look north to San Francisco.

HARRY BRIDGES

Because the shipping companies would have had a hard time defending their treatment of the longshoremen, they took other tacks. Some attempted a we're-hurting-too message, with talk of declining earnings, which was true enough, though most were still profitable, and some ship owners had benefitted from government subsidies. More viscerally, they also tapped into popular fears of communist schemes to forcibly take down the government, leveling accusations that labor leaders were either reds themselves or in cahoots with commies. Certainly there was communist influence in many U.S. industrial unions during the 1930s, and the general public often bought the slippery-slope argument that the unions—no matter how laudable their intentions to improve working conditions—were just one step away from declaring Lenin's birthday a national holiday.

In a particularly clumsy public relations attempt to address the working conditions, the San Francisco–based Waterfront Employers' Union even published a booklet stating that "the [longshoremen], generally speaking, were satisfied." Based on the longshoremen's stories, that wasn't true in San Pedro; and in San Francisco, the West Coast's major port at the time, where conditions were just as bad, it's a good bet the malcontents far outnumbered the "generally satisfied" workers.

Trouble was, any efforts over the years at channeling the workers' anger into organizing a union capable of winning better working conditions and wages splintered into a confusing narrative of one group after another arising and then losing momentum from either internal squabbling or powerful employer resistance. In 1916, the ILA called a coastwide strike, which ended so disastrously that the union was barred from most waterfronts by the employers. The Riggers and Stevedores Union split from the ILA about this time and then tried its own strike in 1919. It didn't go well, either. In the wake of that debacle, the shipping companies decided to set up their own version of a union, one that they could control. They helped to form the Longshoremen's Association of San Francisco and the Bay Region, which promptly signed a five-year, closed-shop agreement with the waterfront employers. It became known as the Blue Book union, for the color of its membership books (and to distinguish it from the Riggers and Stevedores Union, which had red books). The latter union essentially vanished.

Then in 1924, about four hundred longshoremen tried to revive the Riggers and Stevedores Union. It was largely a futile effort, given that in order to work, one had to be a member of the Blue Book union, and membership in the red book union could get you blacklisted. Still, they defiantly marched in that year's Labor Day parade, unaware that among the spectators on the sidewalks were company and Blue Book union bosses taking down their names. Among the men they identified and banned from the docks was Harry Bridges. "I don't know how they got [my name]," he said many years later. "I wasn't anything special."

That was perhaps true at the time, but Bridges had the kind of militant unionist pedigree that would launch him into the forefront of the labor movement a decade later. He made sure the city, if not the entire West Coast, knew that longshoremen were not generally satisfied.

Alfred Renton Bridges was born in Melbourne, Australia, on July 28, 1901. He was tutored in the ways of ultra-rebellious labor unions by his two uncles, who also put in a few good words for socialism and the leftist Australian Labor Party. After leaving school at sixteen and working on local sailing ships, Bridges left Australia in 1920 and crossed the Pacific to San Francisco as a sailor on the *Ysabel*. After the captain ordered the crew to work on Easter Monday, a holiday for Australian workers, Bridges jumped ship and started working American vessels instead.

For two years, Harry (as he was known to American sailors, who called anyone with a British-sounding accent Harry) sailed up and down the West Coast and the Gulf of Mexico. During this time, he joined in a maritime strike in New Orleans, where he was eventually promoted to leading a picket squad. He was arrested, his only offense, as he put it later, "being that of a striker on picket duty." This formative experience (he spent a night in jail and was then released) gave him more credibility than most when he was later involved in the longshore labor movement.

In late 1922, he traded ships for the docks, settling in San Francisco as a longshoreman. A gregarious man, Bridges quickly endeared himself to the other workers, who nicknamed him "Limo," presumably in honor of his Aussie accent. When he was blacklisted two years later, Bridges managed to stay employed by working the many ships that didn't have contracts with the Blue Book union, including Japanese vessels, an occasional "tramp" ship (a freelance ship that operated without any fixed schedule), and the Alaska Packer Line. "It was awfully hard with the goddamn company union officials," he said, "but they were so busy watching card games and catching the chicks and making dough that they couldn't take care of these other things, like the tramp ships. They had a good enough thing without that."

A temporarily less defiant Bridges later joined the hated Blue Book union in order to get work, and for a time he kept a low profile. In a way, he had no choice. In 1925, he had married and needed the more consistent income he got from being a steady winch man. Although he quietly joined an effort a year later to revive the ILA, he somehow kept the bosses from blacklisting him again.

After work, Bridges hung out at Paddy Hurley's, a bootleg joint near the docks in a district filled with bookmaking joints and poolrooms. In what could be considered another way of abusing longshoremen, they were paid in brass vouchers stamped with a number and the boss's name, which they cashed in once a week at Paddy's or another bootleg-ger's establishment. For this service, a worker was required to spend a minimum of 50 cents there, which usually meant two shots of illegal liquor plus a bonus shot. Other places charged 20 percent for cashing the vouchers.

Longshoremen also gathered at the saloons to commiserate over the working conditions. This gave Bridges a chance to preach unionism to a choir of men who, while reluctant to do anything but complain, knew the employers were exploiting them. This was a class struggle, he told them. They needed solidarity among all the West Coast ports and among all the unions—including sailors' unions and the Teamsters—with the rank and file in control, not the corrupt union leaders. Though he seemed a bit arrogant to some, Bridges had a certain authority: he was an Aussie, with his country's well-known reputation for militant unions, and he was a veteran of the New Orleans sailors' strike.

Bridges and other militants needed a better soapbox than a nightly crying over a glass of whiskey. So in late 1932, he became part of the Albion Hall group, named after the place where they met. With overstated confidence, they also called themselves the Committee of 500, even though they were about a tenth that size. It was run mostly by the communist-led Marine Workers Industrial Union and aimed to organize all longshoremen, sailors, and other maritime workers into one group.

For his part, Bridges worked on the MWIU newspaper, the *Waterfront Worker*. This wasn't the grandest example of the fourth estate at work. They produced the bi-weekly paper on stencils that the men, including Bridges, who typed with one finger, cranked out on a mimeograph machine. The ink blurred on the cheap paper they used, and any drawings they added were usually pretty crude.

But the content was powerful, meant to convince workers they were better off joining the MWIU than the Blue Book union. At the top of each issue, it read: "Put out by a group of rank and file longshoremen," and indeed this anonymous group had the inside scoop on what it was like to be a longshoreman in the early thirties. They named names—the bosses, the finks, the pie card union officials (those who didn't carry out the majority's wishes). They reported on speed-ups, chiseling, forced pay-offs. It wasn't anything longshoremen didn't already know, but somehow seeing it in print meant something more—somebody else understood exactly how they felt. The Albion Hall group hired kids off skid row for 50 cents a day to distribute the paper at the shape-up (the San Francisco version of job prospecting), charging a penny and then later 2 cents.

The talk about worker unity that had so often been heard in hushed tones in the bootleg joints started to come out in the open. The newspaper spread from port to port, loaded in bundles in ships' holds, where longshoremen at the next stop would see it and read what was going on in San Francisco. In San Pedro, copies were surreptitiously left at the fink hall for others to see. When men stood around at the dock gates waiting for a job, they increasingly talked about the union.

Still, it wasn't clear which union that would be. In 1933, Bridges decided to join yet another iteration of a San Francisco ILA local, this time backed up by the legislative protections of the NIRA. Longshoremen tested that law on what Bridges called the biggest anti-union company, Matson Navigation, which insisted it would hire only men from the Blue Book union. In September 1933, Matson fired four ILA men for not belonging to the company union, and the workers at the terminal, nearly four hundred strong, walked out on strike. The federal National Recovery Board, which was in charge of union-related business, stepped in to arbitrate and ruled that the men had to be reinstated.

As Bridges put it later, "This battle really got us off the dime. We'd shut down Matson and won our right to have the ILA there. This killed Matson's idea that you'd have to be a member of the company union. . . . Piss on that. So, in no time at all, as a result of this battle, everybody that worked in Matson was a member of the ILA." The ILA tested this even further at Bridges's job site, pier 26, when everybody who worked there wore ILA buttons on their hats for one day. "We marched in there and the company didn't say boo," he said. "They didn't dare."

This was probably more symbolic than anything else, because the employers refused to negotiate with the ILA, saying that the union couldn't prove it represented the majority of the longshoremen and that they already had an agreement with the Blue Book union, to which they were bound. Bridges wasn't impressed with that argument.

"On a certain day, we'd go down to the docks," he said. "The guys used to gather at the docks in a shape-up and we'd say, 'All right. All those guys that are members of the ILA or support the union stand over here outside the docks. And all those that are not, go inside. That's the way we have an election. That's the kind of election we want." With Bridges leading, longshoremen were about to be more aggressive than ever before, to the point of fighting and dying.

THE 1934 STRIKE
The Deaths of Dick Parker and John Knudsen

Harry Bridges had studied the 1916 and 1919 strikes to figure out why they failed. He realized that the companies broke the strikes by playing one port against another. In other words, with a strike at just one port, the shippers simply sailed their cargo to the next one that wasn't striking. So the ILA took up the slogan, "One port down, all down." Indeed, there were signs that solidarity was growing all along the West Coast.

In January 1934, the San Pedro longshoremen voted to have ILA Local 38-82 represent them. The vote wasn't close—1,262 for the ILA, just 32 for the Marine Service Bureau. With that, they set out to establish their own hiring hall. The employers tried to mollify the union rumblings by increasing basic wages to 85 cents an hour for straight time and $1.25 for overtime; hatch tenders and winch drivers received 95 cents an hour for regular shifts and $1.30 for overtime. And, in a concession of sorts to those working dangerous or offensive cargo, hold men were paid an extra 10 cents an hour "penalty wage" for handling such items as fertilizer, fish, blood or bone meal, green hides, and creosote. The ILA local leaders called for more, however, pressing for $1.00 an hour for basic wages and designation of the ILA as the bargaining agent.

The next month, the ILA held a rank-and-file convention in San

Francisco, with official delegates representing fourteen thousand long-shoremen all along the West Coast. They came up with four demands, with one being the most important to them: a union-run hiring hall. If the employers didn't agree to that, they argued, then the other demands—an hourly wage of $1.00, a six-hour day, a thirty-hour week—were irrelevant. They also rejected arbitration as a way to settle the negotiations.

Typical of their responses to the union, the employers called them communists and refused to talk. So the delegates came back with a nearly unanimous strike vote. If this wasn't settled by March 23, 1934, the ILA said, longshoremen would hit the pavement. The public defiance cut both ways. The employers ran a full-page newspaper ad that warned, "Remember that if you strike, it is your own act. It is your own job and your own livelihood that you give up. The ships will be kept working."

Despite the mutual bluster, the two sides did meet. Although the strike deadline was postponed, they made little progress. On May 9, at 8:00 P.M., the men walked out, along with the several maritime unions representing seamen.

For a short time, at least, West Coast ports stayed relatively calm, a product of the solidarity that Bridges preached; the major docks shut down all along the West Coast because longshoremen refused to cross the picket lines. The one exception was San Pedro, where the employers hired thousands of strikebreakers—known as scabs—and formed their own union, the Longshoremen's Mutual Protective Association of Los Angeles and Long Beach. Unwilling to recognize this latest company union as anything but a front for scabs, the thirteen hundred striking longshoremen at the two ports often became violent enforcers, doing what they could to prevent the strikebreakers from usurping their jobs.

In some ways, it was incredibly well organized mayhem. Picket captains selected groups of five or six men to drive to a recruiting office run by the Merchants' and Manufacturers' Association in the Rosslyn Hotel in downtown Los Angeles. There the crew waited for someone who looked like a scab to enter. When he came out, they followed him from there to one of the shipping offices uptown, where he signed up and received money to take the Red Car rail line to San Pedro. With that as proof, they jumped him and knocked him down, took his money, and growled, "Look, don't ever come back here again. You get back to Oklahoma or someplace and stay there! These jobs are for longshoremen!"

For those scabs who avoided an ambush downtown, there were strikers waiting for them at the San Pedro end of the rail line. "Striking seamen and longshoremen continued their campaign of waterfront terrorism" was how the *Los Angeles Times* put it (known to longshoremen as the "L.A. Crimes" for the paper's apparent bias for the employers) when six scab seamen were dragged into an alley, beaten, and robbed. In the most bizarre moment in the assault, one of the victims, minus most of his clothing, which had been torn off, escaped down the street to a Sixth Street office, "where a girl stenographer beat off his [six] attackers with a barrage of inkwells and other office equipment."

To protect the scabs and keep shipping operations running, about seven hundred police were assigned to the port area, aided by hundreds more deputies and private security guards, all paid for by the employers at a cost of $145,000. It could be said that the strikers who went after scabs intended to intimidate them and keep them from working on the docks, not to break bones. But when the cops went after the strikers, they did break bones. There was the Red Squad, a group of police who cruised the streets looking for strikers to club. Workers were arrested—or, perhaps more accurately, kidnapped—and taken to "Seventh Heaven," the San Pedro jailhouse at Seventh and Front, where they were beaten on the elevator ride to the top floor. As only one example, Arthur Jenkins was picked up in a raid on the United Front Committee for Seamen, which supported the strike. The police beat him while he was in their car and then took him to the Wilmington police station, where they beat him again. Then they took him to the San Pedro police station, where he was hit and kicked in the face. Finally they released him.

By many accounts, both from the men involved in the strike and from press reports, the brutal treatment Jenkins received was fairly typical. However, on Monday evening, May 14, the situation escalated to murder.

Not surprising, a small amount of mythology has crept into the story, and even at the time there were several versions of what happened. The *Los Angeles Times* reported that a group of strikers stormed a tented bullpen where scabs were staying, on a pier at the port's West Basin, and set the stockade on fire—a story that, if you go by the strikers who were there, had been pumped up a bit (the article breathlessly called it a "riotous attack by strikers"). According to Joe Stahl, a longshoreman (who had temporarily been a scab before joining the strike), "the longshoremen raided that big tent bull pen . . . " but nothing was said about arson. Later union accounts further toned down the incident into one starting out as "a peaceful demonstration."

In any case, it is clear that a group of strikers, possibly as many as three hundred by the *Times'* estimate, showed up where the scabs were staying. According to an article in the *Nation,* six hundred special cops and private strike-breaking guards showed up and attacked the strikers. Dick Parker, a twenty-year-old longshoreman who had joined the ILA only a few hours before, was shot through the chest by a guard, and Joe Stahl saw John Knudsen take a bullet as well. Ray Salcido, one of the first Mexicans to work on the docks, heard Parker say, "Ray, I'm shot," and Salcido carried him out of the tent. Parker died there, while Knudsen died later of a perforated intestine. Three others were shot in the leg. More had head wounds, including a fractured skull. As for the guard who shot Parker, he was arrested and arraigned—but then released.

Some five thousand people attended Dick Parker's funeral in San Pedro, and even more lined the streets to pay their respects. Over the years, both Parker and Knudsen have been cited as martyrs to the ILWU cause and are memorialized at union events. But during the 1934 strike, perhaps the saddest coda to the deaths of Dick Parker and John Knudsen was the futility of their efforts to stop the scabs: by noon the next day, about twelve hundred nonunion men were back on the docks of Southern California moving cargo.

Bloody Thursday

Known in many quarters as the "big strike," the 1934 labor action saw its share of violence in San Francisco as well. Unlike the situation in San Pedro, where shipping operations pretty much continued throughout the strike, the Bay Area picketers almost completely shut down the port and prevented scabs from getting to the cargo. Matson Navigation, for example, simply shunned the port altogether and took its business to Los Angeles.

Not that the other ship owners didn't try to continue work by sneaking nonunion crews onto the San Francisco docks. As T. G. Plant of the Waterfront Employers' Union put it when the strike started, "It now becomes necessary to load ships with new men and recruiting will begin at once. . . . Those regularly employed longshoremen who have reported for work as usual this morning will be given complete protection and lodged on their respective docks so that they need not go through the picket lines if these form." The new men Plant referred to included football players from the University of California, who lived on a boat tied up near pier 18. But whenever they tried to sneak ashore to go uptown, patrols of strikers found them, dumped them, and rolled them.

"We had a hell of a time because picketing was illegal," Harry Bridges said later. "One of the reasons is the waterfront was state property. We'd get out there with our flag, our union banner, and I think we had a couple of drums to march along. Then the cops would move in and beat the shit out of us."

The first battle in San Francisco occurred on May 28, 1934, when a thousand or so strikers lined up four abreast for a parade running from the Ferry Building toward pier 46. The middle of the group—with Harry Bridges leading—planned to break into pier 38 by charging the dock, kicking the doors down, and scrambling over the dock. Once that was accomplished, the men on the flanks of the group would then follow.

Somehow, the police knew the demonstration was coming, and by the time the strikers reached pier 18, officers were already there, ordering the strikers to stop. "You're breaking the anti-picketing law," they said. John Schomaker, a large man in the front of the parade, asked Bridges what to do. "Let's go," he said. "Move. Just ignore them. No trouble. Keep on marching. Go right ahead."

In the brief brawl that followed, the crowd pushed toward the cops, who charged back, beating up the strikers. It didn't last long, but there were a lot of injuries, and from that point on, it was obvious to the union that the police were determined to protect the employers. Granted, Bridges made it clear his intent was to bust up some property, but given everything the longshoremen had been through, that probably sounded like a good idea.

In mid-June, the ILA's international president, Joseph P. Ryan, arrived from New York and met with T.G. Plant at his home. Ryan believed he spoke for the local longshoremen, but he ignored their demands to include the other unions who had been honoring the strike. So after Ryan quickly signed an agreement with Plant to end the strike, the San Francisco ILA local almost unanimously rejected it. San Pedro also voted it down but narrowly, 638 to 584. In a demonstration of just how united most longshoremen were along the entire West Coast, the other ports refused to even consider the agreement. A clause in that document that read, "We [Ryan speaking on behalf of the strikers] guarantee the observance of this agreement by the International Longshoremen's Association membership," became meaningless.

Ryan declared that the union was in the hands of communists. John F. Forbes, president of the city's Industrial Association, took that notion a step further and telegraphed President Roosevelt on June 18 with this plea: "We understand there is evidence in hands of Department of Labor that Communists have captured control of the Longshoremen's Unions with no intention of strike settlement. We have reached a crisis threatening destruction of property and serious loss of life in various ports on Pacific Coast unless you act to compel performance on the part of Longshoremen's Unions of the agreement signed by their International President."

With the commie epithet hanging over them, all twelve unions involved in the strike formed a Joint Marine Strike Committee, chaired by Bridges, and kicked out the ILA officials. As Bridges put it, "It's up to the employers. We found a way to get together and agree on what we wanted. There is no reason why all the employers can't do the same thing."

Meanwhile, the skirmishes with the cops continued. "By and large, we were all greenhorn amateurs," Bridges said later. "The one who had a little actual past union experience was me. One time we were marching, and the attitude of the guys was the cops would never shoot us. I couldn't convince them otherwise, because they knew all the cops. Then they took all the old cops off the waterfront and sent some new ones down. Suddenly shots rang out. One of our guys falls right down, and he's squirting blood. And, of course, my partner, who was a real anti-communist guy, said, 'Hey, he's been shot!' I said, 'Of course he's been fucking well shot. I've been trying to tell you that.'"

The strikers found ways to cope. They scattered dried peas or marbles in front of the mounted cops to knock the horses over or spook them enough so they wouldn't move. When the cops lobbed tear gas at the strikers, using round glass containers that broke when they hit the pavement, the men tried to whack the balls back at the cops with brooms. If a glass ball did shatter around the men, they had water buckets ready to douse the bomb, although it didn't do much good. For most strikers, their only ammunition came from bricks they picked up at a vacant lot near pier 46, where a building had been torn down.

With the strike some fifty days old, Ryan complained, "Bridges won't go along with anything, but sticks to his original demands. It is my opinion that the time has come for modification. Bridges doesn't want this strike settled and it is my firm belief he is acting for the Communists."

"I neither affirm nor deny that I am a communist," Bridges told the press.

Soon after, the San Francisco newspapers announced the port was opening for business on July 3. Chief of police William J. Quinn warned everyone, "Stay away from the waterfront unless you have business here. The Police Department will have its hands full on Tuesday preventing violence on the waterfront. We do not want any innocent bystanders hurt." As he said this, about two hundred additional men were being added to the waterfront police force, which already totaled five hundred, and new supplies of tear gas and riot guns handed out.

The strikers gathered in the morning, many of them answering a call by the strike committee for all unemployed members of every labor union to join the picket lines. At about eleven o'clock, the police started to move—on foot, on horseback, and in patrol cars—forcing back the pickets to clear an area around pier 38. The crowd was essentially boxed in: empty boxcars strung across the width of the Embarcadero on the south side of the pier blocked off that end of the street. The north end was barricaded by a string of patrol cars, the police armed with revolvers, riot guns, and clubs.

At 1:24 P.M., pier 38's steel doors lifted, and two trucks behind eight patrol cars slowly exited the pier. One truck carried auto tires, and the other was half-loaded with cocoa bean sacks. Police captain Thomas M. Hoertkorn, riding the running board of the lead patrol car with a revolver in his hand, shouted, "The port is open!" The pickets surged forward and shouted curses. Six motorcycle cops following the trucks pulled out and surrounded them as the trucks headed for a warehouse rented for the occasion.

Hoertkorn shouted to a crowd of cops behind him, "Let 'em have it, boys!" He pulled his revolver and fired it into the air while holding a drawn club in the other hand. The police surged into the crowd. Bricks flew, clubs came down on heads, the cops opened fire with bullets and tear gas grenades. Some strikers retreated, choking, while others tried to toss unexploded tear gas grenades back at the police. Picketers dragged several mounted police off their horses and beat them. Heads were bleeding. Workers in the offices nearby had to leave their buildings when tear gas drifted inside. Among the police, one officer was struck in the head, possibly by a flying brick, while another took a brick to the leg. Quinn, who stayed inside his car during the fray, was nearly whacked by a brick that broke through the car's side window.

As the battle continued, the streets were soon littered with fallen men. Eugene Dunbar, a union seaman, was shot in the left ankle and dragged from the fighting, where fellow picketers helped him until an ambulance took him to Harbor Emergency Hospital. Stray bullets crashed through nearby windows, and a Bank of America teller was cut above the eye.

Meanwhile, about ten trucks an hour left the pier, shuttling what turned out to be very little cargo to the warehouse. Going after anything that resembled a scab-driven truck, the crowd overturned five vehicles, not all of them involved with the shipping companies. At Third and Minna, they stopped one truck, beating the driver and his companion. The attackers went after the truck's rice cargo, slitting the bags and dumping them into the street. Unfortunately, the truck was working for J. S. Smith Trucking Company, delivering rice from Sacramento, with no connection to the strike.

Four hours later, the crowd, dispersed and weakened by the battle, finally gave up, running down side streets and alleys. Twenty-five people were hospitalized, nine of them police. Many more strikers simply went home with their wounds, afraid of being arrested if they showed up in the emergency room.

That afternoon, the Industrial Association ran an ad titled "The Port Is Open" in all the papers. It read in part:

> Our action is taken without prejudice to present negotiations for a settlement of the longshoremen's strikes and other associated difficulties.... In our desire that these negotiations succeed, and that the strikes be settled, we have cooperated with all concerned to the best of our ability and we shall continue to do so.... The port of San Francisco is now open to the business of San Francisco.

Well, temporarily. The next day was Independence Day, and the port closed. And then came Thursday, July 5, when eight hundred police showed up at the docks supplied with new riot sticks, longer and heavier than standard issue, as well as sawed-off shotguns, riot guns, tear gas grenades, and vomiting gas, a new product that knocked one down with violent nausea and headaches that lasted a nasty two days. There were even stories of the tear gas salesman hanging about the perimeter, presumably to give handling advice.

Reporters and photographers were on the scene, almost as though they were covering a baseball game (at some points, spectators outnumbered the strikers), although their accounts of exactly what happened that day would later differ. Stories in the *San Francisco Daily News* depicted a morality play of sorts in which the longshoremen—most often referred to as rioters—received a suitable punishment for their attacks on the port and the police protecting it. More sympathetic, pro-labor accounts characterized the strikers' actions as purely defensive, even heroic, and described the cops as overly aggressive tools of the employers.

The battle began early, at 8:00 A.M., after a Belt Line locomotive driven by strikebreakers shunted two refrigerator cars into the Matson docks at piers 30 and 32. According to the *Daily News,* the pickets—a crowd of about two thousand—protested this by setting two boxcars on fire. The police reacted with tear gas, vomiting gas, and gunfire. At one point, so much ammunition was released that workers on the construction site of the San Francisco–Oakland Bay Bridge had to run for cover lest they stop a stray bullet. More gunshots popped against the houses on nearby Rincon Hill. Five thousand spectators gawked at the battle until a gas bomb dropped near them and they ran off, screaming.

One of the picketers, who was shot in the back, was offered a ride to the hospital in a patrol wagon. "Go to hell," he told the police. "I won't ride in that damn thing."

The strikers ran north to Harrison Street, with police radio cars in pursuit. The crowd was driven back to Bryant Street and then from

Beale to Main. Some grabbed rocks they had hidden among the construction materials being used for the Bay Bridge and hurled them at the cops. This ebb and flow in the fighting continued until the crowd found itself at the bottom of Rincon Hill, searching for empty boxes on the bridge that they could use to barricade themselves against the cops' well-armed onslaught.

About twenty police suddenly appeared and started firing toward the crowd. The long nightsticks came out, in a kind of hand-to-hand combat, with cops flailing at the rioters. Injured strikers were left on the ground until a patrol car picked them up. They were first taken to the hospital and then arrested.

The crowd retreated up the hill. One bystander was shot (police later blamed the injury on gunfire from the strikers). Tear gas was hurled into the crowd of picketers. Some of the shells ignited the dry grass on the hillside, and when the fire department arrived, they sprayed their high-pressure hoses not only on the flames but on the crowd as well when some men tried to interfere. Clots of mud and rock were thrown into the air.

The police followed the retreating picketers up the hill, firing their revolvers and swinging their riot clubs. Like a military operation, which in many ways it was, they quickly occupied the hilltop and positioned themselves so no one could retake it.

And then, oddly, at noon, after a full morning of fighting, both groups took a lunch break as if something as uncivilized as all this warfare was merely a job and work rules called for a break.

An hour later, the picketers made their way closer toward downtown, reaching the ILA headquarters on Steuart Street. Away from the isolated Embarcadero industrial area, they felt like they were in neutral territory, but the police staged a surprise attack. One man reportedly fired back at the police with a revolver but escaped after two officers emptied their guns shooting back. With tear gas shells breaking through the ILA office windows, a phone rang at someone's desk, and a striker answered it.

"Are you willing to arbitrate now?" a voice asked.

This almost surreal moment ended when, during the melee, Howard Sperry, a World War I veteran and member of the ILA, was struck by a bullet and died on the spot. Nicholas Bordoise, a native of Crete and a member of the Cooks' Union and the Communist Party, also died of a gunshot wound a short time later. Both of them were reportedly shot in the back.

The fight moved into the downtown district. One striker improvised a slingshot from an old inner tube and shot bricks at Chief Quinn's car; Quinn's attendants retaliated with tear gas and bullets. Dozens lay on the sidewalk bleeding, while others tried to crawl away. A woman coming off a street car was hit in the temple by a stray bullet, and when a man came to help her, he was shot as well.

Finally, in the afternoon, the fight ended. Bridges, dressed in a dark double-breasted suit, complained in person to Mayor Rossi that police were shooting the men without cause. "None of the violence down there was started by our men," he said. "With me are witnesses to police brutality."

Rossi replied, "You refused to arbitrate; now take the consequences."

By the end of the day, two thousand National Guardsmen arrived, under orders from the governor, to which Bridges said, "We cannot stand up against police, machine gun, and National Guard bayonets." True enough. If the purpose was to stop cargo from leaving the docks, the strikers were unsuccessful. About thirty-four trucks an hour left pier 38 and a King Street warehouse.

The day was quickly dubbed Bloody Thursday. The next morning, the two dead strikers were commemorated with chalk marks on the sidewalk along with a few bunches of gladioli and two wreaths. An inscription read, "2 ILA men killed—shot in the back." To either side was written, "Police murder." The mayor called the memorial illegal and police destroyed it, but it was rebuilt.

The two bodies lay in state at the ILA headquarters on July 8 so thousands could pay tribute. The next day, a funeral procession of forty thousand people gathered at the ILA office, where the coffins were loaded on a truck, followed by three other trucks filled with flowers. The procession, in a line nearly 2 miles long, moved from Steuart Street to Market, with a union band playing a Beethoven funeral march. Sperry's casket was left at Dugan's funeral parlor and then buried the next day at the Presidio National Cemetery. Bordoise's coffin continued in a hearse to Cypress Lawn Cemetery. Sam Darcy, regional head of the Communist Party, told the crowd, "We didn't come out here to cry, and Nick wouldn't want us to cry. What Nick wants is, 'The fight must go on. We're just getting started.'"

On July 11, the San Francisco Teamsters voted to strike (nearly a month before, the Los Angeles Teamsters had refused to handle cargo to or from the L.A. port, but this hadn't slowed down the shipping operation). Over the next few days, more than sixty unions in San Francisco walked off their jobs to support a citywide general strike. In Los Angeles, every union in the city voted its full support of the strikers, and each member was assessed 25 cents to provide funds for them.

On July 16, business in San Francisco nearly halted as the general strike began and the working people showed their collective power. No street cars were running, there was little auto traffic, manufacturing plants were deserted and silent, stores were closed. The mayor declared a state of emergency, and heavily armed troops were brought in from around the state.

It didn't last long. Businesses soon found ways around the general strike. After four days, the city's Labor Council voted to end the walkout. By July 26, the longshoremen agreed, by a four to one margin, to accept arbitration, something Bridges had originally opposed. The two sides argued before an arbitration board for five days in an initial hearing and finally agreed to just one of the original demands: that pay increases, to be decided later by the board, would be retroactive to the day men returned to work. Shortly thereafter, the longshoremen were back on the job.

On October 12, 1934, the arbitration board decided that the union would get a six-hour day, a thirty-hour week, and time and a half for overtime. The wage was 96 cents an hour, and $1.40 for overtime hours. A dispatch hall controlled by both parties was established, but the dispatcher was to be chosen by the union, giving it the most control over who got jobs.

The San Francisco ILA local elected Bridges as its president, and later he was named head of the West Coast district. The union eventually became the International Longshoremen's and Warehousemen's Union. There have been no other unions since to challenge the ILWU on the docks, and it's now considered one of the strongest unions in the country.

Of the strike, Bridges said later, "You see, in a small way, temporarily a strike is a small revolution. A strike is a very serious thing. The strike weapon should never be used except as a last desperate resort, when there's no way out. It simply means a form of revolution because you take over an industry or a plant owned by the capitalists and temporarily seize it. Temporarily you take it away . . . " And then he added, without conceding the compromises inherent in any labor action or negotiation, "In this case, we said it to the ship owners of the whole world, 'You might be worth millions or billions—we don't say you own this until we tell you to operate.'"

COMMIES

Every year longshoremen get a paid holiday to commemorate Bloody Thursday and the 1934 strike. With any luck, the thinking seems to be, this annual observance will sober up even the most fat and happy longshoreman with the reminder that anti-labor forces will stop at nothing, including murder, to destroy the union.

This has me wondering if that theme still comes through at the all-day Bloody Thursday picnic held at San Pedro's Point Fermin Park, atop a bluff with a view of San Pedro Harbor and the Pacific Ocean. Dozens of longshoremen and their families blissfully lounge about the grass amid the warm smell of barbecue chicken, while a few people

An ILWU member attends a Bloody Thursday picnic in San Pedro.

with fold-out tables and canopies display photo albums or brochures or sell Bloody Thursday t-shirts featuring a pensive Harry Bridges.

There's nothing strident about the sedate crowd here. Even the parade of politicians, union leaders, and pensioners who speak from a small stage sound subdued as they relate the sacrifices of past longshoremen, credit them for the contented times now, and caution that no one should take said contented times for granted. There's an eat-your-vegetables tone to the whole event. I'm told later that many in the union—especially newer members—have no idea what really happened during the ILWU's first years or how that history affects them today, not just in the contract rules they observe but in the waterfront culture itself. Local 13 even offers classes in union history that explain how the struggles of earlier longshoremen are relevant today.

Perhaps the most obscure item from the past that invisibly affects nearly everyone in the union today was actually one of the biggest issues of the 1940s and 1950s: was Harry Bridges a communist? This wasn't the kind of noble fight that earns paid holidays, nor was it necessarily the kind of personal sacrifice extolled by old-timers at a Bloody Thursday picnic. But running through the union, especially in the upper ranks, among those who are elected to think about these things, is what you might call The Fear. Real or imagined, The Fear whispers the notion that the government and employers have one goal in regard to the union, and that is to expunge it from the docks. And while ILWU leaders cite all sorts of modern examples to back up The Fear, it largely began with the 1934 strike and how men died for the union. But I think The Fear was finally driven into the union's DNA after the government and waterfront employers tenaciously pursued Harry Bridges for his alleged communist ties. The 1934 murders, which were certainly shocking and tragic, occurred in the heat of battle; the protracted, years-long effort to deport Bridges, however, was premeditated and purposeful, which perhaps made it more insidious in the long run.

It would seem that no one among his inner circle knew for sure whether Bridges was a communist, or so they claimed. Although it was clear to all that Bridges's beliefs leaned so far left that he was no doubt a communist in spirit, he always maintained, even under oath, that he had never joined the Communist Party.

In a way, it doesn't matter. What's clear is that the government and the waterfront employers decided that if they could get rid of him—which they were determined to do because he was successfully helping organized labor win such expensive gains as pensions, health care, and better working conditions—it would be through proving he was a member of the Communist Party. At the time, membership implied the volatile presumption that he belonged to a group advocating the violent overthrow of the U.S. government, a crime in itself. Additionally, because Bridges wasn't an American citizen, the Alien Registration Act dictated that he could be given the boot back to Australia. No more Harry. And perhaps no more union, or at least a far less inspired one.

The fight to deport Bridges started when the Immigration and Natu-

Longshore union president Harry Bridges addresses a caucus meeting in Portland in the late 1950s. Courtesy of ILWU Library, San Francisco.

ralization Service first issued an arrest warrant for him on March 2, 1938, accusing him of affiliation with the Communist Party. The INS had been gathering evidence that documented his association with communists as early as Bridges's first labor organizing efforts in San Francisco. Among other things, they had minutes from 1934 meetings that Bridges attended in Seattle, where he and confirmed communist leaders discussed the Puget Sound waterfront labor situation. A written summary of these meetings, dated October 2, 1934, asserted that those in attendance pledged themselves "to do their utmost to bring about a General Strike should the general situation require such a strike" and outlined how such a strike should be engineered and the demands to be made. Nowhere in the document, however, did they mention the overthrow of the U.S. government, although a recitation of communist ideals did creep into the statement's language, like an old habit. Another INS allegation noted that the executive committee of the San Francisco Communist Party approved of Bridges as—according to the INS—"a dictator-to-be on the waterfront and assigned certain named persons [that is, party members] to guide him" during the 1934 strike.

A month after the arrest warrant was issued, Arthur J. Phelan, an INS inspector, finished an investigation that concluded Bridges had been hanging out with the communists for so long that he must have been one himself. Phelan detailed Bridges's numerous contacts with the Communist Party and how various communist publications praised him without reservation for his activities on behalf of longshoremen and presumably communism itself. For example, Phelan cited "the official organ of the Communist party," the *Western Worker*, which wrote what Phelan seemed to believe were mash notes to Bridges: "At page 683, Bridges is again lauded, and it is stated that every proposal he made in the name of the strike committee was carried and that this included a 'rank and file negotiations committee,' and 'the final link completing the original plan for strike committee leadership.' It seems from the foregoing that this 'original plan' was the original plan which the Communist party had formulated before the strike commenced."

In other words, Phelan concluded, Bridges was doing the communists' bidding. Perhaps more damning was a quote from the *Western Worker*, which claimed that Bridges had said, "If my views and policies coincide with those of the Communist party—as those of the [Congress of Industrial Organizations] do—I can't help that."

Bridges never really shied away from aligning himself with communist principles and even admitted that 95 percent of what the government alleged was true. He once gave a speech in Crockett, California, where press reports had him saying out loud to anyone who bothered to listen, "The industrial system under which we operate and live today is headed toward destruction and revolution, a destruction which it is bringing upon itself. In Russia, there is no such thing as competition. The workers own the tools of production. Russia has a planned economy and it is working superbly. We are trying to arrive at such a system here."

All this was too much for Phelan, who concluded, "[There is no] doubt that the Communist party throughout the movement supported, advertised and pushed the efforts of Bridges. . . . It is barely within the realm of possibility that this is all pure coincidence."

All this hand-wringing, however, went nowhere. At the deportation hearing on San Francisco Bay's Angel Island between July 10 and September 14, 1939, trial examiner Dean James M. Landis concluded—even with the help of government witnesses who were later shown to have lied about Bridges's alleged communist ties—that the evidence failed to prove that Bridges was a Communist Party member or even affiliated with the party *at the time of the proceedings,* a stipulation that was something of a loophole in the existing law. As a result, Frances Perkins, the U.S. secretary of labor, canceled the arrest warrant and dismissed the proceedings on January 8, 1940.

But the government wasn't through with Bridges. Later that year, Congress amended the Alien Registration Act so that anyone could be deported "who was at the time of entering the United States, or has been at any time thereafter, a member of, or affiliated with" an organization known to advocate the violent overthrow of the U.S. government. Dubbed the Smith Act, it gave the federal government another shot at Bridges.

A second arrest warrant went out for Bridges on February 14, 1941. It should be noted that during this time the Bridges Defense Committee, among other things, raised money for his legal fees through a recording of "Song for Bridges," by the Almanac Singers (at the time, Woody Guthrie, Pete Seeger, Lee Hays, and Millard Lampell), which sold for 50 cents.

Bridges convinced the Board of Immigration Appeals during oral arguments on November 24 that the evidence didn't actually prove he was a member of, or affiliated with, the communists. But then Attorney General Francis Biddle reviewed the evidence and reversed the board's decision. Another deportation order was entered on May 28, 1942.

The government *again* arrested Bridges. But after three years, the case finally unraveled with the help of the U.S. Supreme Court, which reversed the deportation order, based on the slim but useful enough reasoning that the INS had misconstrued "the word affiliation as used in the statute and by reason of an unfair hearing on the question of membership in the Communist Party."

Before and during this time, Bridges had petitioned for U.S. citizenship four different times, starting in New Orleans on July 13, 1921, though he had always let each declaration of intention expire. Finally, he acted on his fifth declaration, originally dated March 28, 1939, and went to the Superior Court of the State of California, San Francisco, on August 8, 1945, to petition for naturalization.

This wasn't a complicated matter, actually, but once again Bridges ran up against the issue of communism—he was required to swear on September 17, 1945, before Judge Thomas Foley that he wasn't a member of the Communist Party and that he did not advocate the violent overthrow of the U.S. government. He brought in two ILWU officials, J.R. Robertson and Henry Schmidt, to vouch for him. And with that, Bridges became an American citizen, with his Certificate of Naturalization no. 6405274.

For nearly four years, Bridges enjoyed his citizenship in relative peace. But in 1949, the INS once again collared him, along with Robertson and Schmidt, for committing perjury when they had all denied at the citizenship hearing that Bridges was a member of the Communist Party. After a five-month trial, Bridges was convicted and sentenced to five years in prison; his co-defendants each received two years.

Bridges paid bail of $25,000 to stay out of jail while he appealed. In the meantime, the government won a judgment revoking his citizenship on June 20, 1950, which Bridges also appealed the same day. Just five days later, when war with Korea broke out, the government made the strained argument that a national emergency existed and therefore the court should revoke Bridges's bail. Once again, he went to jail until August 24, when the Ninth Circuit Court of Appeals restored bail.

Perhaps in some other industry, all this would have been mere wallpaper to one's daily work, but Bridges was the longshoremen's hero, and they closely followed each intricate detail. Some three thousand San Francisco dockworkers showed their devotion by publicly demonstrating in front of the dispatch hall on September 11, 1952, most of them believing that this wasn't just a pursuit of Bridges, but a vendetta against the union itself.

Out of jail on appeal, Bridges, recognizing an opportunity to show his defiance, grabbed a microphone attached to a sound truck and, standing atop the outside steps to the hall's second floor, declared, "Nobody is worried too much about going to jail here. This is not going to scare us, and we are not going to be pushed around." He concluded, "Putting a few leaders in jail is not going to bust this union! It is not going to change the policies of this union." The next day, longshoremen from the ports of Los Angeles and Long Beach staged a similar demonstration in San Pedro.

Even some in the ship owners' organization, the Pacific Maritime Association, thought this was a phony charge. The doubters went all the way to J. Paul St. Sure, the PMA president, who quietly contributed cash to the Harry Bridges Defense Fund. Others in the PMA attended a Los Angeles fundraising dinner for the Defense Fund. Most longshoremen voluntarily paid $5.00 into the fund, for which they received a stamp (resembling a postage stamp) that went into their union books, to prove they had contributed.

Bridges's complicated saga continued until finally the U.S. Supreme Court reversed the criminal conviction for perjury and the denaturalization order on June 15, 1953, because the statute of limitations had run out. While this may have seemed like a technicality, the majority decision showed just how weary the justices were of the government's pursuit of Bridges. Justice Frank Murphy wrote, "The record in this case will stand forever as a monument to man's intolerance to man. Seldom, if ever, in the history of this nation has there been such a concentrated, relentless crusade to deport an individual simply because he dared to exercise the freedoms guaranteed to him by the Constitution."

Even after that rebuke, the feds took up the prosecution against

Bridges again in 1955 with a trial lasting from June 20 until July 22. Judge Louis E. Goodman decided that the government had not proved its case, and he dismissed the proceedings on August 2, 1955. Finally, the government stopped prosecuting Bridges.

Afterward, Bridges loved to flash the papers that vindicated him—"The court said I'm not a communist!" he boasted. And then, as if to really tweak the government, if not the employers as well, he registered himself as a Republican, or so he claimed.

Bridges died in 1990. It's still possible to find many people who knew him or who say he somehow influenced them. When union officials finally started to open up to me, I met Peter Peyton, who at the time of our first interview in 2006 was Local 63's secretary. When I asked him about The Fear, he told me, "When I met Harry Bridges for the first time, the first thing he said to me—I wasn't even in the union, I was in college, I was taking my grandfather to an event—and he comes up to me and says, 'Good to meet you, Pete. Good to meet you. Just remember: the employer's always wrong.'"

SEVEN

The Employers

THE BACKLOG, 2004

Jim McKenna seems like a decent fellow. From what I understand through secondhand sources, Jim Spinosa, the ILWU international president in 2004, isn't always so thrilled with him, but that's to be expected. An ILWU leader can go only so far in praising the president and CEO of the Pacific Maritime Association, unless it's at the guy's funeral.

As for McKenna, he chooses his words slowly, carefully, whenever he discusses his labor counterpart, preferring mild grumbles over the tirades the ILWU pours out whenever there's a spat between the two. His obvious restraint not only suggests stronger feelings within but also hints that there's more he could say to me—though he won't, because diplomacy prevails. Just the same, he's the kind of guy who won't back away from the kinds of squabbles, some impassioned, some trivial, that go on between Spinosa and himself and, by extension, between labor and employers. Most of the arguments remain fairly private, but when I first meet McKenna in mid-2004, the carping between the two sides is getting very, very public.

That's because, in one of those few enlightening moments when the entire country glimpses how its imports get from Asia to store shelves, incoming cargo is overloading the Port of Los Angeles. The piers are so crammed tight with ships, dozens more are anchored outside the harbor, waiting days for an available pier. The disruption in the usual smooth movement of cargo means that goods aren't reaching stores in time to replace sold items. Factories, dependent on parts arriving just when they're needed, are sweating over their ability to continue production. Most dramatically, fruits and vegetables, as well as other fresh foods, are rotting on some ships rather than being rushed to grocery stores. In the public's perception, both the PMA and the ILWU are partly to blame.

The issue this time is insufficient labor power. The casual hiring hall, which fills the leftover jobs after the ILWU dispatch hall has exhausted its pool of registered union workers, can't keep up with the demand. The number of workers signed up at the casual hall has been reduced through attrition from 6,500 casuals in 2000 to just 3,700, and the rolls have yet to be replenished. McKenna is claiming a certain level of surprise over the situation and tells anyone who will listen that neither side saw this coming.

However, the union's spokesperson at the time, Steve Stallone, tells me Local 13's president, Dave Arian, asked the PMA back in February, during a monthly labor relations committee meeting, to promote 2,000 current casuals to registered longshoreman status—making them dues-paying union members—and to bring in 5,000 new casuals. Stallone implies that the PMA choked on the numbers. After all, the union wanted a more than 50-percent increase in the local workforce. They had already added about 800 registered longshoremen a year before.

When I mention that McKenna says he never heard about the request, Stallone sounds almost resentful: "They're on the record, man," he insists. "There are minutes." Over the next several months, I try to get Stallone to show me those minutes, but he never does. The PMA is equally uncooperative. Five years later, I'm finally able to interview Arian, and he confirms the request.

McKenna, though he had just taken the job a few months before, in March 2004, knows the drill. After nearly thirty years in the shipping business dealing with every industry union, McKenna is well acquainted with the delicate equation that each side tries to work to its favor. The employers want fewer and fewer employees: doing more with less, moving the cargo out faster and cleaner, without having to hire so many people. Labor costs too much, they say. The union, on the other hand, asks for a larger workforce. This potentially puts more people to work and gives the union greater strength in numbers in times of labor disputes; it would also bring in more money to the union's bank account through monthly dues. No matter who's looking at it, as far as McKenna is concerned, the number of longshoremen at the docks is a compromise that makes no one happy.

He tells me that the PMA has based its workforce decisions on such trade reports as PIERS (Port Import Export Reporting Service), an industry database, which the year before had predicted that imports to the West Coast would remain healthy but hardly spectacular. The union eyeballed a different statistic: cargo in Los Angeles and Long Beach had increased 13 percent in 2003 over 2002, setting a pace of double-digit increases for years to come. Screw the outside experts, they say, we're here at ground level, and it's getting busy.

The PMA was also relying on the general principle that shipping, like most businesses, is tied to seasonal shifts in demand. In the first quarter, for instance, work traditionally slows at the ports. Retailers don't import as much after the holidays—they don't need the inventory. Cargo volumes don't usually peak until the summer, fall, and early winter. Exports also dip for many of the same reasons. In 2004, however, the first quarter ended (when the ILWU requested more registered longshoremen and casuals) with volume still higher than usual; and by May, the Los Angeles/Long Beach port complex is already experiencing spot shortages of longshoremen. McKenna admits during our interviews that he and the PMA had slipped up on predicting the cargo tsunami. But when he tries to get the union to join in the mea culpa, Spinosa steps back, his finger pointing to the guys in the suits.

The railroads can't keep up, either, because of their own labor short-ages. Like the PMA, Union Pacific fails to anticipate the volume of cargo traffic. It later announces plans to hire 5,000 employees in the Southwest, add 700 locomotives and 6,500 freight cars by year's end, and lay new track worth about $225 million. But plans that are still on paper or under construction hardly help as the summer approaches. Soon, containers destined for locations outside Southern California are stack-ing up at the terminals with no trains to take them away. The conges-tion and its attendant inefficiency drop production by 9 percent. This also makes it harder for truck drivers to pick up containers for local distribution, and they sit for hours just waiting to get a single container.

Information technology allowed in the 2002 labor contract is sup-posed to be helping. One of the bottlenecks in the shipping industry—and especially at a place as busy as the Port of Los Angeles—is the inability to quickly and efficiently track cargo. For goods destined for the local market, a container is delivered to a spot in the terminal where it waits for a truck to take it out of the port and usually to a nearby warehouse. But the terminal location has too often been buried in paperwork, which is handled by union clerks. The 2002 contract gave the employers the right to install such devices as character readers to record container numbers as the cargo comes off the ship—eliminating clerk positions but allowing the information to be easily retrieved by a few quick keystrokes on a computer. But so far the new systems haven't been widely implemented. Plus, according to Stallone, who takes plea-sure in telling me this, there have been occasional snags in getting the new electronics to work consistently.

As if to prove how important this new technology is, the truck drivers, frustrated with sitting at the port for as long as seven hours for just one load, begin refusing container jobs. And who can blame them? They are nonunion and are paid for each container they deliver, which means they're now losing money on port jobs. After paying for their overhead—truck lease, insurance, gas, registration, and maintenance—one container barely pays for lunch. Stephanie Williams, senior vice president of the California Trucking Association, estimates that between 10 and 20 percent of the 12,000 truck operators are going elsewhere for work.

After twice talking about this cargo calamity on the phone, McKenna and I finally sit down in the PMA's San Francisco offices, separated by a desk. He has an average-size office—hardly an executive suite and, as I learn later, smaller than Spinosa's office—made somber and serious by a preponderance of walnut and mahogany furniture and walls. With short-cropped, reddish-sandy hair and a tall, square body that makes him look a little like a longshoreman, he talks with a faux frankness that belies his occasional evasiveness. It's not that he dodges my questions; it's that he sometimes declares by his tone that he just won't answer them. It makes for an edgy conversation.

As the PMA head guy, McKenna represents the employers at all West Coast ports—mainly the stevedore companies, which the shipping lines hire to load and unload their ships, but also the cargo carriers and terminal operators—in all labor matters. He talks with Spinosa on a nearly daily basis so the individual companies don't have to. He prepares for the next contract negotiations while the shipping lines—who are also PMA members—build bigger ships to keep up with the huge demand for Asian imports. And he's supposed to watch the trends so they'll always have enough labor to unload or load the ships.

Before McKenna came to the PMA, his predecessor, Joe Miniace, was discussing huge cargo increases at the Los Angeles/Long Beach port complex. The 2003 PMA annual report—the last under Miniace as president and CEO—cited predictions that cargo volume would double all along the West Coast in just twenty years. And before that, in a May 23, 2001, statement before a congressional subcommittee, Miniace grimly announced that the two ports did "not have much, if any, available land remaining to handle this growth."

THE NEVER-ENDING SEASON

McKenna began his career dealing with unions. In 1977, only three months after his graduation from Chico State University in California, a friend referred him to Sea-Land, an international shipper hiring at the time. He had never thought of working in the shipping industry before, but it offered a job related to his business degree (at a time when other graduates were waiting tables), so he took it. Sea-Land sent him straight to the docks in Oakland, California, where he became a superintendent. For the next few years, he spent his days out there on the waterfront in the open air, supervising longshoremen, watching ships unload and load as they had for centuries. Imports, exports. Sometimes you were busy, sometimes you weren't. It had become the basic rhythm of life for him.

Harry Bridges had just retired that year, and McKenna found the rank and file as well as the ILWU leaders far more amiable than they would be in 2004. It seemed to him that people on both sides were sensible and maintained their credibility. Oh, sure, there were still shouting matches across the table during contract negotiations, and there would always be guys with long memories for brief insults, but on the whole people just seemed more reasonable then.

After ten years of working his way through the corporation, McKenna was sent off to run Sea-Land's operation in Taipei. From there, he went back to California and then to Anchorage, Alaska; Charlotte, North Carolina; Cork, Ireland; Hong Kong; and Dallas, Texas. At one point, the company paid for his MBA education from the University of Tennessee. He loved the work, the way the industry was always evolving. Indeed, he helped shape that change. He could actually touch it, in a way, watching new ships dwarfing the old ones, the already huge cranes turning into giant praying mantises dangling over the ships, the speed of operations ever increasing to meet demand.

And of course there was the challenge of working with the labor groups. He would get to know the leaders, how they reacted to certain issues. They got to know him. They had a business relationship centered on getting things done, advancing each other's interests while always concerned that their actions wouldn't hurt the industry, all of which made perfect sense. If one side went too far, they could poison the market and shippers would go elsewhere. No matter how strident Harry Bridges could be, he always kept that overriding fact in mind.

McKenna considered himself a fair but firm person, which meant he didn't take crap. If the two sides couldn't come to an agreement on some issue, he wouldn't hesitate to take the matter through the grievance procedure, even if that meant going past the arbitrator to the courts. He didn't want to be confrontational, but he was unlikely to back down.

In 1999, the Danish shipping company Maersk bought McKenna's employer, Sea-Land. However, by law, Sea-Land's domestic arm couldn't be owned by a foreign entity, and it was sold to Horizon Lines, with McKenna as its chief executive officer. Horizon became CSX and was then sold to Carlisle. At this point, members of the PMA board approached McKenna about a chief operating officer position. He first turned them down. But after the sale, Carlisle changed in ways he wasn't comfortable with, so he returned to the PMA and asked whether the position was still open. With his labor-management experience, they quickly made him senior vice president and chief operating officer. When Miniace left in 2004, McKenna was promoted to president and CEO.

Seemingly hardwired to concentrate on efficiency, McKenna tells me he blames the current cargo backup on delays in implementing the new technology allowed in the 2002 contract. After all, section 15.1 of the contract stated in one run-on sentence choked with legalese:

> There shall be no interference by the Union with the Employers' right to operate efficiently and to change methods of work and to utilize labor-saving devices and to direct the work through employers representatives while explicitly observing the provisions and conditions of this Contract Document protecting the safety and welfare of the employees and avoiding speedup: "Speedup" refers to an onerous workload on the individual worker; it shall not be construed to refer to increased production resulting from more efficient utilization and organization of the work force, introduction of labor-saving devices, or removal of work restrictions.

For McKenna, this is the defining paragraph of a new age of cargo handling, even if its theme originally came from the 1960 Mechanization and Modernization Agreement that first allowed containerization. As far as he's concerned, the 2002 contract is the new M&M Agreement, and it makes clear the employers' ability, or right, to install optical character readers to record container numbers or any other device to make the operation more efficient. It means, as he puts it, "the ability to free-flow information." Technology is the new holy grail.

However, before a single OCR can be installed at a terminal, the employers must notify the union in writing—according to the contract's section 10.51—and follow a procedure outlined in the contract. The Joint Port Labor Relations Committee in the port where the new equipment is being installed is required to meet "promptly" to hear whether or not the union agrees with the changes. If the union objects for reasons of safety or because the change is "onerous," a grievance can be filed and heard by an arbitrator. The union figures this is only fair and doesn't slow the operation unnecessarily. But union leaders do complain that they don't always get the opportunity to air their opinion, accusing the employers of charging ahead with new equipment before going through the framework of the contract.

Despite all the potential for technology-enabled efficiency, the ships keep backing up. By the July 4th weekend of 2004, labor shortages are constant, and McKenna and Spinosa are screaming at each other. At one point, Spinosa is in Singapore on a union trip, and he's on the phone at two o'clock in the morning listening to McKenna yell at him to get going on promoting casuals to registered union status as well as hiring more casuals. Spinosa barks back that he had raised this issue the month before, and the PMA hadn't acted.

No one could have foreseen the backup, McKenna keeps arguing. For all its we-told-you-so attitude, he claims that the union stalled his ability to move ahead with hiring more people, something that the contract doesn't allow him to do unilaterally. Nor is this just a matter of the two presidents meeting in an office and hashing out the details. Instead, staff representatives for each group sit on opposite sides of one table or another, and they discuss, debate, and argue. The PMA and the ILWU meet some fifteen times before they devise a means to bring enough people into the workforce. McKenna eventually tells me that new long-shoremen could have been hired a month sooner than they were if the union hadn't nitpicked all the details and asked for more people than the PMA thought they needed.

By the end of July, the PMA and the ILWU finally work out a deal and announce their decision: a lottery for 3,000 casual jobs and the pro-motion of 1,750 casuals to B registrants (that is, union members). The word gets out fast, and in less than three weeks, 300,000 people submit applications. It's pretty clear why people want longshore jobs—the high pay. It might be the only reason they apply. Few probably consider how hard or dangerous the job is; instead, they see dollar signs. The aver-age fully registered longshoreman in 2004 earned more than $89,000 a year working full time, and the highest-paid 72 percent saw more than $102,000. And then, as if that isn't enough to make a 7-11 clerk salivate, the top fifth with the most hours, which typically include overtime, are paid an average of $141,000 and change. Thanks to Harry Bridges and other union militants who came before them, registered longshoremen also earn free health benefits, a generous pension, and an employer-sponsored 401(k) plan. In other industries, some execs pay for their own dental, and here even the guys lashing containers get their fillings for nothing.

So the applications—postcards, really—pour in, so many that they fill a metal bin the size of a small car, which had been specially built by union welders. The applications even come from countries as far away as Serbia, Australia, and Singapore. McKenna tells a *Los Angeles Times* reporter, perhaps a little disingenuously, that he had expected 25,000 to 30,000 applications, but nothing this huge. Half of the cards—marked as such—come from people who have been given applications by long-shoremen. These are separated out so that the mathematics of chance will favor them over the general public: anyone referred by a longshoreman has fifty-fifty odds of being chosen, while the odds for everyone else are one in a thousand. The rationale, wholeheartedly agreed to by both the PMA and the ILWU, is that anyone who knows a longshoreman undoubtedly also understands what the work is truly like. Yeah, we get paid well, they've been told, but look what you have to do to earn it.

As Local 13's Dave Arian tells an NPR reporter on the day of the lottery, with a little bravado leaking out, "Every day we have major injuries, death. A person was killed yesterday on the waterfront. We probably have one to ten deaths a year on the waterfront. On any given day, ten to fifteen percent of our membership is out on an injury. It's like going to war. It's sort of like a war zone when you work on the waterfront." (In perusing the statistics, I was unable to find a recent year in which as many as ten people were killed on the job, however.)

The drawing takes place on August 19 in the Port of Los Angeles administration building and lasts seven hours. McKenna acts as the lottery emcee, watching arbitrator Jan Holmes step into the large mesh container where the general public cards are kept and scoop up an armful of cards, walking over the stack as if trampling on the hopes of so many of those looking for a waterfront job. Several dozen union and shipping company employees sort the cards before putting them into counting machines. By mid-morning, 5,000 are sorted. Altogether, arbitrators select 9,000 cards and mix them in with an equal number of cards sent by those affiliated with union members and casuals. From this combined pool of about 18,000 cards, 3,000 are randomly drawn.

As this process has unfolded over the past weeks, the backlog of ships has gotten even worse. Through August, nearly 8.5 million cargo containers move through the Los Angeles and Long Beach ports, making them busier than the next five U.S. ports combined—a 10.4 percent increase over the same period the year before. By September, there are as many as eighty-three vessels waiting to be unloaded—a flotilla larger than the navy of most countries. McKenna can hardly believe the numbers: volume is up 12 percent, which requires a 23-percent increase in labor. There is no such thing as a slow season anymore. The cargo just keeps coming.

Big retailers like Costco and Walmart compensate for the delays by adding extra stock to each shipment instead of spreading their imports over several months. And then the diversions begin. About twenty-four ships, while still at sea, take a hard left to Oakland or Seattle, while a few even sail south to Manzanillo, a small Mexican port. Other ports to the east form alliances to lure away some of the ships, hoping to secure the business for good once the crisis inevitably ends. The Panama Canal Authority, the ports of New York and New Jersey, Norfolk, Savannah, Charleston, Miami, New Orleans, and Houston all see a chance to prove that the Port of Los Angeles has gotten just too big and that their smaller, friendlier ports are there to help.

On October 11, the backlog is so bad that ninety-four ships are waiting to be unloaded. Diversions increase, now totaling forty ships since the trouble began. More trucks hit the highways, taking cargo from Oakland, San Francisco, and Seattle, originally destined for Southern California, down to Los Angeles, while trains at the other ports haul containers east just as they would from the Los Angeles and Long Beach ports. Another result of the logjam is that empty containers, usually returned to Asia to be refilled, are delayed.

The backlog consumes every moment McKenna spends at the office. He fields phone calls from local government officials anxious over the economic impact of so many containers stacking up at the port instead of going to their intended customers. Major retailers waiting for their shipments beat up federal officials over the delays, and they in turn lecture McKenna on how the situation affects national commerce. Ship owners grill him on when the new hires will finally be on the docks to relieve the congestion. He devotes an entire day in October to press interviews, repeating the same thing over and over: we had no idea this was coming, and we're doing everything we can to fix it. This is in fact the first time I talk with him, and his tone isn't defensive but is a little tired. Without explicitly saying so, his message is clear: we (the PMA *and* the union) screwed up.

And then, finally, in late October, the new casuals, fresh from training, start showing up on the docks. But the union claims that one in four are quitting because the work is too tough, some after only a day on the job. McKenna sees this as a slight exaggeration. Yes, some 25 percent drop out, but he includes in this statistic the many who fail to pass all the tests required to start the job, including drug and alcohol screening as well as lashing and UTR (utility tractor rig) tests. Spinosa calls on the PMA to agree to the promotion of another thousand casuals to the registered workforce. Just another ploy to pad the union's membership, the PMA quips to the *Los Angeles Times*.

By November, the workforce has increased by 35 percent. On November 11, McKenna tells me the backlog is largely over, with only about three ships still anchored in the harbor waiting to be unloaded. He's relieved, but to his mind this is just the beginning. They need to beef up their efficiency through technology, or this will happen again. At this point, the PMA dips into a reserve of 12,000 to 14,000 applicant cards and holds another lottery, which eventually brings the total workforce, casual and registered, at the Los Angeles and Long Beach ports to 15,000, a 50-percent increase.

And that's about what Dave Arian had originally asked for the previous February.

THE BIG TABLE, 2008

The big table is a private stage where the PMA and the ILWU negotiate labor contracts for the West Coast ports. The negotiations are a combination of tedium and drama, witnessed by an audience of perhaps thirty or forty people. In the case of the 2008 contract negotiations, Jim McKenna sat on one side of the 30-foot table, close to dead center, and the ILWU's international president, Robert (Big Bob) McEllrath, faced him from the opposite side. Flanking both of them were negotiating committee members, and behind them, sitting along the wall, were mostly silent invited parties, including the occasional local union leader who might have asked to peek in on the proceedings.

The meetings can last all day if the two negotiators are making progress, that is, constructively grinding through one issue or another, both presenting their cases, occasionally over and over, until each finds just where the other will give a little. On more complicated disputes, some of the more esoteric details are hashed out in separate committee rooms at much smaller tables by people who specialize in such minutiae.

During the six-month-long process, the separate sides also meet among themselves, continually developing strategy as well as generally bitching about the other side's perceived recalcitrance. There are, in fact, two big tables, one at each side's headquarters, and the PMA and the ILWU alternate between the two. Despite the occasional hostility that goes on during negotiations, there's an unwritten rule that when the visiting side wants to meet privately, they will get the big table for that conference while the hosts adjourn to a smaller room. This kind of quaint civility is rarely, if ever, reported. Instead, we hear how one side decides it's not going to back down and the other resorts to shouting in response.

In preparation for the talks, McEllrath and his committee developed a list of so-called demands, a rather severe term given that this is merely a wish list of contract changes suggested by the rank and file or local leadership during a pre-negotiations caucus held in San Francisco in late January. McKenna did the same thing, but without the caucus. Over about three years, he and his staff explored what they believed needed to be changed. They consulted PMA subcommittees from the different ports as well as the PMA board of directors. Then a coast steering committee took all the PMA proposals and whittled them down to the items they deemed most important.

In honesty, neither McKenna nor McEllrath expected the other side to accept *all* their proposals, but both had priorities that they fought for with varying degrees of success. In the 2008 negotiations, the PMA's top priority was to control the cost of healthcare by more clearly defining who could be covered under the longshoremen's health plan. The PMA had decided that, in exchange, they would be willing to extend the union's jurisdiction over future maintenance workers at the docks. At the time, those who repaired vehicles, dock facilities, and so on were either ILWU workers or members of the International Association of Machinists. The PMA conceded language that gave the ILWU jurisdiction over maintenance at any future facilities. As McKenna told me the following year, "We got some of the things we wanted. You never get everything you want."

What the two sides did during their talks, which lasted from March 17 to July 28 in 2008, affected just about everything that happens at all twenty-nine West Coast ports. The longshoremen may say they're lords of the docks, but what really controls their world is the contract. And however boring the topics of contract negotiations might be to the outside world—and, trust me, reading the minutes from these affairs can be a tremendous snorefest—the outside world feels the impact, in small or large ways, of what happens at the big table.

The most significant example of this impact dates back to the 2002 negotiations between the PMA's Joe Miniace and the ILWU's Jim Spinosa. The talks did not go well. Miniace had made it clear for months—no, years—before the April 2002 launch of the talks that the employers were the rightful lords of the docks and that he wasn't about to be pushed around by Spinosa. This, among other statements that reflected Miniace's belief that the union was trying to slow the introduction of technological improvement, peeved Spinosa enough that he decided to push through increases to healthcare coverage, pensions, and pay largely without compromise; if Miniace wanted greater efficiency, which would eliminate a great many clerk jobs, the employers would pay dearly.

Contract negotiations typically begin several months before the previous contract expires; in this case, the 1996 document ended on July 1, 2002. By that date, after three months of negotiations, Miniace and

Spinosa had agreed to little, so they decided to extend the contract on a day-by-day basis. The looming threat was always that, if for some reason the PMA or the ILWU refused to renew on a particular day, the union was free to call a strike vote (which is a complicated process and doesn't happen right away).

This made for a lot of tension, and eventually the stubborn Spinosa showed his anger over what he perceived as Miniace's refusal to compromise and called for a one-day slowdown at the ports. In retaliation, Miniace threatened to lock out the longshoremen if they repeated what he called a "strike with pay." The union went back to the job and again worked at a glacial pace. The PMA shut down the ports and locked out the workers.

It should be noted that every longshoreman I talked with about the slowdown maintained they didn't deliberately decrease production but merely paid more attention to safety regulations. As Peter Peyton, who acted as an occasional ILWU spokesperson during the talks, puts it, "We have always been a production union. Production means you push the limits on moving things, meaning you take safety to its edge. You push the speed limits to their edge. Guys are racing everywhere. When you say work by the rules, it's a little different than saying you slowed down. It's semantics, I understand. . . . Slowing down is a hardship. To me, it would be sabotage going beyond that, and we didn't do that. We worked by the rules."

However, Spinosa doesn't parse his words quite so carefully, calling the slowdown a way to "turn up the heat." He added, "[Miniace] knew it was coming. That was our tactic, one we did. He was threatening to shut us down. It wasn't going to be something where we were intimidated, afraid of that."

The lockout lasted a total of ten days, during which no cargo entered or left the West Coast ports (the one exception was goods headed for Hawaii, which depends on shipping for most of its food), costing the U.S. economy an estimated $10 to $15 billion. Food rotted on ships. Factory orders arrived late. And then there were the smaller losses:

souvenir items ordered for the World Series, for instance, didn't show up until after the games had been played. Every corner of the United States learned firsthand just how important the West Coast ports were, especially the biggest one, Los Angeles.

With neither side giving in, the Bush administration hauled out the Taft-Hartley Act, which mandates that workers go back to work and sends in a federal mediator to help both sides iron out their disagreements during an eighty-day "cooling off period." The two sides finally signed the contract just before Thanksgiving but not without first traumatizing the country for a few weeks.

In 2008, McKenna and McEllrath weren't about to repeat the 2002 confrontation (McEllrath had been the ILWU vice president during that time). Given the weak state of the economy in 2008, a strike or lockout would have drawn little sympathy from anyone. Many shippers—who were just beginning to forget the heavy losses they had suffered during the 2002 lockout—would have considered taking their business to other, theoretically more reliable ports in Mexico or Canada, on the Gulf Coast, or farther east, bypassing the West Coast altogether. The union could have lost thousands of jobs. And so, with far less drama this time around, the two sides quietly—and with such privacy the nation barely even noticed—settled on a contract that will last until July 1, 2014.

That's not to say there weren't a few scuffles along the way to the settlement. On May 1, 2008, while negotiations were still in progress, thousands of ILWU members along the West Coast took the day off and set up picket lines protesting the Iraq war (while members of Local 13, which includes longshore workers from both Los Angeles and Long Beach, didn't show up for work, they refrained from demonstrating at the port). This was also meant as a show of unity; as McEllrath put it in the ILWU's newspaper, the *Dispatcher,* in a "President's Message" summarizing the contract negotiations, "it sent a powerful message to the employers that we were united and willing to take action to back up our beliefs." In other words, bad economy or not, the strike threat remained.

Along the same lines, the ILWU had refused to extend the contract after July 1, which meant they would have been able to hit the bricks if the union membership voted to do so. "Obviously, it gives the union more leverage if they don't sign an extension," McKenna says. "Whether they take advantage of that, it's up for discussion at all times. But you really have an open contract, that says you don't have a grievance procedure in place, arbitrators aren't in place—so what happens, happens. Now certainly there's a lot of public scrutiny, a lot of media scrutiny on what's taking place, so nothing got absolutely out of hand. But certainly slowdowns were experienced during the twenty-eight days that the contract had not been resolved. They weren't to the same degree that happened in 2002, where you saw significant decreases. They were twelve, fifteen percent, and I think they were teed up as, 'We're not going to work continuously, we're going to take our breaks.' So operations were down for the fifteen-minute break, which really meant about a half hour by the time the guys got to the coffee room, you know, out of the coffee room and back on the job. So it had an impact on operations. There wasn't a mechanism to say [the employers] have the right to have continuous operations, now go back to work. So it's, again, a ploy used by unions in negotiations to leverage employers to reach an agreement."

As McEllrath said, "This and other strategies were enough to push us across the finish line and get a good agreement—without provoking a lock-out or federal intervention."

"When you go into contract discussions," McKenna says, "both sides know what they have to come out with—what they would like to come out with and what they have to come out with. And I think we worked through the process. I think there was—again, business-like dialogue. I think everybody conducted themselves in a reasonable manner. There wasn't pounding on desks, jumping on tables. Very candid discussions. And certainly we don't see eye to eye on a number of issues. I think at the end of the day both sides could look at each other and say what they needed, and you had a contract."

EIGHT

The Importer

A wine tasting is supposed to be a cultured affair, with dainty pours of selected vintages barely puddling the bottom of your glass. The host, usually a vendor looking for future customers, lovingly describes the vineyard—its grapes, soils, age—to establish the wine's quality lineage while you swirl the liquid and hold it to the light to see how it drains down the sides of the glass. The host tells you what flavors to anticipate just before you swish the wine over your palate, hoping that your taste buds will actually detect the peach undertones. And if you really know what you're doing, you spit out the wine after tasting.

Jeremy Wilkinson's life is a constant string of wine tastings. At the moment, in May of 2006, his Great Wines International has seven tables set up end to end among the 134 wine sellers at a massive wine tasting in the Paris Las Vegas Resort and Casino ballroom. His 60-foot bit of enologic heaven cuts a swath around the globe from South Africa to Austria to Spain to Australia. This annual event, called UNLVino, after its sponsor, the University of Nevada, Las Vegas, has been grinding on for two hours, and the cultural pretensions are draining faster than the Austrian wines he's serving. People swallow here, and they've been swallowing since 3:00 P.M.

Wilkinson towers over most of the people in the room, a tall explosion of enthusiasm whose grandiosity seems sincere, though a little too energetic for this crowd. He wears a loose-fitting, short-sleeve shirt with martini glasses and other alcohol accessories printed all over it. "It's my party shirt," he tells a woman who asks. "I got it from Nordstrom's."

I'm standing beside Wilkinson because I want to know what it's like for a small importer to run a business when the ILWU and the PMA squabble for weeks over workforce size or other issues while the ship on which his product sits is anchored outside the Port of Los Angeles with nowhere to go. In such situations, Target and Walmart manage to take care of themselves. But small companies like Great Wines can get socked in the gut when the port they depend on is clogged to the point of chaos.

That conversation is going to take awhile. Right now, I'm watching the patrons at the tasting, the people who might understand wine enough to pick up an import or two. Compared to the sweaty sampling of t-shirted middle America on the streets outside, this crowd is reasonably well dressed. The women drift about in airy, desert-elegant dresses with heels. The men, with their executive guts poking out under polo shirts, wear the bored looks of people who would prefer to sit down with a *full* glass and do some serious imbibing. Hey, they paid $58 a head and all they're getting are sips of wine and a noisy rock band. Screw culture.

Wilkinson realizes that, for all the edifying wine rap he throws at these people, it's hard to tell what good it does. Part marketing, part education, a wine tasting helps plant the seeds of desire for a particular brand. In this case, however, nothing is for sale; patrons must seek out that magic bottle later, at a retail outlet. In fact, because Wilkinson imports the wine, he's prohibited by law from retail selling. So he peddles his libations to stores or restaurants, who add their often huge markups, and the only way he can gauge whether or not the general public is willing to explore something besides that comfortable Napa Valley number they've been drinking for years is if the orders for his more esoteric brands continue to rise, as they've been doing lately.

Just the same, even with four assistants pouring samples, he rarely

Importer Jeremy Wilkinson shows off a wine bottle at the 2006 UNLVino event in Las Vegas.

exits the room, leaving only to take a bathroom break. I ask him if he conducts market research on the other vendors while he's here. "I can do that any time," he snorts. "If I leave my spot, I could miss the food and beverage director of the Bellagio."

"I've been living on expenses," he admits to me, pausing between tasters as we stand behind the Austrian wines; he draws only enough money to pay his family's rent and food bills. "But, you know, I have a passion. I'm building the world's best portfolio of wine." He turns away from the crowd and mentions to me in a conspiratorial tone that he's working on a deal with a megabucks financier that could catapult Great Wines to $100 million sales in a mere three years. (A few months later, he's still working on the deal and isn't about to concede that it might be anything but on its way to completion.)

In his late forties, Wilkinson has had several careers up to this point, but this is perhaps the only one that began, in a way, when he was still a boy. Growing up in Durban, South Africa's third largest city, he had

Wilkinson pours a sample of imported wine at the UNLVino event.

once visited the nearly three-hundred-year-old Lanzerac vineyards in the Stellenbosch region, the country's Napa Valley. Apparently, no one saw anything wrong with an eight-year-old participating in a wine tasting as long as it was properly conducted with a healthy swish in the mouth before spitting out the sample. It's not that the moment became an enologic epiphany, but when children get to enter the adult world in such a way, the experience sticks with them.

At the time, however, the country's hated apartheid system got in the way of further explorations. In the 1950s, Wilkinson's father, an attorney, had helped to found an organization that opposed the government's racial policies and advocated universal suffrage. When he was banned from speaking in public, and it became clear that he risked jail, the family packed up for Barcelona, Spain, in 1968 and then finally ended up in Australia when young Jeremy was thirteen.

Soon Jeremy was shipped off to Bath, England, and a monastery boarding school. From there, he went to the London School of Business and became a chartered accountant. He got a job at Bank of America's London office and learned how to work with money and contracts, two handy skills for importers. He moved to San Francisco, where he first fell in love with America and then with the world of extreme risk known as venture capital, which requires someone both overly self-confident and obsessively optimistic who can pursue big payoffs while risking colossal failure. At the end of the 1980s, when the economy took a dive and risks indeed turned to busts, Wilkinson did the one thing that could be considered even riskier than venture capital investments—moviemaking. Let's just say this didn't go so well, either.

"Maybe I'm unemployable," Wilkinson tells me in his San Pedro office in a jovial tone that makes it sound like a virtue. "I love the challenge of creating things. When I was young, if anyone ever told me that something was impossible, I would try and achieve that. So I always liked to push myself in new directions."

Fortunately, near the end of his three-year Hollywood phase, he remembered visiting those Lanzerac vineyards. By then, trade sanctions against the new South Africa, finally free of the apartheid system, had been lifted. So he contacted several vineyards to ask whether anyone represented them in the United States, and the answer was always no. Wilkinson figured he knew a few things about wine, and he saw it as a product with the kind of proven appeal that made moviemaking seem like the crapshoot it was. And he had another thing going for him: he could approach the South African vineyards as someone who had been born in the country and who drank the product. He told Lanzerac he had visited the vineyards as a child. As Wilkinson puts it, "They said, 'You've got the passion, and you also talk like us, so you can go and sell the wine.'" Just like that. So he created Great Wines International in April 1999.

He discovered that importing is in equal measures about personal relationships and bureaucracies. This towering, outgoing man with the kind of can-do confidence to which everyone responds nailed the relationship part with ease. Government regulations took a little longer. There was the matter of labels. The U.S. Food and Drug Administration had to inspect the labels that would be going on the bottles to make sure they contained all the information legislators deemed important for American drinkers to see. And once those labels were on file, the only pieces of information that could be altered without going through the whole FDA approval process again were the alcohol content (which changes from vintage to vintage) and the UPC bar code. In addition, each U.S. state has a unique set of arcane laws governing how alcohol can be brought across its boundaries and thus requires separate arrangements with wholesalers in that state.

After signing up four South African vineyards and dealing with the government regulations, Wilkinson began taking samples to restaurants and hotels to determine how much they might buy. He then found investors to pay for his first wine order. When I ask if he was worried at the time about his prospects, he says, "I've got three containers on the ocean, and I figured I'd either sell them or have a party. And I was hoping I would sell." This is as close as the man gets to admitting anxiety of any sort.

Wilkinson has two offices, one at home in a converted den and another in a loftlike former department store in San Pedro. His day starts at 4:30 A.M. when he gets up to call or e-mail the vineyards and wineries in South Africa and Europe before their staff goes home. He does this either with a cup of coffee in his home office or at a laptop while on the road, where he spends much of his time going to wine tastings, promoting his product to retailers, and taking the occasional trip to a foreign vineyard. In the evenings, he's once again on the horn to Bethany Wines, his Australian supplier.

The unique logistics involved with wine imports are a major concern for him. Many companies order to fill inventory "just in time" so that the items arrive at the last minute and therefore don't take up costly warehouse space. But Wilkinson's wine needs are handled at the speed of a nineteenth-century Sears, Roebuck mail order. Given the mountain of paperwork that must be completed both in the exporter's country and for U.S. Customs, as well as the often slow shipping schedules, Wilkinson must typically wait two or more months from the time he places an order until the arrival of his next shipment of wine.

Once Wilkinson decides on an order—he is the only one among his small staff who makes that decision—he e-mails it to the vineyard. Specifying the details of an order requires a logistical balancing act: he must order enough cases to fill one, two, or three 20-foot containers while maximizing space and minimizing shipping costs per bottle. A typical container runs about $3,000 in shipping charges alone. In the beginning, he once tried to shave freight costs by stuffing his wine in one 40-foot container rather than two 20-footers. It made sense—just take that one box off the ship, throw it on a truck, and you've saved a lot of overhead. Not exactly. Seems the 40-foot container of wine was so heavy that it exceeded the 80,000-pound highway weight limit for commercial trucks. He had to hire a crew to unload the larger container and split the wine between two smaller boxes. (I'm told later by a trucking company that this happens to a lot to greenhorn importers.)

For its part, once the supplier receives Wilkinson's order, it prints up the FDA pre-approved labels and slaps those on the bottles. This usually takes about two weeks. During the same period, the supplier has to go to its own government for certificates of analysis, attesting to the wine's quality. After those are obtained, another two or three weeks could be spent just waiting for an available ship to take the containers. And once the cargo is loaded, the ship may well be at sea for another three weeks.

The lag time between placing an order and the wine's arrival doesn't give Wilkinson much time to decipher, let alone satisfy, new trends in a timely fashion. Will the spike in chardonnay sales continue, or will sales unexpectedly slump just when the warehouse has hundreds of cases? Does anybody know if pinot noir will leave the shelves or not? How can he get people to experiment a little more and pick up a bottle of shiraz? Plus, the vineyards may have their own ideas, pushing one varietal over another because the vintage is a good one or they have surplus stock. More important, decisions about what wine to order and how much aren't entirely a function of pre-orders or even an inventory management system that determines what to buy based on previous sales or demand, as if wine were soap or dish towels. It's all about public taste and what the wine drinkers believe will make for a good glass.

For Wilkinson, selling focuses on educating wine drinkers more than anything else. Although the United States imports about five times as much wine as it exports, making it the world's third largest wine importer, it is nevertheless true that about two out of every three wine bottles sold in the United States come from California. That brings us to Wilkinson's main concern as an importer—getting people to toss the Gallo for a good ol' glass of, uh, Landskroon. American wine drinkers may understand how to pair wines with food for the best effect, or they may know only the name Beringer or Mondavi and simply go with the brand. An Austrian wine, for all its quality and value, might seem so exotic or, ahem, foreign, to some customers that they'll hesitate to drop a twenty-dollar bill and risk a bad experience.

"I call myself sometimes the Wine Doctor because I ask for the symptoms and then prescribe the medicine," Wilkinson tells me on another day, sitting on the back patio of his Rancho Palos Verdes home. That means he tries to draw out his tasters' wine preferences, which are often no more complicated than red or white.

"They say, 'I like chardonnay,' or 'I like cabernet.' And then I say, 'How about a verdelho or a shiraz?' It's amazing how many people haven't traveled around the world in the way of wine. Shiraz is a very popular grape. A lot of people still stick to what they know, and this is why these tastings are so educational."

Not a lot of people even knew South Africa made wine, but once they tried the stuff at dinners and wine tastings, Wilkinson quickly built a clientele on the West Coast. He traveled to restaurants, wine schools, hotels, and, to his mind, the most obvious market, Las Vegas. "I figured Vegas would be a marketplace where if you established the products in top restaurants," he explains, "the product branding migration would help travel the country and [restaurant patrons] would ask for the product."

Because he cannot sell his wines through retail channels himself, Wilkinson has wholesalers in various states who will take the wine and then distribute it to retail outlets. With eighty-five thousand different wines competing against his lineup, he figures that if he ever takes any of his distributors for granted, they'll drop him not because the relationship has gone flat but simply because they forgot about him in the crowd of competitors. He also has to worry about where his wines are seen once they've been distributed. An upscale restaurant would take it as a business insult to see the chardonnay they're selling to diners at $75 a bottle at a local Costco for $20. So he has to divvy up the product, making sure the vintages he positions as top quaffs never get discounted.

In contrast to his experience in the movie business, Wilkinson was actually seeing money flow back to him as his business got off the ground. The twenty-four hundred or so cases (28,800 bottles) he first ordered were leaving the climate-controlled warehouse in Ontario, a city east of the Port of Los Angeles, and it began to seem that he had found a passion that would also pay the bills. And then Osama bin Laden put a cork in his nascent success.

The September 11, 2001, al-Qaeda attacks on New York and the Pentagon destroyed the tourism industry for months, as people canceled trips and vacations, particularly ones that involved flying. Las Vegas, where Wilkinson had put so much effort into selling wine, was especially hard hit, and his new hotel and restaurant clients canceled their orders before they found themselves with wine cellars full of bottles and no one to drink them. Business tanked for five months. Sales fell 90 percent.

No one, including Wilkinson, knew how long this would last. But then that part of his personality that was so well insulated from discouragement took over, and he continued. "The thing is," he asserts, "there are people who get out and people who don't. I don't."

New security rules went into effect as well. Every vineyard he worked with had to apply for a special security number before they could continue shipping to the United States. And they had to specifically appoint Great Wines as their agent, making Wilkinson responsible for them. In the long run, these were minor issues and, because he had no orders to place, certainly didn't delay his business.

The wine tastings and cold calls continued. To keep the business afloat, Wilkinson needed someone who would buy a lot of wine all at once—and he got that with United Airlines in 2003. Many first-class passengers got their first taste of Lanzerac chardonnay, while business class drank Van Loveren sauvignon blanc, both South African wines. In 2005, the airline bought about twenty-five thousand cases. By the end of 2006, Great Wines had established itself in about thirty states.

We finally get around to talking about how his business is affected by conflicts at the Port of Los Angeles, including the infamous 2004 backlog and the disputes over workforce size. In the midst of that backlog, he managed to divert his cargo to a East Coast port. This was not a simple process, but it did let him avoid the immediate complications of having his wine sit on a ship in the harbor. Given the extra time and effort it took to make these arrangements, it's easy to see how importers like Wilkinson can develop a lingering distaste for both the union and the employers. He shrugs. "I probably have shipped much less to the L.A. port as a result, because of those issues. And because you get used to shipping through Houston and New York with certain companies and containers, and if you are forced to entertain those options, and you do, and they work well for you, then it becomes a good solution."

His implication is that, as an importer, he's entirely comfortable going elsewhere to bring his goods into the United States. And if the Port of Los Angeles becomes too much of a problem, he's got alternatives in place that may become permanent. Harry Bridges, for one, was always mindful of that threat and on occasion diluted the more radical, less business-friendly impulses he and his union members felt so that shippers such as Great Wines wouldn't bolt for ports elsewhere in the country. As evidenced by Wilkinson's attitude, the balancing act doesn't always work.

At the UNLVino wine tasting, the crowd starts changing as the hot afternoon wears on, turning into something you might see at a suburban cineplex. People look a little bewildered, as if they might have bought tickets on impulse, not realizing just how many wines are out there to sample. Wilkinson is hoarding a couple of Bethany GR6 shiraz bottles, pouring them only for those who seem to recognize a good wine when they sip it. This Australian wine comes from vines that are 80 to 120 years old, and the winemakers sell the wine only when they feel they have a world-class product, or so goes Wilkinson's patter. Just six hundred bottles went to the United States through Great Wines, and the local Whole Foods store got a measly twelve. So he's not about to waste the good stuff on just anybody.

A worker comes by to empty the gallon buckets placed along the table, where patrons can deposit the ice water they use to wash out their glasses for another taste. "The funniest thing I ever saw at a tasting," Wilkinson recalls, "was a maid pushing a forty-gallon vat of expelled wine when the wheel caught on a tablecloth touching the floor. The whole thing went over. A tidal wave of spit! Everyone was running to get out of the way!" His voice is a slurred baritone, and when he laughs at the end of his story, it comes out sounding so hearty, I can imagine him playing Santa Claus in a few years if this wine thing doesn't work out.

Back in San Pedro, he holds another wine tasting at his offices a few weeks before Christmas, once again trying to drum up more sales and investors. But it's that one big investor—the one who could bring in millions and truly make Great Wines International great—who still hasn't signed up for that one big swallow. And yet, when I ask what's happening with the deal that's taken months and months to complete, Wilkinson quickly says, with both impatience and hope, "We're still talking."

Not long after that, Wilkinson's company ran into one of the more ironic aspects of importing: sales were excellent, orders for wine kept rolling in, but he was having trouble coming up with the funds to pay his foreign suppliers. And because the suppliers don't ship until they've been paid, he had to scramble around the finance world looking for investors so he could buy the wine and fill the orders. He did manage to snag a big European partner in 2003, who promised $1.5 million to capitalize the business, but only about a third of that ever went into Great Wines' bank account. To make matters worse, the money was doled out over the course of three years, so that Wilkinson rarely had enough cash at any one time to buy an adequate supply of product. This meant he was working just as hard, if not harder, to scrounge up cash for the wine deals as he was to sell the wine.

"It was a start-stop operation," he tells me, more than three years after we last talked. "We got some very substantial contracts with some of the airlines for a lot of wine, but then the investment partners didn't produce the goods."

He finally realized that "if you're undercapitalized, you will not be able to succeed." His investors failed to produce the promised funding and, in frustration, Wilkinson resigned as CEO. The company filed for chapter 11 bankruptcy as a means to reorganize. His erstwhile partners continued for two years, but they couldn't sell the wine and eventually filed for chapter 7 bankruptcy. Great Wines no longer exists. "The caveat," he says, when I ask if he learned any lessons from all this, "is beware of your partners. For me, it was eight years of really hard work gone down the drain."

Not one to completely give up, however, Wilkinson is paying the bills by consulting for companies that hope to import or export wine or other products. At the same time, he is plotting his own return to the business. "I'm very keen on looking at what potential there is to export some of the U.S. wines to foreign marketplaces like India, China, places like that."

NINE

The Shipper

For small importers such as the late Great Wines International, a shipment's punctuality usually has little impact on profit margins so long as the product doesn't hit the shore more than a few days late. All things being equal, the costs are the same whether the wine arrives on Tuesday or Friday. Larger companies, however, employ an inventory strategy known as "just-in-time," which means that being late and being early are equally bad. The idea is that a retail item or a factory part, for instance, will arrive exactly when it's needed, whether it's going to be stocked on a store shelf or installed in a factory. In the case of retail goods going through the Port of Los Angeles, this means calculating the amount of time it will take for a product to leave an Asian factory, cross the Pacific Ocean, be loaded on a train or truck or both, briefly see the inside of a central distribution center, and then hit the store shelves just as the last of that particular product is about to be sold. Think of the cost savings: no real estate to buy for a warehouse where the items just sit, no big hulking building to maintain, no employees who must be paid to put the boxes away and then to take them off the shelves. The fiduciary brilliance should bring tears to a stockholder's eyes.

Well, only if it works. Geraldine Knatz, executive director of the Port of Los Angeles, tells me about cargo coming off a Maersk ship that was delayed at the port because of a crane fire that held up the discharge operation by a measly thirteen hours. But that was all it took to miss the train leaving for Dallas, where the containers filled with items for a department store chain's Labor Day sale were headed for further distribution in the Midwest. Because the shipment had been scheduled for just-in-time delivery, there was no way to catch up. The products were too late for the store sales, and the corporate office had to yank the sale ads before they were published. And while it's entirely possible that no one in Kansas City cares about what happens at the port, as Knatz puts it, "If I lived near that store and I was going to get my kids' school clothes right before Labor Day and I went in there and they didn't have the school uniforms, I would have really been pissed off."

The large retail chain that brought this delayed merchandise from Asia is known as the shipper (or, in current corporate parlance, the "beneficial cargo owner"). The shipper negotiates prices with the steamship line, the railroad, and the trucking company so that its product (usually) gets to its stores right on time and at the cheapest cost. Shippers treat their line of work with a level of secrecy worthy of the Pentagon. As much as I wanted to talk to a shipper and as many interview requests as I submitted, they had all been lying low, afraid that I might inadvertently leak some minor, esoteric detail of how they move cargo and thus give the competition a new way to, say, shave a fraction of a penny off each box sent through the distribution center (which might mean that the competition could then sell its sweaters for a slightly lower price). The methods involved in this are so proprietary that I wonder if even the lubricant they use on their conveyor belts might be considered a competitive edge.

But then I get lucky. Through contacts I talk with only on the phone, I'm steered to a woman high on the shipping food chain, someone whose identity I can refer to only as "the Shipper," whose employer—we negotiate how I can say this—is a "major retailer" with headquarters in the Dallas area. Also, as a prelude to our interview, I'm given the narrow parameters of discussion, designed to deny her competitors even a whiff of how she moves boxes.

The Shipper's secrets are so juicy, and her reluctance to speak to me so great, that I decide not to mention what I know about her company's just-in-time Labor Day sale debacle, fearing that it might make her squeamish enough to cancel the interview. I end up confirming the information through someone in the company's advertising department.

I figure if I'm going to interview the Shipper, I might as well follow the 1,200-mile route her cargo takes from Los Angeles to Dallas. If nothing else, I'll learn over the long, three-day car trip what it's like to be a container. While the railroad stiff-arms me in my request to watch its operation at the start of the line, the rest of the rail line is easily seen from various freeways that share the route. And that route, by the way, isn't what I would call scenic. After leaving the coast, the rails make their way to Interstate 10, through the Coachella Valley (home of Palm Springs, among other cities), and swings south to the desolate, putrid Salton Sea, which is partially fed by agricultural runoff and all the fertilizers that come with it. As I'm trying to photograph a train blasting by the lake, I'm attacked on the neck by a praying mantis.

The railroad passes Niland, California, where a public thermometer on this October day reads 94 degrees, and eventually swings east a few miles north of the Mexican border. I can see why this desert route was chosen: no real mountains to slow down the train and few weather-related closures (that is, except during some summer days when the rails can get so hot they actually soften, to the point where they're unsafe to use). This is Union Pacific's 760-mile Sunset Route, which has been around since 1881, when it was built from Los Angeles through the Mojave Desert to El Paso, Texas. From there, lines lead south to Houston or farther east to Dallas. The stretch from Los Angeles to Dallas accounts for 24 percent of all the freight Union Pacific handles and more than 90 percent of its cargo leaving the Port of Los Angeles. Union Pacific is spending hundreds of millions to double-track the entire length, which will help accommodate the growing cargo volume coming through the Los Angeles/Long Beach port complex and will make train movement back and forth more efficient.

As I drive across southern Arizona, New Mexico, and the flat plains of West Texas, the cargo never seems to stop. Two-mile-long trains loaded with piggy-backed containers pulse over the tracks like heartbeats, some only a few minutes apart. I stop in Deming, New Mexico. At one end of town I notice mildly jingoistic signs touting "American Owned and Operated" stores, while at the other end Walmart and Kmart (also American owned) compete, with their shelves full of Asian-made products. This is the kind of symbolic irony I can't resist, and it gives me something to think about for miles: we've become so dependent on goods coming through the ports of Los Angeles and Long Beach that those kinds of signs are meaningless now. Yeah, sure, we might feel good about buying something from locally owned stores, but when it comes to socks, we go to Walmart.

The containers land at a rail yard 12 miles south of Dallas, a tightly controlled facility surrounded by high fences, barbed wire, and cameras. Security seems tighter here than at the port. Trucks coming in to drop off containers—usually empties at this point—or pick up loads must first drive through a barnlike structure where lights illuminate the rig from all angles and cameras scrutinize every inch, including the underside. A team inside the Union Pacific office, adjacent to the truck lane, watches the resulting television show for anything suspicious.

After clearing that hurdle, the truck goes to a gate, where the driver's fingerprints from two fingers are checked against a database. Only drivers who are registered with Union Pacific are allowed on the property. The truck is also weighed to confirm that it matches the manifest. Inside the yard, trains stop on one of seven long tracks, and the containers are unloaded or loaded using top loaders. The place seems clean and efficient. It lacks the port's noise and chaos, plus it's so hidden from the main roads that I wonder if anyone nearby even knows it's there. If nothing else, it's doubtful anyone has complained about diesel ultrafine particulates in the air.

This is as close as Leslie Jutzi, a PR person with Allen Development of Texas, can get me to the facility. Union Pacific isn't crazy about reporters hanging about its yard, and so we're limited to what I consider sneaking about the perimeter in order to get a view of the action from a nearby hill. Jutzi's firm is developing the Dallas Logistics Hub, a massive, 6,000-acre distribution center, where cargo from Los Angeles/Long Beach, Houston, or smaller ports will wind up before spraying out to the rest of the country, mostly by truck. Allen Development hopes to take advantage of the huge cargo increases predicted for the next ten to twenty years and turn Dallas into a major freight hub for the rest of the country.

At the time of my visit in 2007, the land is mostly wooded or being leased to farmers, which brings with it an agricultural tax break. The hefty brochure Jutzi gives me is full of nice charts of how cargo flows into, through, and out of the country (to Canada, mainly). Allen Development makes a compelling case for the hub, arguing that cargo is more efficiently distributed away from the port in a central location such as Dallas, which is connected to the West Coast and the rest of the country by rail or interstate freeways.

Beyond that, my eyes glaze over. Somehow, with all this geeky talk about intermodal point exchange, cross-dock this or that, and logistics something-or-other, I've lost the reason why I'm here in Dallas. I want to know how companies, their employees, and plain old consumers are affected by what happens at the Port of Los Angeles, some 1,200 miles away by road or rail. When the longshoremen and employers squabble, or if the Coast Guard shuts down the port because a suspicious package turns out to be a bomb (or not), what happens to places where the port is barely on anyone's radar? Perhaps the Shipper can tell me.

Three days after leaving Los Angeles (a container would have taken about half the time), I'm about to meet the Shipper on a park bench at the major retailer's headquarters, located on a large wooded campus where the manicured gardens outside flow through the doors into a long central atrium. As I search out our meeting point—the three-story atrium is so long that there's a receptionist on either end—I pass through an indoor park, a wooded workers' paradise. Associates, as employees are known these days, casually stroll past the greenery, talking shop with a kind of cool, satisfied calm. For the moment, business is good (though in a few months, the major retailer will lay off thousands of its workers when the economy goes south). People dress in jeans or casual slacks. A few women wear summery dresses and sandals. The only men wearing ties seem to be vendors, who sit on benches below the indoor trees checking their notes or talking on cell phones. Just as I find a receptionist, she calls to three women walking by, "Hey, ladies! Twenty percent off jewelry down the hall!" Gosh, what a fun place to work.

A few minutes late to our appointment, the Shipper shows up at my bench, apologizing several times for her tardiness. A petite, attractive woman in her mid-forties, she's hardly the image of a corporate executive trying to wring every fraction of a penny out of the shipping process. And even that vague description is more than she would prefer people to know. Beyond preventing her competitors from learning anything about her company's operation, the Shipper has two concerns about our conversation: she doesn't want the average consumer equating her employer, the major retailer, with cheap Asian imports, which these days is a slippery slope to her second concern, the outsourcing of manufacturing jobs overseas and the bad image it presents. She is, in fact, adamant that I refer to the products she's responsible for importing into the United States as "widgets" so that no one will be able to determine the identity of her company.

Since I'm thankful that someone in the tight-lipped shipping industry is finally talking with me, albeit minus any significant identification, I'm not going to be ungrateful and make the argument that the major retailer's customers are well aware they're buying something made in another country, probably China, Vietnam, or Pakistan, and don't seem to mind. (Then again, they most likely don't realize that the major retailer imports from fifty-five different countries and that none of its private brand offerings are actually made in the United States.)

The larger issue here is that the country's trade deficit, especially with Asia—and most people pick on China as the most egregious example—has been out of whack for years. In 2005, the U.S. trade deficit topped a record $725.8 billion. To put it another way, for the same year, about 70 percent of all containers leaving the Port of Los Angeles were empty. In 2009, however, with the dismal economy depressing even imports, the deficit declined to $378.6 billion.

While many people bemoan the consequences of a high trade deficit—the loss of manufacturing jobs in particular—you'd be hard pressed to hear a whimper of discontent out of carriers, longshoremen, truckers, warehouse workers, or the City of Los Angeles, which owns and runs the San Pedro port.

Trade unions do castigate Walmart and other companies for depending on low-paid Asian workers, and certainly the ILWU has added its voice to that chorus on occasion. But that's not saying they aren't just a little ambivalent. "We are against outsourcing, and we've been against outsourcing, the loss of American jobs, since the beginning," Peter Peyton, an ILWU clerk and one of the union's most erudite analysts, tells me when I gingerly bring up the idea that perhaps there's a contradiction in being against something that has paid many a longshoreman's check. To his credit, he doesn't even bother to rationalize the issue: "Despite the fact that we benefited from [outsourcing], we've been against it since day one. There's never been any question about that.... We're blessed because [cargo] happens to be coming. We win whether it comes out or comes in. It's just the nature of our business."

(As for goods going out of the country, food products account for more than half of all U.S. exports. But many of the outgoing containers that are actually filled with something carry a most unglamorous item—scrap paper. Four of the top ten U.S. exporters sell paper, mostly to China.)

None of this seems terribly important to the Shipper. Her true concern is time. Time means everything to her. The major retailer—with more than a thousand stores in the United States (and more being built) and nearly $20 billion in revenue in 2006 brings new goods from design to store in just forty weeks. Trendy items, which used to take nearly a year to cycle, can now be moved in seventeen weeks.

Once we adjourn from the park bench to a glass-enclosed conference room, I ask her what would happen if something drastic were to take place at the port, say, a shutdown such as the 2002 lockout or the 2004 traffic jam. "You would want to be going to your store shelf and stocking up," she says with the slightest of Texas accents. "I really think that's what you would want to do. It's not to say the country would go dry immediately, but most people don't realize our dependency on imports."

Wearing jeans and a white shirt, the Shipper describes her profession as one that, for all the stress of saving time and money, has always been exciting and a little exotic, given that it involves exports and imports. I ask her if it's fun, and she says, "Love it. Love, love, love."

I can certainly see the challenge that apparently energizes her. In a job that she cautiously boils down to "We just pick up [the widgets] when they're ready to move," the complexity of details can be withering, and, as in the case of the late Labor Day sale items, success or failure turns on seemingly small events. What are those details? Ha! Don't even ask. Well, okay, in a nutshell—but remember, we're talking about *widgets*—much of her job comes down to negotiation, working out deals with carriers to have her product reliably shipped to her stores on a schedule and at a cost that keeps the price tags competitive.

There's a lot to keep track of. Maybe one carrier is great on one route, but so-so on another. And maybe you don't want to always use the same carrier; it's useful to have a backup in case one carrier has labor problems or something else goes wrong. You try to figure out a compromise between more costly customer service and a cheaper transportation price without all the friendly extras. Then there's tracking the shipment to make sure it's running on time. Perhaps you need to punt and put the shipment on a truck to speed things up. It costs more, but you must keep in mind that having empty shelves instead of shelves filled with a popular item can really hurt in the long run, creating angry customers. (It should be pointed out that smaller importers don't have the muscle to negotiate competitive costs for getting their cargo delivered once it hits the port. Most often, they deal directly with the shipping line, which uses its power to get better prices on delivering containers.)

And let's not forget security, which in this case means keeping cargo from being stolen. The Shipper nearly giggles at the thought of how clever they've been on this point. But, of course, she adds, "I can't say what it is. It's good stuff, let me tell you! If you were me, you'd go, 'That's pretty cool.'"

After my stultifying drive across four states, this is as revealing a look into the Shipper's world as I can get. I'm not surprised. The world surrounding the Port of Los Angeles is secretive and press-phobic. The longshoremen largely steered clear of me. The terminal operators? Forget it. The steamship lines? Nope. Everyone, it seems, has some secret that they'd rather keep to themselves, while perhaps ignoring the biggest one—that their industry has become so intertwined with the U.S. economy that all it takes is a small fire at a crane or a single labor dispute to ripple across the country, potentially costing the nation billions.

On my way back home, I visit the major retailer's store in Dallas and browse through the shelves. The place overflows with "widgets," most of them no doubt hitting the shelves just when they're needed to replace purchased merchandise. I pick through a few labels: "Made in China," "Made in Pakistan," "Made in India." Granted, these are hardly life-and-death items whose absence would cause a crisis, but that's not the point. If something happens at the port so many miles to the west, sales associates might be out of work. Given Americans' flirtation with extreme debt, that loss in pay might mean a lot of unpaid bills adding up. Those in the shipping industry could find themselves out of work as well. Stockholders, many depending partly on the major retailer's fortunes to keep them afloat, could lose money. All these people could experience some minor to serious financial grief.

As I'm driving west, once again along the Sunset Route's tracks, the locomotives dragging hundreds of containers pour past me, going east. But instead of tons of metal, I'm seeing more than a few Americans unaware of what it all represents to them.

TEN

Los Troqueros

THE DRIVER

It's ten minutes before 6:00 P.M., and outside the Evergreen America terminal, parked trucks choke the shoulder of the road as though they've been abandoned—2 miles of tractors, tractors with empty containers, and perhaps a few with cargo, strung bumper to bumper in the kind of grinding gridlock that must look like money thrown into a bonfire to the drivers sitting there. After all, they get paid only for delivering a container, not for the time they spend in line—and some of them have been there for three or four hours. They won't be moving soon, either. When the gate opens at 6:00 P.M. for the longshoremen's night shift, the security and administrative processes required just to get inside the terminal could take another hour or two.

Four drivers bunch up around a truck's front bumper like office workers at the water cooler. At first I imagine them commiserating over all the wasted time, but since this happens nearly every day, only the newest of rookie drivers would even bring up the topic. Instead, the all-male group projects a collective resignation, bringing a purgatorial feel to the line-up, as though no one has any option but to wait and wait and wait.

Anthony Branch points out the grim scene below us as we descend on a freeway off-ramp in his truck, and he sounds like he pities these drivers. "I was here on Monday. I got in this line at three-thirty. I got out of the terminal at nine-thirty." I ask him why the terminal is so slow, and he can't offer a reason other than "that one is pretty bad." So bad that he can literally sit there for five hours doing little but worry about whether he'll be able to get in three moves that night. A move includes picking up a container at the terminal, delivering the load, and then bringing back an empty. Doing fewer than three moves means a smaller than usual paycheck—an unfair penalty on the truck drivers for the terminal's inability to get trucks in and out efficiently.

Then again, it can't all be blamed on Evergreen. There's also a somewhat ironic reason for the congestion. In 2005, marine terminals in the ports of Los Angeles and Long Beach instituted a program called PierPASS, which was designed to thin out the long truck lines during the day and encourage container pick-ups or drop-offs in the evening by charging a "traffic mitigation fee" of $100 per container during the peak hours, between 3:00 A.M. and 6:00 P.M. So now drivers queue up in the afternoon to wait for 6:00, when they can avoid the surcharge. Given that the shippers pay the fee—the same people who scrutinize their costs down to the fraction of a penny—it's not surprising how successful that incentive to redirect truck traffic has been: during the program's first four years, 11.5 million trucks were diverted to the off-peak hours, which overall has helped to reduce pollution because fewer idling trucks have been sitting in even longer lines during the day.

Branch continues on past Evergreen America to the Yang Ming container terminal. He gets to the gate unimpeded, just as an ILWU clerk arrives at a small booth, where the clerk apparently has nothing but attitude with which to stop a scofflaw truck. Branch drives up in his rig, a reasonably sleek, low-emission diesel 2010 Mack Pinnacle with sleeper compartment and GPS; though it's a shiny white monster with ten gears and a 16-liter engine with more than 500 horsepower, it's surprisingly quiet. He's owned the truck barely a month, but he seems largely unsentimental about it, as if it's nothing more than a wrench. For a simple tool, it's already well used, with 11,000 miles collected on the odometer (by the time he replaces it, he will probably have put on more than half a million miles).

Branch calls himself an owner-operator, a rather fuzzy description that fits about 90 percent of truck drivers at the port, who are technically self-employed but generally work for only one trucking company. From the standpoint of, say, the IRS, that's slippery enough, but there's much more to it. The system has turned the fairly simple procedure of drayage—picking up cargo and short-hauling it to a nearby location—into a complex battle over who really owns the trucks, who really works for whom, what constitutes fair pay and working conditions, and, above all, who is really responsible for the tons of air pollution coming from diesel trucks.

Ernie Nevarez, a tax advisor by day, has devoted years to trying to organize the drivers into one defiant force strong enough to overturn the current shortcomings of the owner-operator system at the port, including the non-income-producing hours in line. He prefers to call the drivers he organizes *troqueros,* which is his attempt to apply a little more dignity to what is at best a difficult way to make a living. "I won't use the term 'truck driver,'" he says, calling it too suggestive of cowboy truckers—"mainly white guys," he tosses in—who haul cargo coast to coast, as opposed to the people working in drayage, many of whom bear Spanish surnames. Thus far, Nevarez has had two successful demonstrations of potential *troquero* power: the drivers boycotted both ports on May Day 2006 and 2007. This stung the shippers for only a few hours, however, and overall didn't seem to elicit that much sympathy for the drivers, especially the ones who made their point by blocking traffic on the 710 freeway, which leads into the ports.

Branch doesn't call himself a *troquero.* On the surface, about the only thing that belies the owner-operator appellation he prefers is the green and dark gray Fox Transportation logo that swooshes like a vapor trail from the front grille of his truck to his door, as if to evoke an impression of speed. This isn't the name of a company Branch owns; rather, it's the trucking operation to which he reports five nights a week. While Fox classifies Branch as an independent contractor, which makes him responsible for his own expenses (gas, insurance, truck maintenance, and so on) as well as income taxes, Branch cannot take his truck to another company and work for them too. That's because Fox also owns the truck until Branch pays off the approximately $30,000 he owes on it.

This is actually a $100,000 rig, but there's a rush at this time to dump older, polluting trucks for new, lower-emission vehicles ("clean trucks," as defined by the U.S. Environmental Protection Agency), which the two ports will require of all truck operators after 2012, as part of their plans to fight pollution. So Fox offered Branch a no-down-payment, lease-purchase deal subsidized with $20,000 from the Port of Los Angeles and another $50,000 that an unnamed customer pitched in. After five years of $200-a-week payments, which include a total of about $20,000 in finance charges, Branch will own the truck.

Much has been made of these lease-purchase deals (many of which aren't as sweet as Branch's) because the drivers who enter into them can't drive for other companies. How could they be independent, some ask, if they're stuck moving cargo for only one company? Unfortunately, the complexities of federal law make the answer rather messy: in order to operate a commercial truck as well as negotiate contracts with shippers, one must be a licensed motor carrier (LMC). The reasoning is public safety—an LMC has to meet certain requirements that theoretically protect other vehicles on the road, including a public liability insurance policy of $750,000 to $1,000,000 per truck. Most owner-operators don't take on the paperwork and expense (about $10,000) to become an LMC, and instead they work under a trucking company's motor carrier license. The company does the legwork in securing clients and then dispatches the owner-operators to move the cargo. For that reason, a 2007 Port of Los Angeles economic analysis of port drayage described LMCs as "actually not trucking companies but rather brokers that arrange for the movement of cargo."

In some ways, this rather confining relationship between owner-operators and LMCs is mandated by the Federal Motor Carrier Safety Administration's regulations, which state that the LMC leasing the truck "shall assume complete responsibility for the operation of the equipment for the duration of the lease." In what is known as a captive lease, this regulation is interpreted to mean that the so-called owner-operator can't drive the truck for anyone else. (The law does provide exceptions to this rule, but it's clear the LMCs aren't taking advantage of them.)

So far, none of this is especially onerous, and it's fair to say that the owner-operators leasing their trucks pretty much accept the laws governing their careers as unchangeable. But peel back a layer or two, and you start to see why people like Nevarez want to protest the current system.

According to Joe Rajkovacz, director of regulatory affairs for the Owner-Operator Independent Drivers Association (OOIDA), many of the LMCs operating at the port will work only with drivers who lease trucks from them. That's because in order to encourage early adoption of the latest crop of clean trucks, both ports provided purchase subsidies of $20,000 to $50,000 to the LMCs. (Through mid-2010, the Port of Los Angeles helped fund 2,087 trucks, for a total of $41.6 million.) The companies now have a fleet of new trucks that they want to lease to the drivers for eventual purchase, thus recouping their investment. "They don't want to dink around with a guy with his own truck," Rajkovacz says, "when they're sitting there with fifty, sixty, seventy of these subsidized trucks."

He adds that this has turned into an unsavory situation in which some of the trucking companies haven't passed on the subsidy to the driver, who ends up paying the full price for a truck, about $100,000. Mike Fox, CEO of Fox Transportation, and Branch's client, if you will, contends that most companies do pass along the subsidy, which he does with his drivers, but the grant may be masked through a company's bookkeeping methods. "Some make it more complicated than they need to," he says.

In order to make truck leasing an even bigger profit maker, Rajkovacz says, some companies also charge the driver for the required public liability insurance. This is indeed legal, but instead of making it a simple charge-back—that is, having the driver pay the exact amount of the premium—the LMC tacks on an extra fee, "charging anywhere from $150 to $250 per week," he tells me, a total of $7,800 to $13,000 for a year's worth of insurance. Considering that the OOIDA offers a $750,000 policy for $4,200 per year, Rajkovacz calls the practice "an illicit charge-back."

This gets us back to the question of driver independence. If the company from whom a driver leases a truck turns out to be a bunch of scoundrels, the driver's only recourse is to bail on the lease contract and return the truck. Some companies aren't quite so forgiving about the break-up and will bill the driver for the remaining balance on the lease. They then turn over the predictably unpaid bill to a collection agency. "They will harass these guys to the gates of hell," Rajkovacz says. "These [trucking companies] are bad actors."

To be fair, not all LMCs engage in these practices. Mike Fox says his company isn't so vindictive: "If that owner-operator says, 'Look, I'm just not making enough money under this program,' they give us thirty days' written notice, walk away from the truck, and owe us no money at all."

Nevertheless, some have called the owner-operator system as it now exists a sharecropper arrangement or even serfdom. At a May 2010 congressional hearing on the subject, driver Jose Covarrubias told the U.S. House Subcommittee on Highway and Transit, "We're called independent contractors, but all we are is employees with expenses. Our bosses tell this lie so they can make us pay for the company trucks."

Fox agrees that the drayage industry has a bad reputation. "There's been some trucking companies that—as painful as it is, I need to say it—they need to go, because they're not doing it the right way. They're not treating the drivers the right way. They're giving a bad rap to the industry. They're not making sure these guys are making enough money so they can maintain the trucks. They're not making the investment in the future they need to. They don't have the right mindset."

For his part, Branch seems content working exclusively for Fox, because, essentially, he's able to come and go with no set hours. Fox Transportation and its clients are happy as long as he manages to pick up the three loads at the Yang Ming container terminal that the Fox dispatcher has assigned to him and bring back three empties. (A "load" is a container with cargo inside; an empty is usually headed back to Asia for more cargo.) He's limited from doing more only by the often lengthy wait times and the 2:00 A.M. closing time when longshoremen and clerks go home.

Branch, a jovial fifty-year-old with gray whiskers easily visible against his black skin, calls being an owner-operator "the only way to go.... You have your own freedom. Naturally, you make more money [than an employee driver]." He pauses and then adds a note of ambivalence: "You're responsible for your fuel, all your maintenance, and upkeep. Being an owner-operator, you have more responsibilities than a company driver. You have a little more freedom. You come in when you want to. You can go home when you want to. Sleep when you want to. But it's not that glorious. When you work for yourself, you're going to work harder.... You're not going to cheat yourself."

Not all truckers are quite so satisfied with their positions as owner-operators. Covarrubias showed the House subcommittee how dismal the job can be by producing his weekly pay stubs, one for $96 after his truck lease payment, insurance, and fuel costs were deducted, and another for minus $200. Yes, he *owed* the company, Southern Counties Express, after what he implied was a fifty-hour work week.

This testimony was no doubt atypical and presented for shock value, but the take-home income for owner-operators is hardly reassuring, either. According to the port's 2007 economic analysis of the Clean Truck program, the bosses Covarrubias referred to pay their independent contractors a median gross income of $75,000. Not so bad until you factor in the $46,000 in operating costs that the drivers pay out of their earnings, leaving them with $29,000, or about $12 an hour. The median household income in California in 2007 was $63,932. (According to one national survey, drivers who are employees of a company and thus are not independent contractors make between $14.63 and $20.07 an hour.)

There are other shortcomings that chip away at the job. As independent contractors, drivers must pay for their own health insurance, plus they receive no vacation pay, workers compensation, unemployment benefits, or employer contributions to Social Security and Medicare. Most worker safety laws don't apply to them. Because most of the drivers aren't registered with the U.S. Department of Transportation as LMCs, they are prohibited from negotiating directly with the shippers for contracts or fees. So they work for an LMC and earn a percentage of the shipping charge (around 80 percent going to the driver), although they rarely know exactly how much the shipper is actually paying for the delivered container. Rajkovacz says he's heard of cases where the LMC collected far more than what they told the driver they charged.

If any of this concerns Branch, he isn't saying. Once he stops beside the Yang Ming guard shack, he abruptly tells me to leave the cab, a 5-foot descent on small metal steps, and then says to wait for him under several sooty madrona trees on the other side of a large, momentarily empty swath of asphalt about the width of an eight-lane freeway. I'm being ejected because I don't have the required Transportation Worker Identification Credential, or TWIC card, that federal regulations require for anyone entering a port facility without special escort. Terminals also don't allow passengers in trucks. As some have demonstrated, it's possible to hide in the sleeper compartment and enter illegally, but Branch seems concerned with following *most* rules—although he doesn't wear a seatbelt this night—and perhaps wisely fails to offer this skullduggery as an option.

So I trot across the pavement, aware that the trucks that have been stuck inside the terminal waiting for the gates to reopen after they were closed at 4:30 for the end of the day shift, will soon be pouring out, with few expectations of a pedestrian in the way. (Yes, that's right—drivers who can't leave the terminal before it closes are locked inside, losing more time.)

While I wait at the exit, Branch shows his TWIC card to the guard and then continues 100 feet over two speed bumps to painted lanes divided by concrete barriers. To the side is an orange windsock hanging limply with no apparent function. Posted signs that I guess haven't been read by the drivers suggest an attempt to rein in chaos: "SEAT BELT REQUIRED"; "NO SOUNDING OF TRUCK HORNS, VIOLATORS WILL BE DENIED SERVICE AND DISMISSED FROM PROPERTY"; "OUTSIDE TRUCKERS STAY IN YOUR TRUCKS." Branch pauses for a wooden arm to raise, and he continues through.

Even with the warnings, there are drivers—Branch calls them harbor rats—who aggressively ignore the rules. "They don't care 'bout nothin'," Branch says, sounding annoyed. "Safety doesn't matter to them. They will pull out a unit that has a flat tire, no lights. They have no respect for nobody. They will cut you off in line. And they do speed."

I see examples of that as more trucks leave the terminal. For no apparent reason, the drivers gun their engines just as they exit the gate and race 100 feet to the red traffic signal at John S. Gibson Street, where they have to hit their brakes hard to stop. They slide alongside other trucks as though challenging the drivers for a race through the intersection. From my position, I see nothing but testosterone so thick and obnoxious, I step back a few more feet from the truck lanes just to be safe.

Trucks continue entering the gate, many with bright logos announcing their greenness. Swift Transportation calls itself "The Clean Fleet"; Southern Counties Express is "The Green Fleet" (which they've trademarked); and then there's Green Fleet Systems. In contrast, a dirty, blocky chunk of steel drives by, looking like it might have been built in the sixties. "Powered by Jesus" is painted on the cab, but given the ultra-fine particles invisibly pouring out of the black-tipped exhaust pipe, this might be an insult to Jesus.

While I watch the parade, Branch has halted, stuck in a line that creeps toward a speaker at another gate stop. After about thirty minutes, he talks to a clerk at a remote site, who confirms the number of the container he's here to pick up and tells him where to find the can—at location Y211. The Fox dispatcher has already told him that a load on wheels is waiting, meaning that a container with cargo is parked on a chassis at that location. At other times, the container may be piled in a five-high stack where it has to be retrieved by a longshoreman driving a "strad," or straddle carrier. This spindly-legged contraption straddles the container stack, picks up a can, and sets it on an empty chassis that the truck driver has picked up. (Later, Branch talks to another driver who complains that all three loads he's there to pick up aren't where they were supposed to be—not an uncommon occurrence.)

Branch gets a gate pass and a ticket with the container location and continues down a lane just inside the fence. Piles of empty chassis stacked five high line the other side of the lane, looking like a trucker's bone yard.

Branch finally arrives at Y211. One problem. Well, actually, three problems. Even though the chassis are supposed to be checked as part of a Biennial Inspection of Terminals (BIT), required by state law, Branch is still responsible for ensuring that the equipment is working properly. So he inspects the chassis for working lights, among other things, and discovers one tire is completely flat and two others are deflated enough that they should be replaced. So he hooks up to the chassis and pulls it to a maintenance shop, which is fortunately near by (in some terminals the shops are located in remote corners of the yard), where new tires are installed while the container still sits on the chassis.

With repairs finished—I'm standing in the dark cold with no jacket—Branch leaves the yard, first driving through radiation detectors and then stopping at the final guard booth, where the man inside stays in his chair and languidly holds up a long stick that reaches to Branch's window. Branch attaches his gate pass to the stick and then leaves to pick me up, ninety minutes after he first entered the gate. Apparently, delays like this are common enough that Branch doesn't feel like complaining about it, but later he admits that hauling containers out of the port is far more stressful than other truck jobs he could take.

I can see why. If he spends two hours or more to pick up just one container, and it takes, say, an hour or more to deliver the cargo and come back, he risks being unable to fill the three-move quota assigned to him before the gates close at 2:00 A.M. Each container, filled or empty, represents about $170 in pay (the total charge to the shipper is around $200). And from that, expenses chisel away the dollars.

There's the weekly truck loan payment, and about $230 in fuel that goes into the 129-gallon tank every other day, totaling about $700 a week. Insurance is $200 a week. Tires, which last about two years, cost anywhere from $350 to $450 each to replace, and there are ten of them. To maintain his five-year warranty, Branch must take the truck in for a quarterly check-up that costs about $175. At the nickel-and-dime end of the spectrum, Branch washes the truck once a week, either at a truck wash, which charges $28, or at a do-it-yourself place costing a pocketful of quarters.

According to *From Clean to Clunker,* a report put out by a coalition of groups including the Sierra Club and the Teamsters, routine maintenance on a new truck can run about $2,200 the first year for such items as oil changes, filter treatment, truck valve adjustments, and so on; over the life of a seven-year lease, the coalition estimates, truck maintenance will cost $60,000. Mike Fox calls that "simply not true." Routine maintenance for a new truck, he says, will cost about $800 a year, and the warranty takes care of many of the other repairs.

(It should be noted that many *troqueros* with older trucks were able to scrape by with lower maintenance expenses because they drove vehicles they could repair themselves. The newer trucks are far too complicated for shade-tree mechanics to even attempt diving under the hood to fix something: they have to go to a qualified shop. Thus many drivers have lamented that the ban on so-called dirty trucks has burdened them with maintenance costs that are higher than their weekly lease payment.)

Given all these expenses, it's no wonder that Branch sometimes spends the night in his truck. If he is running late and gets to the terminal gate with his last container after the terminal has closed, he'll stand in line with all the other drivers who couldn't squeeze in three moves and nap in the sleeper until the 6:00 A.M. opening.

"I don't have too many bad nights," he says without emotion. "When I have good nights, I am happy. When I have bad nights, I don't complain. There's not too much you can do about it." Just the same, these long nights keep him from seeing his wife, daughter, and son or sleeping in their West Los Angeles home.

The uncertainty of each evening is nothing compared to his previous job as a welder. "I had a buddy who was driving a truck," he says when I ask how he got started, "and he was telling me how much money you can make and how glorious it is. And where I was working, I was working for a company called Southwest Marine. . . . It got to a point where they would lay us off, hire us back, lay us off, hire us back. It got to the point where they could lay you off in the morning and hire you back that evening."

So in 1993, he took his buddy's advice and enrolled in a truck driver school. Once he completed the training, and with $6,000 in the bank, he went looking for a job, but no one was hiring. Finally, a company offered him a position, but he needed his own rig; and, as it turned out, they had a used Freightliner for sale for a down payment of $6,000. Branch was now broke, but he became a working *troquero*.

More than fifteen years later, he's reasonably happy with his independence, however limited it might seem. But now the Port of Los Angeles has come up with a plan that would eliminate most owner-operators altogether from the port's terminals. No more *troqueros*. No more *reyes del camino*.

THE CLEAN TRUCK PROGRAM

Sometimes a person's body language says more than his or her words. At the May 5, 2010, congressional hearing before the House Subcommittee on Highways and Transit, the room is so packed, both with other drivers and with trucking company executives, that the overflow crowd has to watch the proceedings from another room's closed-circuit television. Driver Jose Covarrubias is shifting around in his seat for reasons other than nervousness. He and six other witnesses are sitting in alphabetical order along several long tables, and his closest neighbor is Robert Digges, vice president and chief counsel of the American Trucking Association (ATA), the guy who is the most outspoken defender of the current driver system at the port. Covarrubias, wearing a light-colored suit, moves as far away as he can from Digges, hugging the end of the table as though caged. Digges, in a dark business suit, tightly crosses his arms anytime the driver slams the ATA's position.

The main purpose of the hearing is to dig into the Clean Truck programs offered by the ports of Los Angeles and Long Beach as a means to cut back on truck-related diesel pollution. But the testimony becomes more of a debate over how those programs will hurt or enrich the drivers.

The Port of Los Angeles announced its Clean Truck program in March 2008. This followed a 2007 plan, approved by both ports, to ban all pre-1989 trucks and to eventually, by 2012, prohibit all trucks with engines older than the 2007 model year (when federal emissions standards were mandated for diesel trucks, creating a class of vehicle known as "clean trucks"). However, the port wanted not only to scrap older trucks—eliminating an estimated 80 percent of truck-related pollution at the port—but also to have motor carriers enter into concession contracts to service the port. (When a government entity grants permission to a private company to do business on public property, the arrangement is referred to as a concession.) With contracts to be phased in over a five-year period, the port would begin providing concessions only to licensed motor carriers. This would eliminate most owner-operators: truck drivers would be allowed inside the terminals only if they were employees of an LMC.

The port's stated rationale had little to do with reengineering the drayage industry; it was more about economics. According to John Holmes, the port's deputy executive director of operations and one of the speakers at the House subcommittee hearing, the LMCs have greater financial resources with which to buy the new required trucks—especially after the port offered subsidies—as opposed to owner-operators, some of whom may have trouble qualifying for a credit card, let alone a truck loan. "There's a reason why our trucks were twelve years old when we started this program," he told the hearing. "It's not because the drivers didn't want to have new trucks, it's because the drivers couldn't afford new trucks."

Several environmental groups, including the Sierra Club and the Natural Resources Defense Council, backed the idea of improving air quality by making the companies, rather than the owner-operators, responsible for the new trucks. The Teamsters also approved, for the obvious reason that they would have an opportunity to bring the employee drivers into the union fold. The Teamsters' Fredrick Potter, vice president at large and port division director, contended in written testimony to the subcommittee that the LMCs could easily adapt to the new rules. He cited three companies that "converted thousands of drivers from nominal 'independence' to legally recognized W-2 employees overnight." One company, Total Transportation Services Inc., he said, turned one hundred previously "misclassified contract drivers" into employees and, according to TTSI drivers, held onto only twenty contract drivers. TTSI's president, Vic LaRosa, calls that "grossly overstated" and says the numbers were the other way around.

LaRosa also takes issue with the proposed rules themselves. "By the ports making it mandatory that you only put an employee driver in that truck, they've now discriminated against a whole pool of independent owner-operators," he says. In what might seem like an odd joining of forces, the OOIDA agreed and was poised to sue the port should it apply the concessionaire requirements to long-haul drivers—who make up most of the OOIDA's membership—bringing in containers from elsewhere in the country. The port conceded the point concerning the long-haul drivers and, for a $30 pass, allows the visiting drivers into the terminals.

The ATA agreed with LaRosa's sentiment—one shared by most trucking companies—and proceeded to sue the port in July 2008, seeking a preliminary injunction against the concessionaire requirements of the Clean Truck program. The ATA, based in Arlington, Virginia, and representing 37,000 members (although not many of the trucking companies who work at the port belong to the group), argued before the U.S. District Court that the Federal Aviation Administration Authorization Act (FAAA Act) prohibited states and local governments from regulating the "price, route, or service of any motor carrier." (The Port of Long Beach avoided similar litigation by settling with the ATA out of court, agreeing to a plan that allowed access for both owner-operators and LMC employees as long as they met the port's truck standards for low emissions, among other criteria.)

The ATA didn't convince the judges, who decided in September 2008 that the port's rules fell under the act's exemption for preserving the "safety regulatory authority of a State with respect to motor vehicles." After the decision, the port asserted in a press release that the ruling had "[cleared] the way for the October 1, 2008 launch of the landmark environmental program."

Not so fast, the ATA said. Following the tortured legal route that these things take, the U.S. Court of Appeals for the Ninth Circuit then heard the case. Among that court's conclusions, announced in March 2009, it didn't buy the port's argument that all the owner-operators out there driving possibly poorly maintained, diesel-belching vehicles constituted a safety concern. "We see little safety-related merit to those thread-paper arguments," the court wrote, "which denigrate small businesses and insist that individuals should work for large employers or not at all."

And so the case went back to the U.S. District Court, which, in a forty-two-page decision, granted the ATA's motion for a preliminary injunction against the non-safety-related provisions of the concessionaire requirements, including enforcement of the truck ban against motor carriers. The case then went to a full trial on April 20, 2010, and four months later, U.S. District Court Judge Christina Snyder dismantled many of the ATA's arguments as not applying to the FAAA Act. "Drayage truckers do not have to sign the Port's Concession Agreement to operate in California," she wrote. "Instead they can operate anywhere in California, including other ports within the state, without signing POLA's Concession Agreement."

While Geraldine Knatz in a press release put this down as a victory for the Clean Truck Program, Mike Fox—who is against the concession requirements—is depending on the ATA's follow-up appeal to end any talk of him being required to hire the owner-operators working for him. And if that doesn't work, he predicts an insurrection by the drivers themselves: "I think the independent contractors could file their lawsuit against the Port of Los Angeles, because I think they have a constitutional right to be in business for themselves."

At the congressional subcommittee hearing, several people argued that the Clean Truck program had successfully reduced air pollution without the concessionaire requirement. Putting aside for a moment that the owner-operators are rightly or wrongly paying for the new, low-emission trucks responsible for this, a report released about a month later confirmed that levels of air pollution had indeed dropped: the port's 2009 Inventory of Air Emissions showed that diesel particulates had decreased by 47 percent between 2005 and 2009; in 2009 alone, the diesel particulate emissions were reduced by 26 percent. (This statistic is based on emissions per 10,000 20-foot containers and thus takes into account the more than 20 percent decrease in volume due to the recent recession.) However, responding to the arguments that the port's proposed rules were unnecessary, Covarrubias asked the subcommittee a pointed question: "Why are the laws set up so families like mine are forced by our bosses to pay for cleaning up the air?"

There's also an ominous scenario suggested by his words: if some drivers can't afford to pay for the clean trucks, they will have to leave the drayage business behind, and that could—if the numbers are large enough—slow the movement of cargo in and out of the port. With fewer truck drivers, containers could potentially pile up at the terminals, waiting for someone to deliver them. Without enough trucks to pick them up, the cans might have to be stacked to conserve space, which makes it more time-consuming to retrieve any particular container.

As port official Holmes told the subcommittee, offering an oblique warning, "We are concerned that we are setting up a system that's eventually going to fail because the independent owner-operators, without the company buying the trucks, are not going to be able to buy the trucks on their own."

THE TRUCKING COMPANIES

Vic LaRosa is a compact, intense man who exudes such competitiveness that even during our two interviews, he's fiercely selling his product. In his case, the angle is simple: his company, TTSI, is driving nothing but green trucks, either low-emission diesels or the even cleaner liquefied natural gas–powered rigs. That's 150 of the cleanest trucks this side of electric. Yes, he's committed to green, he says with both apparent sincerity and an eye toward good PR and how that attracts customers.

"[In 2007], we decided we don't care what the government does," he says. "We don't care what regulations come down. We are going to make an investment in green trucks. We are going to go to our customers and ask for our customers' support. The big guys got it. They got it. They said, 'Clean air. We want it. What's it going to take? And can you do it?' Yes. This is what I need. Ba-boom, we signed the contracts, we signed the agreements, and we moved forward. . . . So now the demand for our clean trucks grows every day because as people realize that they're getting hit with a seventy-dollar fee [for 40-foot containers pulled by "dirty" trucks] and there are alternatives in the market, our phones ring."

He also jumped into an incentive program offered by the port in

October 2008, which paid $20,000 for each newly purchased clean truck. It would appear that LaRosa wasn't the only one who figured it was best not to wait until 2012 to drive clean trucks; in total, the incentive program received subsidy applications for 7,500 trucks to be purchased by LMCs, when the port had expected to see about 1,000 applications.

Throughout our conversations at his Rancho Dominguez headquarters, LaRosa paints himself as a diehard environmentalist who would rather be hunting or fishing at his house in Montana. Just the same, he clearly knows how to be green and profitable at the same time. TTSI has operations in Seattle, San Diego, Atlanta, and Norfolk, and its Web site lists twenty-seven major clients including Target, Pioneer, Polo Ralph Lauren, JVC, and J. Crew, some of whom LaRosa lauds as just as environmentally savvy as he is.

Following a dissertation on what he considers the trucking industry's emancipation from federal regulation in 1980, which opened the nation's roads to more competition (the new deregulation laws also brought to the market more companies who hired only independent contractors to haul cargo), LaRosa endorses the owner-operator system. "This is why it works—it's this simple," he says. "[The owner-operators] get paid for productivity. The incentive is on how many moves do you make? Not how many hours do you work. How many moves do you make? The more moves you make, the more money you make. Okay. When you go to an hourly employee—and I've got tons of statistics to prove this, the productivity drops in half. The hourly employee is just not motivated to work on a number of moves. 'I'm on the clock. I'm going to put my eight, ten hours in. I'm going to get paid.'"

Joe Rajkovacz says this may be true on paper, but there's more to it. First, an employee driver and an owner-operator are equally productive standing in line at an inefficient terminal. Neither can pick up a container any faster than the other. It just looks like the independent contractor is accomplishing more moves, he claims, because by law drivers are limited to eleven hours of road time before they have to stop for ten hours, and so they sometimes underreport the time they're driving so they can get in that last move, legally or otherwise. "'I've got fixed expenses I've got to meet,'" he says, speaking as a hypothetical owner-operator. "'I'm going to lie my ass off on my logbook about how I account for my time. That's why I discount the delays in loading and unloading from my daily service record. That's why I get this bogus view that somehow I'm much more productive as an owner-operator.'"

For this reason, Mike Fox is convinced it's the delays at the terminal that are at fault, not the owner-operator system. He has a point. For its part, the drayage industry is becoming more sophisticated, and it would seem that the terminals haven't kept up. LaRosa shows me his dispatch office, where, with software called E-Modal, they're able to track a container while it's still on the ship, allowing them to update the customer on the status of the cargo. After a driver picks up the container, the dispatcher can pinpoint the truck's location through GPS, so if a shipper wants to know where the can is, they find out down to the street corner. The terminals could easily catch up, say LaRosa and Fox, with an appointment system, which could thin out the long lines, but the terminals have resisted because it would involve hiring more ILWU clerks.

So in the meantime, the congenial Fox believes the issue comes down to LMCs treating their independent contractors better than the advocates for *troqueros* claim they do. "You've got owners much more concerned about treating drivers correctly—and they should be, because they're making a $100,000 investment per truck," he says. "It doesn't do us any good to go out and buy all these trucks and then have drivers quit on us. So we have a real stake in this whole thing now. More than ever before. So there's a dramatic mind change here about—let's treat the drivers real well. Make sure they make their money."

THE DELIVERY

As Branch and I drive along the 605 freeway through the City of Commerce, Branch compulsively glances to his side-view mirrors watching for cars trying to get around him who don't seem to understand or care that they're about to cut off some 50 tons that can't stop until their car has been crushed. If he knows he has valuable cargo, he's also more alert to anyone trying to squeeze him off the road and then hijack the truck, which has happened to other drivers.

He points to a string of brightly lit malls. "The good thing is I get to drive all over so I can see, like, a lot of the spots [to eat]." He starts pointing out the restaurants he's tried as a result of his travels. "I know the places where I can go and park. And hopefully there's not another truck or cars parked there. There's plenty of times where I'm, okay, when I get to Carl's Jr. or some place to eat and I get there, and the parking is all full. So you know, I have to keep on driving."

After about thirty-five minutes on the road, we take an exit and rumble into an industrial park, pulling into a dark, deserted parking lot at Coaster Furniture Company. Branch drives up to a guard, who is ready to take his paperwork and open a gate to the back end of the warehouse, where containers are already parked in a row against a series of closed docks. The guard tells him where to take the container, and we enter, no other ID necessary, which is a relaxed change from the port.

Branch finds the parking spot, a narrow slot between two 40-foot containers, and deftly backs up his load. After jockeying back and forth twice to maneuver about the narrow lot, he's able to straighten the container, and he stops just as it hits a rubber bumper below the dock. "What you do is," Branch says, after explaining that this was the hardest thing to learn in driver school, "you have to turn your steering wheel the opposite way. Even when I learned to do it, when I'd get in a car, I would sometimes, you know, think I'm still in the truck."

Branch gets out, lowers the landing gear—two heavy-duty stands under the front end of the chassis—and then releases the hitch, known as a fifth wheel, a large, slotted metal plate with a locking mechanism inside that holds the chassis to the tractor. He then walks along the row of parked containers, banging on each, listening for the bong-bong sound that rings back. He's looking for an empty to bring back to the terminal. Most sound too low-pitched and are probably filled. Finally, the sound comes back with a hollow, higher-pitched boom-boom. He's found his can. After calling the Fox dispatcher with the container number to make sure the can is okay to take, he hitches it to the truck, pulls out, and speaks to the guard for a moment, who opens the container to make sure it's indeed empty. From entering to leaving takes just fifteen minutes.

Without wasting a moment, Branch heads back to the port. I watch him as he shifts gears with such fluid ease that he could be flipping on a light switch. Clearly it's the "independent" part of his job he likes the most. "What's nice is I'll put on some jazz. Meditate," he tells me as a way of explaining the working conditions he values as part of driving a rig for a living.

ELEVEN

The Hold Men

ART ALMEIDA

Like most longshoremen in the 1950s, Art Almeida was a hold man. The men who worked with him were soldiers, gladiators, the sweaty, muscled foundation of shipping. They toiled in the pits, down in the ship's shadowy lower decks where the real work was done, all backs and elbows. This made the hold men the most important guys on the waterfront.

At a time when cargoes were loaded and unloaded almost entirely by hand, a typical ship required five to eight gangs of eight hold men each to discharge cargo. On a good day, they might pump out 15 tons of cargo per hour. They confronted everything from cotton bales to lumber to heavy oil barrels to poisonous cyanide in drums and DDT insecticide in leaky sacks. As soon as one gang cleared out enough space in the hold, gangs of six were brought in to fill the spot with the next load of outgoing cargo, and the first gang climbed into the next hold. The entire process could take more than five days to complete, before the ship steamed off to another port.

Here was a world where Almeida could feel good about his work. He felt strong working down in the hold, like the muscles in his arms and shoulders meant something. He went to the waterfront each morning looking forward to another day and came home dead tired, barely able to take a shower before hitting the bed, but proud of what he had accomplished, the emptied holds and the warehouses full of cargo that had ridden on the Pacific Ocean. And the variety—he worked on all kinds of ships, usually for no more than five days before he was assigned to another. Each ship had a different cargo and a new gang to work with. It was the greatest experience he had known in his young life. It's not that Almeida couldn't have done something else—he had the smarts— but this is what he unapologetically enjoyed.

Almeida first entered this world before he graduated from San Pedro High School in 1947, walking onto the docks as a casual, or sportie (a nonunion worker who got the leftovers after union members were assigned jobs). This was the most common way for someone to get a taste of dock work without jumping through any hoops to become a union member. When he started college, he attended classes for just two weeks before he ran out of money and found himself leeching off his parents, and you just didn't do that. He really couldn't earn a decent living as a sportie with limited hours, and there were few other jobs unless he wanted to fish or work in the cannery. So he believed his only choice was to enlist in the army, where he spent his next three years. The army sent him to Germany and trained him in telephony and telegraphy.

When he came back, he joined the reserves, but he also needed a job. He first applied with the telephone company to put his military experience to use. Hired, they said, but then he penciled out the pay and discovered he could earn $40 a week working with those snooty phone guys, or make $19 a day at the docks and get to hang out with the men he liked. Being a gregarious kind of guy, that camaraderie meant a lot to him. So he chose the waterfront, and it was the best decision he ever made.

Getting a union card required a longshoreman sponsor, which showed that you were trusted by association and that the union could assume you were okay. It was also how the union filtered all the people who des-

perately wanted the relatively well-paid waterfront jobs. The sponsorship system started about the same time the ILWU began. The union's
charter members could bring in blood relatives, and it was the primary
way the labor rolls were fed. That exclusivity eroded over time, and
it eventually took ten union guys—and not necessarily an applicant's
kin—to endorse an application. (It was not unheard of for sponsors to
take payoffs, occasionally as high as $2,000. Sometimes other motiva-
tions prevailed: once, some guys backed several athletes just out of the
navy so they would play on the union's football team.) When an application was endorsed and tentatively accepted, it went to the membership
committee. The applicant stood before the committee for an interview,
facing such easily answered, loyalty-related questions as, "Have you
ever crossed a picket line?"

Almeida didn't have to pay a bribe to get in. On July 7, 1953, after three
years of working as a casual and a year after he had married his high
school girlfriend, Irene, he earned his Class B union card, and he was
later promoted to Class A status, number 3202. He could work just about
anytime he wanted as long as there was a job. The Class A status was
important because it meant that a worker had piled up some substantial
work time and was in good standing with the employers. Even if someone was in good graces with the union, the employers could say, "We
don't want him. He's a drunk. We're not going to take him." Almeida,
who didn't drink and thought of himself as a hard worker, had it made.

The ILWU dispatch hall, where he got his work assignments, operated with egalitarian simplicity. At the beginning of each quarter, each
longshoreman started with zero hours. One guy could work all day
and earn eight hours. However, the guy next in line might get a job
that lasted only the six hours per shift guaranteed by the contract. At
the end of their shifts, they would both check in and let the dispatcher
know their hours. The next day, the worker with six hours was assigned
a job ahead of the one with eight hours. "Low-man-out" dispatching, as
they still call it today.

Almeida started out as a hold man because union rules required him to work inside a ship's hold for five years before he could do anything else. And if he didn't like it, tough. But hold work was okay with him because going into the hold meant learning how to be a longshore-man, how to be a man. He began his day at the dispatch hall, where he checked in before 6:30 A.M. by writing down his union number and the previous day's hours at the hold board. (Each board represented a work category, and if you worked the hold board, your name rotated only among others who were also working that board.) Any later than 6:30, and he wouldn't get a job. After all, the union—and the employers, for that matter—kept order on the chaotic waterfront through its simple but rigid rules, all of them codified in "the book," the contract. There were always some workers who were trying to tip the system in their favor by sidestepping the rules. But if you wanted to work, then damn it, you got to the dispatch hall on time. That was the rule.

By 6:45 A.M., the dispatchers, who had already sorted the men on each board by how many hours they had worked, started calling the boards. Crammed shoulder to shoulder in the crowd, Almeida waited to hear his number yelled out. Once called, he usually grabbed the dispatch slip with its job information and simply reported for work at the assigned dock and shipping line. He did, however, have the option of flopping, that is, waiting for another job assignment instead. But if he made that choice, there was a penalty attached—he would have to add six hours to his day's total. So, if he took another job that day and worked eight hours, he would be required to report fourteen hours. This, of course, would mean that he might not get a job the next day because he had more hours on paper than others. Another rule.

Naturally, there were those who had bad memories and "forgot" how many hours they had worked. Writing down six instead of eight might mean the difference between working the next day or not. But longshoremen who suspected a cheater could challenge that worker's report. Also, the dispatchers periodically cross-checked reported hours against dispatch slips, and if they discovered a cheater, they could pull that worker off a job in the middle of the shift.

At the beginning of each month, longshoremen were also checked to make sure they had paid their union dues on time. The night before, the secretary would post a list of delinquent members at the dispatch hall. Many read the lists not to check their own status but to make sure the guy next to them wasn't getting a job without first plunking down $20. "Hey, dispatcher! This guy hasn't paid his dues!" they would call out. No dues, no job. One more rule.

Almeida was always cleared through the dispatch hall without a problem and reported to his ship. Like most longshoremen, he wore clothes that fit the hard, nasty work. His striped hickory shirts were heavy cotton, made for all the abuse. The shirts came long-sleeved, but he cut off the sleeves at the shoulders so they were a little cooler in the dank holds. Everyone wore Frisco jeans, made of heavy black denim reinforced with metal rivets. And you couldn't show up without a cap called the "Harry Bridges Stetson." Most longshoremen, especially hold men, also had variously shaped hooks in their pockets, which they used to drag unwieldy or small boxes they couldn't grab with gloves on. The hook became a symbol: if you put a hook in your pocket, it meant you were going to a job or working. When you retired, you put away your hook.

On paper, unloading a ship wasn't a complicated process. Say you were discharging whisky from a ship called the *Bridges Bottom* out of Liverpool. The ship would dock, and the clerk—a union member— would tell the boss (who worked for the ship's company) that, according to the manifest, the cargo was in the ship's aft in hold number two. Longshoremen would then rig the winch boom over that hold's hatch and get ready to lower the first lift board to the hold men, who had climbed down a ladder to the deck. Lift boards looked like pallets but were much sturdier, made from two-by-sixes bolted together as reinforcement to sustain all the weight and knocks.

With the lift board lowered into the hold, the hold men would then load cargo on it. From there, the cargo was raised out of the hatch, known as "topping the boom," and swung over the ship's deck onto the dock, where the other half of the gang waited to unload the lift board. They piled the cargo on the dock, where clerks counted the boxes and confirmed that the cargo matched the manifest.

A jitney, a truck with a small cab, waited to take the cargo away to the warehouse for temporary storage. Jitneys, sometimes called Fordsoms, had magneto engines that made an incredible racket when revved up, but they were powerful little trucks, able to pull a four-wheeler loaded with cargo. To support the load, the four-wheelers had heavy rubber wheels and were connected to the jitney with a hook called a stinger, named for the obvious pain it would inflict if it landed on someone's foot. Once they took the cargo to the warehouse, the jitney drivers brought back an empty four-wheeler for another load.

It may have been a simple process in theory, but it was backbreaking enough to grind down the hold men over time until, even if they needed the work, their bodies had nothing left. The older men, age sixty or more with twenty-five years on the waterfront, didn't have to work in the hold if they didn't want to. It was one of the perks for hanging around so long, and the younger men respected that, even rewarded it. If an older worker was feeling the pain, he could go on the swampers' board. These were some of the easiest jobs on the docks. Some swampers did little more than add stickers—strips of wood—to lumber to separate the individual loads as they were stacked. That was the thing about the union—it had ways of taking care of the longshoremen who still needed work but were too old to handle the heavy loads.

Working in the hold could kill you. Down in the ship's lower deck lit by bare lightbulbs, where if the blowers weren't running the stale air could stiffen in your lungs, Almeida heard about a 1,200-pound roll of newsprint that got away from Freddy Negrete. Perhaps Negrete pulled too hard on the rope he used to maneuver it, and the gray paper, hard as wood, crushed him against the floor. His dazed partner and everyone else working on the ship went home for the rest of the day, a somber practice when someone lost their life on the job. Who could continue discharging the now irrelevant cargo knowing Freddy's broken body

Hold men watch a lift board loaded with cargo leave the ship. Courtesy of ILWU Library, San Francisco.

left the hold on a stretcher? As Harry Bridges said, borrowing from another union, "An injury to one is an injury to all." Yes, you could get hurt just about anywhere on the docks, but a hold man, moving cargo by hand, had the greatest chance of shutting down the waterfront for a day and earning a memorial.

It wasn't just accidents that made the job dangerous. A hold man could earn extra pay for working hazardous cargo, but it's hard to say that dime an hour was adequate compensation. Bone meal, or crushed bone, used for fertilizer was nondegradable and could lodge in one's lungs. For that reason, it required a mask, supplied by the employers, which was just flimsy cotton held over the mouth with a metal frame. Hold men also wore masks when they handled DDT insecticide.

Then again, no one wore a mask with asbestos—they didn't know it could make you sick—and it didn't earn you extra wages. The same was true for rubber bales. It wasn't the rubber itself that could harm you; it was the talcum powder used to keep the rubber sheets from sticking together after being compressed over the weeks in the often hot hold during the passage from Indonesia. Almeida was one of the smart ones who requested a mask anyway to combat the talc flying in the air as he separated and loaded the 350-pound bales.

After working hazardous cargo, longshoremen had the option of what they called shirt time, a ten-minute additional break just before lunch so they could leave the hold and shake off the dust, whatever it might be, from their clothes. Unfortunately, they still brought plenty of the dust home with them and exposed their families to the same poisons they came in contact with in the hold.

The hold men had other ways of taking care of themselves. In a less-than-efficient practice known as "four-on, four-off," each eight-person gang that discharged cargo split itself into half, one group in the hold, the other on the dock. After the hold men had loaded a lift board, they sat waiting until the workers on the dock had unloaded it. While this translated into some down time—according to a union analysis, these individuals worked about 70 percent of the time for which they were paid—no one, not even the employers, could fault the practice because the work was so strenuous.

As work rules evolved over the years, eventually a gang of eight could sit out half the day—two men in the hold working, two men on the dock working, while the others watched. In the same vein, long-shoremen embraced the concept of multiple handling, which stipulated that cargo coming off a ship must actually touch the so-called skin of the dock. Thus once a loaded lift board was set down on the dock, the cargo couldn't go anywhere until it had been hauled off the pallet onto the dock by longshoremen and then onto a jitney's four-wheeler by Teamsters, who had jurisdiction at the time over loading and unloading trucks and trains.

In fairness, this also allowed clerks to easily check the cargo against their manifests before it went to the warehouse. But even the union recognized there was something less than efficient about the practice, and it no doubt occurred to everyone involved that a lift board could be loaded directly onto or off a four-wheeler. To be sure, the employers grumbled about the double handling, and yet they didn't do much about it.

Even as talk of containers and mechanizing the docks reached the point where the union and the employers were making it a contract issue, the system continued. In a September 18, 1960, memo to Harry Bridges, ILWU analyst Lincoln Fairley wrote after touring the San Pedro port facility, "I was impressed by the fact that shippers can avoid double handling any time they choose, simply by putting their shipment in containers." He then added with a touch of sarcasm, "That most of them do not do so seems to indicate that there are technological reasons for shipping the way they do, or that the economic advantages of changing are not sufficiently great."

Long before this, Bridges, and indeed the entire industry, had recognized that the additional labor costs involved were starting to make the waterfront industry look less attractive to shippers. Whenever possible, some were taking their cargo to the road on trucks or rails instead of sending it up or down the coast on ships. Bridges also foresaw that the employers—embodied by the Pacific Maritime Association—would sooner or later start pushing for ways to decrease those labor costs through the one weapon they had: the container. As he told a caucus convened in Portland, Oregon, in October 1957, change would take place, "the easy way or the hard way."

His negotiating counterpart, Paul St. Sure, president of the PMA, believed Bridges also understood that the industry was more vulnerable than some realized. After the 1957 contract talks, in which the PMA shrugged off an ILWU demand for higher wages as retaliation for longshoremen habitually calling wildcat strikes to make impromptu changes to work rules, St. Sure wrote, "[Bridges] now sees the movement forward of mechanization. . . . [H]e knows that unless something is done to correct the situation on the docks, there isn't going to be any work for longshoremen. I think he's in the mood right now to do something about it."

In other words, the hold men were about to lose their status as the waterfront's linchpin. Almeida saw it coming in the late 1950s. First came the forklifts, able to pick up 40,000 pounds. The cargo was still stored in holds, but now it took less labor to bring larger and larger boxes to the hatch, where a winch would haul them out and onto the dock. Then, the once-dangerous rolls of newsprint paper that killed Freddy Negrete were being strapped ten to a board, called a whaleback, and lifted out of a ship all at once. Ships such as the *Coast Progress* were retrofitted to make the hatches wide enough to handle the bigger loads. In San Pedro, longshoremen discharged whalebacks at a rate of 69 tons per hour, nearly three times what they could do with individual rolls.

Clearly, this was just the precursor to cargo going into containers and being lifted out by huge cranes. The process of unloading holds by hand would soon be crushed—an hour of manual labor compressed into a few minutes. Or, as the union's newspaper, the *Dispatcher,* put it in 1957: "We would be fooling ourselves if we didn't agree that in many ways the shipping industry has been long operating with very old fashioned methods compared to other industries."

Longshoremen have always been pretty astute observers of their world, and this was perhaps one of the most clear-eyed statements they've ever made. In 1960, the ILWU and the PMA signed a contract dubbed the Mechanization and Modernization Agreement (M&M). The contract's bottom line for all involved was the union's agreement that the employers were free to introduce containers, thus largely eliminating the hold man position, and that they could hire only the number of workers necessary to do the job. Work stoppages were now contract violations, with a penalty as high as $13,650 a day. In return, the ILWU won expanded jurisdiction over both cargo and jobs on the docks, as well as substantial increases in wages and pensions. The PMA began paying into a "jointly trusted fund" that was designed to compensate longshoremen for lost wages when their jobs were replaced by machines and containers; the fund was calculated to total $27.5 million after five and a half years.

When I first met Almeida in 2004, he had been retired for ten years. Then in his seventies, he had a large midsection that hinted at how much easier life was these days. He wore a loose, short-sleeve shirt that draped past his belt line, the signature outfit for many longshoremen in their off hours. His thinning gray hair hung over his ears and collar in an almost boyish manner. His voice was strong with just a hint of gruffness. "The real progressive and great advances came with the M&M," he said at the beginning, when I, the neophyte in union lore, admitted I knew nothing about the seminal contract. "What came of it?" I asked naïvely.

A lot, as it turns out. By 1964, as containers were showing up more and more, there had been a 34 percent rise in productivity over 1960 and a labor cost savings of nearly 7.5 million work hours. It took gangs just twenty-four hours to send a ship on its way, compared to five to six days before the M&M. This was all great for the employers, but as Bridges put it in a 1961 speech before the American Association of Port Authorities, "At best, we have secured the livelihood of the present registered workforce. But in so doing, we recognize we have been forced to shift the impact of the machines to those workers who might have found employment in this industry but for mechanization; they are the victims of silent firing, or no new hiring."

By the end of our three interviews, it's clear that Almeida relished his days as a hold man. Sure, he embraced mechanization as a practical matter: he became a crane driver in 1964. But he was also on the strike committee during the 1971 strike, a rebellion of sorts against some of the M&M's provisions that longshoremen felt didn't go far enough to compensate them for lost jobs. He served as Local 13 president between 1976 and 1978 and still maintains a high profile today as the local's unofficial historian. He later helped push for a monument to longshoremen killed on the job (Freddy Negrete is among those listed), which now sits on San Pedro's Harbor Boulevard overlooking the port.

Yet he talked about his accomplishments in an almost academic manner. But whenever I asked about working in the hold, he became more animated, especially recounting his memories of his fellow workers. "The important thing you had in common was, you were a hold man," he said. "You worked hard in the hold."

DAVE ARIAN

Dave Arian would take a bullet for his union, the ILWU. Granted, labor struggles are usually fought these days with legal briefs or contract negotiations, not the violent confrontations that accompanied the union's first years. Just the same, as he puts it, "When push comes to shove, I guess the workforce will be there. They will defend what they have with their lives. I believe that."

It's one of the fundamental differences, he thinks, between the workers and their employers. All those CEOs and managers would rather walk away from their jobs than march down the street toward a phalanx of well-armed police (a fascinating image, to be sure). "I think that's true," he says of the rank and file's willingness to lay down their lives for the union. "And I think that's true not to the man and woman, but to the majority, they know if they don't have [the union], they don't have anything."

When I first talk with Arian in mid-2006, he has a greater chance of being killed on the job as a hold man than in a battle with police or scabs. A load of scrap metal could pop loose and crush him. Or someone in a truck could be driving too fast, lose control, and nail him to the skin of the dock. At this point, with nearly forty years as a hold man, Arian works at night moving pipes, lumber, and anything else that's normally shipped as break bulk cargo, items that must be moved individually rather than in 40-foot metal containers. In that way, he's an anachronism. There are few hold men anymore. The docks are so mechanized

that you're unusual if you don't spend most of the day gripping a steering wheel, isolated in a truck cab from the rest of your coworkers.

But when Arian goes to work, he joins his gang, that throwback to the
pre-container days. Arian figures his gang's pedigree extends back to
the 1930s or 1940s; it's had the same ID number—110—for about seventy
years. Whenever someone retires from the gang, another worker comes
in as a replacement, getting the same gang number. It's that connection
to the past that means so much to him. At the moment, he leads the
gang along with his partner, Norm, and they choose who they want in
their eight-person group, which is composed of four in the hold, two
winch drivers, and two front men who work on the dock.

Almost every weekday, Arian calls into the dispatch hall and gets
his assignment for that night, issued by different employers, depending
on who has a ship docked with break bulk cargo. Occasionally, only
three of the four gangs on the rolls are needed. Because jobs are rotated
between the gangs to ensure they all work more or less the same total
hours, his group may be idle on a given night. In that case, he often opts
to visit the hall and seek work as an individual; when volume at the two
ports, Los Angeles and Long Beach, is high, he'll no doubt get a job.

This freelance status makes him different from about a third of
the workforce, who prefer steady jobs with the same employer rather
than working out of the dispatch hall. It's a choice the union reluc-
tantly allowed in the 1960s in return for certain benefits. Employers
want steady workers because they believe they're more apt to arrive
on time and to know the company's system better than those coming
from the hall. Also, steadies are less likely to attend union meetings or
get involved because they get comfortable, as anyone would with job
security, and start looking to the company for which they work as the
provider of that security and not the union. But for a self-described
lefty like Arian, working as a steady is anathema to the whole idea of
the dispatch hall, which was created so jobs would be equally distributed among willing workers. It's also a place where people can meet and
befriend other members, discuss the day's issues, or compare notes on

the employers. But even that function is disappearing as the phone-in system, which allows workers to simply call in to check on job availability, becomes more prevalent.

Once Arian gets his ship assignment, he meets his gang at the dock at 6:00 P.M., and they tackle whatever break bulk cargo is coming off or on the ship, often scrap steel or fruit. Two people in the hold work the 25-ton Hyster forklifts—almost all break bulk cargo these days is far too heavy for a person to lift and carry—and maneuver the cargo so that the men on the winch can haul it out and land it on a truck at the dock. There, Arian and Norm, the front men, unhook the load. Two additional people, often coming out of the dispatch hall, clean up the hold afterward.

"You know you have a group of workers that you can trust," Arian says of his gang with an even-toned affection. "You know they're going to show up for work, you know they're going to do a good job. You know they're going to work safe. You know they're going to back you up. There's more of a camaraderie. And you get to work with the same guys. My partner, Norm, we've been working together on and off for thirty-five years. He's somebody you can absolutely depend on. That's important on the waterfront."

It's both that camaraderie and the job's physicality that connect Arian to the hold men he first knew and admired as a kid. He began his longshore career while in high school in late 1964, working out of the casual hall. At a time when longshore jobs weren't popular, he stayed at the docks to become a hold man, like his father. He carried banana stalks taller than he was, weighing more than 100 pounds. The guys in his gang moved 500-pound cotton bales as a team or carried 100-pound-plus sacks by themselves. He came home so worn out that he couldn't help wondering what it would be like to work in the shipyard building navy vessels and making just as much money without getting beaten down by the loads he carried. Or perhaps he could become a fisherman, conceivably earning even more and working only seasonally.

"It took me a lot of years to understand exactly why you felt good when the day was over," he says. "And just like a brain surgeon when he finishes a successful operation, or a scientist who succeeds at a certain experiment, or an athlete who perfects the fastest time because everything clicks for him that day—the technique, all the speed, all the energy, and he's accomplished something. Workers do the same thing. When a worker loads a ship or unloads a ship—back then, it was like a jigsaw puzzle to load and unload ships. It took a different kind of skill, and when you got done, you looked to see what you got accomplished, and you knew you accomplished something that day. The winch drivers have their skill. The hold men have their skills. The people who drive forklifts have their skills. And everybody worked together. There was camaraderie."

He stayed on the docks because he could choose his hours, which was another advantage of working out of the dispatch hall. If he had something more important to do—perhaps regarding his increasing involvement with the union—he simply didn't show up to get a work assignment. No one wondered what happened to him, no one expected him to call in and explain why he wasn't at the hall. The steadies may have had their job security, but he had the sort of freedom that is so rare in the workplace.

Arian's involvement with the union started almost at the beginning of his career. He first ran for the union's executive board in 1969, but lost. He found his way onto the district council in 1970. He won election twice as president of Local 13, starting in 1984. He took the top international spot, as ILWU president, between 1991 and 1994, only the third person in union history to hold the job, after Harry Bridges and Jimmy Herman. He served one term, losing in 1994 to Brian McWilliams.

In 2004, he once again won the Local 13 president's office. As near as he can tell, his views were probably to the left of about 80 percent of the membership, but he won anyway because voters figured he could do the job. Unfortunately, they didn't like the job he did. According to Jim Spinosa, Arian's friend and himself a past international president, Arian concentrated on increasing pensions, which at the time were barely adequate to survive on, instead of boosting wages. However, the younger longshoremen were more concerned with fatter paychecks and weren't thinking ahead to retirement. An apparently unforgiving, short-sighted bunch, the Local 13 rank and file booted Arian out. (It's hardly unusual for Local 13 officers to have short careers.) In subsequent contracts, wages indeed went up. But thanks to both Arian and Spinosa, longshoremen eventually also got better pensions and medical packages covering them and their surviving spouses until they die.

Through all of this, Arian developed an appreciation for how his views—sometimes more radical than the mainstream—were tolerated within the union, if not always agreed with. "And that was the beauty of the union," he says, telling me of his strong views about the Vietnam war, the government, and corporations (none of them exactly positive). "Not that people agreed with me, but people allowed you, and the union allowed you, pretty much any beliefs you wanted. Two things Bridges said: number one, the only thing we can guarantee when you get into this union is the right to get in a fight—not to win, not to lose, but you had a right to get in the fight. And the second thing is your point of view will be respected even if not agreed with."

These days, it's unclear if the rank and file has the same familial feelings toward the union. The newcomers may not even realize how much they owe to their underpaid predecessors who negotiated those first contracts, not to mention to anyone who marched during a strike rather than taking the employer's lousy excuse for a pay increase, pension, or medical coverage. Mention Harry, as in Harry Bridges, and some of the newer folks think it's the foreman over at the Maersk terminal. Say you're taking out your hook, and they haven't a clue what you're talking about.

"Today, people make so much money, it's not like it was before," Arian says, appearing to walk a fine line between disparaging his fellow workers and just explaining the reality of the current situation. "People are more in it for the money now, not the job or the union, but that comes with financial success."

Local 13 even offers classes in union history so the rookies will realize that their relationship with the employers is not to be taken for granted, with the past full of examples of betrayal, subpar working conditions, and attempts to weaken or break up the union. Generating such suspicion toward the members of the Pacific Maritime Association is a subject I gingerly take up with Arian and his cohorts, not wanting to denigrate their sincerity, but hoping to at least get them to explain why they still rely on the extremes of what is now fairly ancient history to characterize the employers of today. If nothing else, they all look at me as though I'm more than a tad naïve.

You want modern examples? they ask. How about Joe Miniace, the former PMA CEO and president, who, they believe, was under orders from the employers he represented to dismantle the union by, among other things, outsourcing union jobs to out-of-state companies. It eventually got so ugly that Miniace shut down West Coast ports for ten days during the stalled 2002 contract negotiations.

Miniace, for his part, denies he was a union-buster: "I think there are certain things that are realities in life, and the longshore union, absent of something colossally stupid, is going to be around. You know that. And you work with that. No one was ever trying to bust the union. Never."

The present PMA CEO and president, Jim McKenna, repeats the same sentiment: "Nobody that has been around the industry, the waterfront, for any length of time gives [that idea] any credence whatsoever. It's a sound bite that might play well in Washington or somewhere, but they're a regulated monopoly and they're put in existence by the [federal National Labor Relations Board]—one union will represent all dockworkers on the West Coast of the United States."

At first glance, it appears that the union, as embodied by its leaders, doesn't believe it. Jim Spinosa, perhaps the ILWU's strongest international president next to Bridges, has used language in the past to suggest the union was under duress from outside forces out to dilute its power.

"The employers continue to lie and cheat in every way they can to use technology to outsource our jobs," he told the ILWU's 2006 international convention. "They try to overwhelm us with paperwork and deadlines. But our Technology Committees are up to the challenge and the [union] has the money and the will to continue to fight for our jurisdiction." But when I ask him if Miniace was a union-buster, he isn't so definite: "I don't know what his thinking really was, but my perception of Miniace is [he was] coming in to change the way we worked on the waterfront."

So I ask Peter Peyton, one of the most astute observers of the waterfront, if the employers are out to destroy the union. "No. No, I think— first of all, it wouldn't be to their advantage," he tells me. "I mean, you don't just pick up a workforce [after eliminating the union]. It just doesn't happen. And this job is becoming more specialized, [with] crane drivers, people on computers. You have to have people who can do this stuff. And I don't know, in the true sense of busted—no. Does that mean they would like change? Well, they always want change."

Clearly, Arian has given this a lot of thought, and he approaches the subject from more of a big-picture angle. It's really nothing personal, he says. It's just that the workers and the employers will always be at odds with each other.

"The absolute rule of capital [that is, the employers] is to maximize profit. It has nothing to do with greed. It has nothing to do with oppression, or repression. It has nothing to do with any of that stuff. . . . Either you become efficient in your competition with other capitalists, or you go under. You have to be the best at what you do. And the way you make money, you know, is by the exploitation of labor," he explains.

"You know, you've got a labor force. That labor force is creating everything you're making a profit off of, so you've got to keep them happy. But you can't give them too much because it cuts into your ability to expand your business. If you just make enough money to pay your workers and pay yourself, you will fail under capitalism. Can't be. There's got to be a surplus profit. There's got to be additional money for future investments, because you just borrowed money from the bank to produce two thousand more shoes. So the question of exploitation is objective. And it's antagonistic. It's natural to the system."

In a way, all the table pounding about union-busting comes down to maintaining an adversarial relationship between the rank-and-file workers and the management. Arian says that's necessary for those times when the employers attempt some maneuver that could hurt the workers, such as cutting back on benefits during contract negotiations—in a situation like that, if the union doesn't appear unified, its position is weaker. "Even though it may seem to be demonizing," he says, "it's at a point in history where you're really trying to get across to the membership what the real issues are. 'Pay attention. What's going on with our health and welfare plan? What's going on with our pension plan? What's going on with those things? Pay attention.'"

So I ask him if the PMA is out to destroy the union. "I don't think the PMA knows what they're doing," he replies.

The last time I see Arian is mid-2009, a few months after his retirement. His current position in the ILWU family is as a kind of labor wise man, able to boil down the choices being faced in any given situation into understandable chunks. Reflecting that image of union guru, Arian has authored a booklet, *The Right to Get in the Fight*, published by the Harry Bridges Institute in 2009, which details his life and labor philosophy.

He's relaxed as we talk, and it appears that life is good. Money is no longer an issue for him. His two kids are grown (his daughter is an ILWU member, his son an attorney). The house in San Pedro is paid off, he has no car payments and no credit card debt. Best of all, he has a healthy pension, nearly equaling his past pay, and health benefits.

"It's a beautiful position to be in," he says with the calm, satisfied look of someone for whom money is almost another natural element, like oxygen. "But I planned it that way. It's not like it just happened. I planned it that way. I've always been very, very militant and progressive in my thinking, and very conservative in my economics. I'm not a big spender. You could almost call me a minimalist. I live simply. Always have. So it's a good position right now. I don't have any money, but I don't need any money. My pension will more than take care of me."

A pension, he might have added, negotiated by the union.

TWELVE

The Women

ANGER MANAGEMENT

As she speaks, I'm trying to picture what it was like to be Gretchen Williams back then. In my imagination, she's standing on the broad asphalt field outside a cargo ship, a clerk's clipboard in hand, directing an all-male parade of longshoremen driving new Toyotas out of the hold and to the parking spots she assigns them. She's in her early twenties, five-foot-one, a self-described "voluptuous surfer chick" with sun-bleached hair. As far as the lead-footed yahoos joyriding past her know, she's the only woman out there, or, for that matter, anywhere on the docks. Small, alone, an easy target. She watches them as they spin about the lot like overstimulated schoolboys playing chicken with each other and circling her.

In a moment that she might have anticipated, one of the drivers brushes near her, too close to call it an accident. No, wait. Why would some guy, his face obscured by the midday glare on the windshield, run her down? That's an easy one to answer if you're the lone woman on the docks. *You know.* You're absolutely certain at least some of the men out there hate you enough, *fear you enough,* to turn a simple discharge operation into a little physical intimidation. Here's an opportunity for them to make the vindictive point that she's not only unwelcome but currently as vulnerable as anyone could be.

Wary, she watches the cars more closely. They keep coming off the ship; the space around her feels as though it's shrunk to a few inches instead of the wide, flat area the size of a stadium parking lot. She wonders if this shithead will take another shot at her. Perhaps, she thinks, he doesn't have the balls to actually try to run her down again, and this was just a dim-witted, brief impulse that gets his impotent anger out of his system.

And then once again he deliberately veers toward her. She leaps aside, perhaps a little unhappy that her reaction is so visceral, so emotional, so fun to watch. Perhaps he wouldn't get so much cruel satisfaction if she were calmer, not so jumpy. Again he comes as close as he can to running her down. And then finally he steers directly into her body. Williams runs across the asphalt toward an 8-foot chain-link fence and scrambles up it. In my imagination, I can hear the fence rattle as she grabs at the wire, but I doubt she even hears any sounds in her shock. The toes of her high-top boots slide in and out of the wire mesh, and I can feel the inevitable cuts to her fingers that she won't notice until it's all over.

This should have been considered assault with a deadly weapon, but Williams seems to shrug it off as an atavistic, territorial reaction. After all, she was trying to push her way onto the docks as a longshoreman, and no doubt the guy carried such a distorted image of masculinity that he believed waterfront work was uniquely suited for men.

As Williams tells the story some twenty-five years later, I want to be angry for her. I want to reach inside the car and throttle the bastard. But she's merely academic, as though reading a paragraph in a dissertation: "I find it interesting that in the days that I was trying to integrate the union, people tried to kill me," she tells me. "This was an extremely unpopular position to be in."

This doesn't seem like nearly enough resentment. Then again, I'm probably reacting like a typical male, wanting to protect the delicate blonde woman, when it's clear she did pretty well without me or anyone else. Besides, she's already poured out her own warranted anger so many times since then that it's barely visible now when she talks.

"Who knows what lurks in the mind of an idiot?" she says. "Who knows why? They had a beef with their old lady that day. Or they don't like their mother or their third-grade teacher. Who knows?"

She talks about that time with an almost amused demeanor, as if she's trying to say, "No hard feelings." But her face is taut, her eyes narrow. She tries to sound intellectual but admits, "One of my personal problems is instead of getting afraid, I get angry," as though conceding it's still difficult to calmly tell her story. "And that's not always safe."

We're talking over lunch at one of San Pedro's nicest restaurants, a warehouse converted into an Italian eatery, which she's reviewed in the past for *Random Lengths,* a local newspaper where she works as a food writer when she isn't organizing cargo on ships, a union job she describes as a cross between solving a jigsaw puzzle and sorting out air traffic control. She claims she was the first woman casual clerk, starting out in 1974, and, as such, the direct catalyst for women now working on the docks. The title of "first woman" is disputed; I'm told others may have started sooner, but they remained more low-key. Either way, women would have gotten the waterfront jobs eventually, but it usually takes someone with enough rage at injustice to jumpstart the process. And Williams was the one who did that.

She hasn't advertised her status as the first—or second—woman on the docks for years. But I get the feeling that after keeping a low profile all this time, she now wants to publicly tell her story, unafraid of any retaliation that might befall her, and I happen to be the one who crossed her path first.

It's not that Williams started her longshore career seeing a need for fairness and then pursuing that equal opportunity ideal. She just needed a job to sustain her college studies. In 1974, she envisioned herself as an academic, although, at nineteen, she was a little hazy about which topic she wanted to pursue for a doctorate—something in international relations, maybe, or political science. But universities charge for their services, and there are no discounts just because you're simply picking at their offerings, like attending some cerebral buffet. So her stepfather, who had been a clerk on the waterfront since 1946 and who perhaps should have known better, suggested she could pick up some extra cash by applying for casual work at the clerks' hall. After all, her stepbrothers made five times the piddling two bucks an hour she earned washing poodles or bartending (both among her various subsistence ventures).

With a hint of sibling rivalry, or perhaps with the view from her highly educated perch, she figured that if they could do it, she was no doubt overqualified. In the end, this bifurcated life of college studies and waterfront work did more than plant her feet in two different worlds. It produced one pissed-off intellectual.

That rage had a chance to surface early. Becoming a casual meant taking a written test. She had tutored her stepbrothers a few years before in their rookie days, so she already knew the exam treated math and other topics with grade school simplicity, and she had few trepidations about passing. But when she entered the clerks' hall for the first time in November, escorted by her stepfather, she endured the kind of grumbling from those in charge that comes more from fear of change than a perception of any actual threat.

"They didn't dig it," she says, "but I took the test and I passed." At least on paper, a woman had infiltrated the clerks' Local 63.

In a moment of relative naïveté, Williams later went to the Wilmington office of the Pacific Maritime Association in January 1975, just to see about getting registered with the employers. With the smug condescension one might use in talking to a child, the man in charge told her that he couldn't hire her because the longshoremen's wives would object (as if the PMA had ever worried what the little ladies thought before).

On the union side, the dispatchers assigning casual jobs had all the necessary power to keep her from working, as they did with anyone else they didn't like. The system made rejection easy. Casuals got jobs by calling in. When Williams was connected to a dispatcher, he would tell her, "No work for girls today." She would then hand the phone over to her brothers, who, with the dispatcher still on the line, easily picked up jobs for the day. (Occasionally, there were exceptions to this, when the port was so busy that they had no choice but to give her a job.)

Perhaps the dispatchers were incapable of realizing how each reference to her sex clearly defined their actions as discriminatory in the eyes of the law. Or maybe they paternalistically figured she would see her mistake in wanting to work a "man's job." Either way, it gave Williams plenty of legal fodder when she filed a sexual discrimination complaint in 1975 with the Los Angeles office of the U.S. Equal Employment Opportunity Commission. About the same time, a shy woman named Deborah Golden had also signed up for casual clerk jobs and was getting the same treatment. Williams didn't know her at the time, though the two met some eight years later; she believes Golden used the application to set up a legal confrontation.

At first, neither woman got much of a fight. The EEOC gathered the initial paperwork and then notified the PMA and the union of the two separate complaints. Williams says from that point on, nothing happened. For eight years, she waited, while the agency repeatedly reassigned her case or lost the paperwork.

"It was a nightmare all the way around," she says, implying with the kind of paranoia that sometimes comes with such crusades that somehow the fix was in. It seemed to her that the union or the PMA had some leverage over somebody at the EEOC, and that's what stalled her complaint.

So when it was clear her complaint was growing mold at the EEOC, she started multitasking. She figured the National Organization for Women would jump at the chance to help, but instead, "they didn't even bother to talk to me. They wanted nothing to do with it." I suggest that elitism on their part might have played a role, that they might not have been interested in working-class women, but she looks at me as if I've just mildly insulted her. I realize later how proud she is of her longshore career and suspect that my analysis implied my own elitism toward blue-collar workers, even if I would prefer to think I'm not such a snob.

Williams next tried Gloria Allred, then a budding attorney who later became famous for civil rights cases involving women. But, according to Williams, Allred "wanted four hundred bucks to walk in her office, and I didn't have forty bucks to spend on that. I was barely making it as it was. So there was no way she was going to help me."

Older longshoremen—some of whom Williams knew as fathers of her school friends—acted hurt as much as angered by her EEOC complaint. Art Almeida, who had started out in the early fifties as a hold man toting cargo (his story is told in chapter 11) and was now a stalwart on the waterfront, brought Harry Bridges to Dominguez Hills University in Carson for a speech. When Williams, an undergraduate there, came up to shake the great leader's hand, Almeida ignored her. A little later, while she studied in the cafeteria, the two men sat at a table near her. Almeida got up to buy some coffee, and Bridges started talking to her in a flirtatious way, telling her how cute she was. But it was clear that he knew who she was, and he quickly got to the point. "Why the hell do you want to be on the waterfront?" he asked. He followed this by reiterating his standard philosophy: if you want to be a longshoreman, you spend your first five years in the hold—as though the threat of hard labor would dissuade her.

I can tell Williams doesn't want to implicate the revered Bridges in the misogyny she's endured, and so she interprets this as receiving his qualified blessing. "[But] he didn't come out and make any kind of [public] statement to that effect," she adds, aware of the implied hypocrisy. After all, over the years Bridges had proudly promoted the principle of equal opportunity, showcasing the union's democratic nature by insisting that workers of all races were welcome to join the worker brotherhood—apparently as long as they were male. Perhaps he was a victim of his time, when most people believed it made no sense to have women down in the hold hoisting sacks of rice. Then again, what woman wanted to?

Well, Williams, for one. Although she preferred the less physical clerk jobs, she took on jobs in the hold, tossing 40-pound boxes of bananas, as well as other muscle-popping work whenever it was available. However, given all the resistance, the casual jobs were too rare for her to survive on dock work alone—she worked six days her first year and ten days the second year, all of them, she figures, the result of labor shortages. She eventually compiled a resume of some thirty temporary occupations, from chief cook on a ship to belly dancer in a Montana ski resort bar to artist's model. Even in her relative poverty, she regularly cooked spaghetti dinners for her fellow graduate students at the University of Southern California. Among the students at these simple chow affairs was Geraldine Knatz, the future executive director of the Port of Los Angeles.

Finally, in 1980, with 360 clerks in Local 63 and only one of them a woman (while the ratio in Local 13 was three thousand male longshoremen to seven women), Williams—and Golden on another occasion—discovered the Center for Law in the Public Interest, a law firm that specialized in cases involving Title VII of the 1964 Civil Rights Act, which prohibits employment discrimination. With three other women, including her sister-in-law, Williams met with an intense, compact attorney with thick black hair and dark eyes named A. Thomas Hunt, who enthusiastically greeted them.

With a successful racial discrimination case against the PMA and ILWU Local 13 already on his resume, Hunt knew the industry was ripe for more litigation. In fact, for years various groups had sued the union and the PMA to peel away the restrictive rules the old-timers loved so much. It had started before Hunt's time, when the sponsorship system began to break down little by little: first, the union was no longer allowed to give applications only to selected longshoremen; instead, when there were open positions, applications had to go out to everyone on the union rolls. Eventually, the docks opened up even more, to the point where a man walking in off the street had a shot at a union card. Later, workers had to earn their way into the union by racking up hours as a casual: once the union local and the PMA reckoned they needed more longshoremen, they decided how many and took that number from the top of the list of casuals, which meant those with the most hours.

In 1977, Forest Bates and five other black men—all union members—
filed suit against the PMA and the union, alleging racial discrimination under Title VII. They believed they had been refused skilled and
higher-paying positions, such as that of crane driver, because of race.
Hunt was one of the signing attorneys in that case. The groups settled
the next year despite a boilerplate disclaimer by the defendants—"The
defendants, and each of them, have denied and continue to deny the
claims of the plaintiffs." The settlement involved a court order that,
among other things, singled out crane driver positions and decreed that
"for every one hundred longshoremen selected for training, a number of
[crane driver] positions equal to or exceeding the percentage of blacks
in the labor pool shall be offered to black longshoremen." To Williams,
the logic behind the Bates case was easily applicable to a sexual discrimination case.

Precisely, Hunt said in his 1980 court papers, going after Local 13,
Local 63 (marine clerks), the ILWU, and the PMA for a "pattern of employment discrimination against women." A 1965 Harvard Law School
graduate, Hunt had spent most of his career litigating employment
discrimination and fair-housing class actions. While working for the
Justice Department between 1971 and 1972, Hunt was the lead attorney
in the first Title VII case brought against a public entity, the city of
Montgomery, Alabama. When Williams found him, Hunt had earned a
reputation in Los Angeles as a civil rights lawyer with big guns, winning
discrimination lawsuits against the Los Angeles County Fire Department, the county Sheriff's Department, and the City of Los Angeles
Police Department. If anybody could get the ILWU and the PMA to
pay attention, he could.

Williams says she asked not to be one of the recorded plaintiffs in
the lawsuit because she had been getting death threats, and she didn't
need her name on what promised to be a monumental legal decision.
So Hunt put Golden down as the lead plaintiff. When I ask him why,
Hunt says he can't recall but that it was probably because she had the
oldest complaint among the seven women whose names ended up on

the original court filing. Williams theorizes that Golden possessed the double appeal of being black and having a name that went so well with the eventual judgment—the Golden Consent Decree, as it's largely known today. The title just exudes a moral superiority and abundance.

During the resulting two-year litigation (the case never went to trial), the ILWU resisted any kind of settlement. Hunt believes that "the union had political concerns. Unions always have political concerns. Whoever the officers of the union are, they are concerned that if they make a deal like this, they're going to get voted out of office for having done it." As for the PMA, Hunt figures they wouldn't settle the suit on their own out of fear the union would retaliate in some way. What finally brought the case to an end, he tells me, is that the two sides put aside the possibility of back-pay awards, which could have sullied a few profit reports on the PMA side. The union was more concerned about the prospect of legal fees continuing to pile up if a trial were to take place.

Before the various parties settled the lawsuit, the union finally registered Williams in January 1982 with an offer of "big money to bail" on the litigation. She took the union card but refused the cash.

U.S. District Court Judge Robert M. Takasugi's final consent decree, issued on May 25, 1983, took a blunt axe to the old, male-dominated waterfront culture. "The defendants," he wrote regarding Local 63, "shall adopt the long range goal of employing women as marine clerks at the Port in sufficient numbers to eliminate the continuing effects of any possible past discrimination." Overall, he ordered that by 1998, 20 percent of all registered longshore workers at the ports of Los Angeles and Long Beach and 25 percent of clerks must be women. But then he went further and required that starting in 1983, "no less than 30 percent of the persons transferred from longshore to clerk registration at the port shall be women." He also specified short-term goals: of the next nine hundred persons registered as class B workers (those promoted from the casual hall), at least 35 percent had to be women. And then of the next one hundred persons, 25 percent were to be women.

It's not that Williams was thrilled with the final quotas. She insists that early drafts of the settlement mandated half of all clerks and 35 percent of all longshore workers be women, but that Hunt and his team backed off on such parity as a way to settle the lawsuit before it went to trial, where presumably the legal fees could have bankrupted the union. "They were making a deal," she says cynically. "[But] I was happy to be alive at that point."

While the union and the PMA publicly maintained a posture of innocence, they were also privately relieved the decree didn't go any further. Local 13's attorney, George E. Shibley, told Local 13 president Lou Loveridge and the local's secretary, Louis Rios, in a letter dated June 6, 1983:

> All in all, in my opinion, the Consent Decree and its approval by the Court represents a substantial victory, especially for Local 13. It is true that after a fabulously expensive trial we may have had a fairly even chance of winning the litigation, but the converse is also true: after expending a fortune in money, time and effort, we may have been faced with a very oppressive judgment in favor of the women, which could have included large sums of back pay, enormous attorneys' fees for the opposing parties and Court interference with the selection of transferees and registrants. As it is, not one Class A Longshoreman has, by virtue of the Consent Decree, been deprived of his right to transfer from Class A Longshore to Class A Marine Clerk registration. Nor do we have to be seriously worried about an undue influx of registered women Longshoremen who are either unable or unwilling to perform the same Longshore work as the male registered Longshoremen. . . . Further, now that the facts have become known to women in this area generally that registration as a Longshore worker requires a full time commitment to Longshore work . . . it is doubtful if as many women will be attracted to Longshore registration as were attracted when the myths circulated by the Media led women to believe that Longshore registration meant a fortune with no arduous responsibilities attached.

This might have been grandstanding on Shibley's part to soothe a wounded client. Longshore work, while still physical, was becoming more and more mechanized. No doubt just as many men believed the so-called media myths and bolted from the docks once the work got too sweaty.

As soon as the Golden Consent Decree took effect, the nepotism began, in particular among those men who had been the most dead-set against hiring women. Talking about a PMA official, Williams says with enough intensity to reveal just how deep her resentment really resides, "He worked hard against—really hard against me. Did nothing but lie to my face. Completely manipulative little jerk. As soon as [Golden] was settled, his mother left the L.A. Unified School District after twenty-five years [for a union card]. His sister dropped out of a third year of law school. His wife and his mistress—they all got jobs as clerks."

THE MAILMAN'S DAUGHTER

Predictably, other women eagerly grabbed at the open chance to work on the waterfront, with the high pay and benefits these jobs promised. In 1984, about forty thousand applications for casuals were printed. Some went to union members to be handed out to friends and family; some were distributed at a public event, held at a San Pedro movie drive-in because so many women and men showed up. In all, the union gave out every single application.

Connie Chaney's neighbor, a longshore foreman, told her about the job openings. Along with the neighbor's wife, Chaney filled out the application just for the hell of it. After all, she had been working for the County of Los Angeles, and she needed a change. Not that she expected to be hired—she didn't know about the Golden Consent Decree and what seemed like a nearly automatic ticket to the docks (as long as she passed the tests). Well, there was also that lottery business: of the thousands of eligible women, only 350 would be chosen for longshore and clerk jobs—and they wouldn't even have to go through the casual hall first. Under the provisions of the consent decree, they would get union cards right away.

Chaney applied in September. Then in January, with marine clerk

George Love pulling names, she got lucky. The union called. Report to Memorial Hall on February 1, the caller said, you've been accepted as a longshoreman. As it turned out, about a third of the selected women were "outsiders"; the others had fathers, brothers, or other relatives already in the union. Chaney paid her first month's dues and registration fees, totaling $300, and the ILWU gave her a union number. She was to start work the next day.

And so she found herself driving to Terminal Island on a Sunday morning, watching the berth numbers get lower and then higher, not sure where her assignment was—TI 228, it was called. Once she found it, she and another woman, a registered nurse who had been working at Cedars Sinai Hospital, were told they would be swingmen. Not a tough job, or one that took a lot of training. As the trucks drove under the crane, swingmen made sure the locks on the empty chassis were popped open so the container could sit squarely on the chassis.

At the end of the day, Chaney and the nurse sat on the long ledge of the dock and looked across to the cruise terminal. The nurse said, "Yeah, I think I like this." Chaney happily agreed. She took a leave of absence from her job, exhausted all her sick leave, and then quit her county job. She was going to be a longshoreman.

Two days later, she got a banana job, meaning she tossed 40-pound boxes of bananas, one of the few remaining break bulk cargoes, from the hold to a conveyor belt. Next was an auto job, which her friend the nurse found hip but Chaney decided was a screwed-up assignment. Walk up into a ship, drive a new Honda down. Walk up, drive down. All day, breathing car exhaust and feeling bored.

That first week, she saw men peeing on the dock. Some guy would be talking with other men or women and then suddenly turn around, unzip, and do his business. Some pissed off the ships or off the edge of the dock. Others smoked pot or drank beer while on the job. Cursing surrounded her. Someone wore a t-shirt that read, "Don't ask me for shit." Prostitutes prowled the gates at the end of each shift. She had left her genteel county job for another planet. It was hip, really hip.

Chaney tells me this while we sit in her Carson home, a modest, two-story house filled with a grandmotherly clutter. Among her stories, one concerns a boss near retirement and a utility tractor rig with a broken air hose held together with a rag—a typical example, she says, of how poorly maintained the equipment was. At first she drove it, but it kept losing air. So eventually she just pulled off the rag and announced she couldn't drive it anymore. The boss, a small man, didn't take it well. She told him to bring out the maintenance records to see the last time the truck had been worked on.

"Who do you think you are? You're fired," he retorted. So Chaney called in the union business agent and again asked for the maintenance record. The boss backed down and said she could work there. Then she asked for a decent truck.

The way men gossip, pretty soon they all knew about this wild black chick with the long fingernails and attitude. She had actually read the rules, and you had better watch it. Worse, she stood up for other women who were being jammed for no reason. They got the worst equipment, junk trucks with bad brakes, steering, or air hoses.

"You don't have to put up with this," Chaney lectured them. The rules stated so clearly that it was their responsibility to protect their safety and health. "So just stop the job for safety and health. The rules say you can." And she'd challenge the men: "Why don't you be a good union man and take a stand for what's right?" (Unfortunately, this ethic didn't prevent her life-changing accident when the UTR she was driving was lifted in the air by a crane and then dropped to the ground, as detailed in chapter 3.)

"I love rules," she tells me, as if we all should feel the same way. "What's the next rule?" Perhaps realizing this sounds a tad rigid, she quickly adds that this is about fairness: "Just make sure everybody adheres to the rules."

Her improbable inch-and-a-half-long lacquered nails click together as she counts off story after story of how she applied the rules from the two books that she carries with her, the union contract and the safety regulations, and smote the offenders. She has the rules on her side, and it's a good thing, since she doesn't have the family connections many of the women dockworkers do. At the Port of Los Angeles, she notes, you're either descended from longshoremen or you're not. And her father was a mailman. She doesn't have the luxury of calling on an uncle, a father, or a brother to take on some jerk who's harassing her.

"I wouldn't call anyway," Chaney declares, with such bravado that you can imagine her waving a gun in the air at the same time. Instead of asking for family backup, she returns fire with words. Goes toe to toe. Blasts them with some smart mouth chased by a recitation of the union rules they've just broken. And after more than thirty years on the docks as a longshoreman and now a marine clerk, she knows how to leave tormentors gulp-sputtering for a comeback.

Careful not to put too noble a point on her self-assigned role of forcing fairness where it may not exist, she brings up her father's accounts of bigotry in segregated army barracks. "I'm very prejudiced," she says, with a shrill conviction that approaches verbal assault. "It's called right and wrong. That's what I worked for to come to the waterfront. That's what I'll leave the waterfront with."

LITTLE BABY DRESSES ON THE WALL

As Chaney learned her job and how to apply the rules in her favor, men started showing up in the courts, claiming their own versions of discrimination. For example, the PMA, the ILWU, and Local 13 were accused in 1992 of denying registration to complainants Mark Flores and others. The employers and the union, the suit alleged, "hired in a discriminatory manner with the goal and aim of favoring members of their respective unions, members of the families of said members and in violation of their contracts with others and federal law." With a gusto that can come only from a lawyer's fertile mind—in this case, Steven J. Freeburg—the filing threw in a reference to RICO, the anti-racketeering law aimed at organized crime, as a new twist on an old subject. The plaintiffs claimed, "The actions of the defendants in fostering and continuing in their endeavor over the years to run the Union and industry to suit their own purposes based upon favoritism, bribes and nepotism is [*sic*] a corrupt act based upon conspiracy and a violation of RICO." The lawsuit fizzled.

Gretchen Williams wasn't always aware of the litigious cottage industry that grew from her simple but naïve desire to get a casual job at the clerks' hall. Instead, she was busy surviving, both on the job and off. Even using the restroom at work had its risks. At the time, there were restrooms only for men, so typically some of the guys would offer to watch the door while she went in. "As soon as I was inside, they were trying to take my jeans off." She reported the attempts at rape to a supervisor who gave her the "standard answer"—"Don't worry about it, little lady." Facing a deluge of threats, she had to move a half dozen times; she changed her phone number eight times. On top of this, she was twice diagnosed with cancer and endured a hysterectomy and chemotherapy treatments. (She's now fighting several melanomas from her days under the sun both at the docks and sailing.) Her first marriage lasted only one year and three weeks, partly, she says, because of the stress. She gave up her beloved academics in the middle of writing her master's thesis so she could make sure the fight for women at the docks was done right. She passed up an opportunity to study in Sweden for a year.

Her anger fueled her, kept her strong. "I had other things in mind that I wanted to be doing. [But] I had to be here and now for this thing. And to be threatened at the same time. So by then I was hot." And yet incredibly, in the end, Williams tells me without a hint of irony, "This has been the most successful affirmative action program in the country. Ever."

As for the Golden Consent Decree, Judge Takasugi ruled in 1999 that his 1983 court order had done its job. Women were now a permanent part of the waterfront workforce. Williams agrees. Now a ship planner, working in an office before a computer for the most part, she says women have been largely accepted at the docks. She tells how once at the Matson Shipping terminal, a group of men threw a baby shower for a woman coworker. There in the equipment room where they worked, they set up a barbecue, served food, and hung little baby dresses among their stacks of pornographic magazines. A creepy picture, to be sure, but Williams realized the job she had started nearly thirty years before might have been completed. "I thought, 'We're integrated now.'"

THIRTEEN

The Clerk

When he was young, George Love wanted to be an accountant, but he became a marine clerk at the Port of Los Angeles instead. That's not to say his second career option turned out all that badly. The responsibility for monitoring the flow of containers at a terminal gives the job a certain weight; a clerk is an important pivot point, a traffic cop of sorts in the movement of cargo. Still, as we eat lunch at a restaurant frequented by dockworkers, it's clear he would have been just as happy taking a sharp pencil to the withering array of numbers that go into, say, a company's balance sheet and having it all come out correct in the end. As Love tells me about his fifty years at the docks, he reveals the complexities that can arise from making just one choice that affects your entire life, while you try to balance out the regrets and joys that came with it.

It's fair to say that if Love had stuck with accounting, he wouldn't have seen the periodic tribal uprisings against the employers that go on at the docks. When he tells me about the current workplace protests, his face brightens with a wry smile, and I get the feeling this is part recreational rebellion for a guy who's seen every employer attempt possible to chip away at the clerks' and longshoremen's power, income, and benefits. In 2009, when I last interview him, that has meant cutting back hours because traffic at the ports has slowed, as the economy reels. Or perhaps, he wonders, the motivation is more spiteful than budgetary: the union had recently put the kibosh on an employers' proposal to delay making pension fund payments—more than $350 million a year that's put into a special account—until 2011, with a promise to pay the deferred amount more than a decade later.

"We can't help it if things have gone sour," Love says. He adds a few minutes later, "There's so many people on the employers' side that are dislikable. It's the arrogance factor. For me, personally . . . you get your licks in."

From here, what that means gets a little fuzzy. For three days during the third week of April 2009, clerks at the Yusen Terminals were somewhat casual about getting back to work after their meal hour, milling about the gate a little too long for the employers to see this as anything but an illegal work stoppage. Love wasn't involved, but he seems delighted any time an employer gets such a poke in the eye, retribution for all the years of one slight or another.

This includes the previous October, when he and five other clerks, all steadies at the Ports America terminal, called in to notify their employer that they would miss work on a Thursday night because they had other plans. For his part, Love was going to a funeral that afternoon.

"But they got a hair up their ass," he grumbles. "When they called me and I listened to his spiel, [I said,] 'Listen, I told you I'm not going to work today.' I didn't even give him—it was none of their business. See ya. Click. And nobody went in because we all had things to do."

As far as Love is concerned, the employers—notice I didn't say the people in charge—could have easily ordered up replacements out of the Local 63 clerks' hall and let the incident pass. Instead, "they were looking for an excuse," and the group got busted. They no longer had jobs at the terminal. It was back to working out of the hall.

As I listen to his story, I think about mentioning how this might have gone in other work worlds where the tolerance level for missing days is low to begin with and how he might have risked losing his job altogether if he were, say, an accountant. But he speaks with such conviction that it hardly seems to be the most important point. No, the larger issue is the continuing conflict between employers and the union that most dock-workers see as a fact of life. This isn't just about Love getting bounced out of his steady job of ten years and being forced to freelance out of the hall. It's actually about technology, the natural enemy of all blue-collar workers and the apparent fuel for so many waterfront grudges these days, as it has been, for that matter, for the past fifty years, ever since containers started showing up.

After all, it's no secret that the employers intend to eliminate as many clerks as possible from the docks and replace them with machines. The process seems inevitable, a consequence of computer and GPS systems juggling a thousand numbers and other information faster than the sixty-eight-year-old Love can cough. Just the same, it saddens him that his career is going the way of the hold man's, that, although a few clerk positions uniquely requiring eyeballs and a brain will remain, a computer's binary breathing will mostly do the job instead.

Already, one of the more interesting jobs, the supercargo position—deciding where and how to load cargo in a ship's hold—has gone to computer-operating planners who work in an office and move container icons around with a mouse (granted, these are also union jobs). It's a lot more efficient and less labor intensive for someone to do this work on a computer screen rather than on the dock. Also, much of the paperwork that clerks once handled now whizzes from one computer to another; they once retyped cargo information that arrived in emails, but the 2002 contract wiped out that usually unnecessary step. One of the clerk's most basic jobs—recording container numbers as the cans come off or go on a ship—now goes to scanners at each crane that can read the can's ID and send the information to a central computer. In the case of cargo coming off the ship, once the container is delivered to its temporary resting spot in the yard, a GPS system on the utility tractor rig that delivers it sends the location to the same computer system.

Union leaders have protested some of the changes. Between 2003 and early 2009, Local 63 and the employers have tussled over forty-two different technology-related disputes, which were heard before an area arbitrator, a judge and jury of sorts who is selected by both the union and the PMA to handle conflicts over the contract at the local level (if it's decided that the case has an impact on other ports, the issue goes to the West Coast arbitrator instead). Of those cases, twenty-eight decisions went in favor of the union, covering what seem on the surface to be the most nit-picking items. But for the ILWU they all come under the slippery-slope category: one lost job leads to two more, and so on, until clerks are wiped off the docks altogether.

Many of the complaints concerned employers implementing new technology without first running it by the union, a somewhat tangled procedure first instituted in the 2002 contract. The arbitrator usually sided with the union in these dust-ups, although this probably didn't prevent the eventual implementation of the technology. However, a grievance involving transtainers—mobile cranes that straddle container stacks—brought out a kind of turf battle between clerks and longshoremen (though the change in procedure had been initiated by the employer, SSA Marine). The transtainer operators had been told to input trucker information into an electronic database—a job that clerks would typically perform. The arbitrator ruled in favor of the employer, reasoning that because this was "new" technology, clerks didn't have exclusive rights to its implementation. It's hard to say whether or not this eliminated any of the higher-paid clerk positions, but it was clearly one more example of how the job is becoming more obsolete.

Love is realistic about the ongoing computerization and concedes that, after a few bugs, it's working pretty well. So he directs his ire toward the slights that take place on a more human level. His voice rises with the periodic frustration he expresses during our interview when he tells me about the employers sending more of their superintendents to the docks to watch over clerks, to question their decisions, and to question the traditional ways of doing things.

"In the old days, you might have one, two, three ships alongside,"

Love tells me without sentimentality. "You have one, maybe two superintendents. They would let you do your job. You, the professional. . . . So
[their attitude today has] put a little more stiff on the job."

It's a mild tirade, as though the resentment and hot temper of his
youth have been somewhat dissipated not so much by age but by acqui-
escence to change. Nothing to do but retire in perhaps a couple more
years, with the substantial pension and lifetime health coverage. By the
end of the current contract, in 2013, he'll receive $180 per month for each
year he's worked, up to a maximum of thirty-seven years, or $6,660.
It's a decent reward for time spent. But in some ways, it still feels like a
just-in-time escape from the inevitable withering of the position rather
than a triumphant end to a satisfying career.

Love looks at me with clear gray eyes, shifting from annoyance to
amusement over the employers' alleged foibles or, for that matter, the
stupidity his fellow workers exhibit on occasion. Other times, he punc-
tuates his complaints with a laugh, as if he's stopped caring. He has
an honest, I-don't-need-to-lie manner that makes me want to believe
everything he says without confirmation.

Underlying this calm umbrage is something deeper, more familial.
Love reveals that his father had pushed him into the clerk job fifty years
ago. So I ask if he thinks his life would have been any better if he had
stood up to his father, the late George Love Sr., and said, "No. I want to
be an accountant." He shies away from a straightforward answer. As with
many father-son relationships, I'm not sure he can pin down his complicated feelings quite so easily, or perhaps he doesn't want to get too
deep into the subject with a stranger who's just placed a digital recorder
under his nose.

He tells me that when he turned eighteen, his father offered him
and his brother, Marvin, what other sons of longshoremen would have
considered an enviable proposition—their uncle Seth could get them
into the clerks union. No working in the hold for five years. No getting
dirty. A good job right from the start. Not interested, Marvin said. He
had already applied to be a sheriff. So George's father looked at him and

said with the kind of guilt-inducing voice that only sons respond to, "You're not going to let me down, too, are you?"

Love tells the story stiffly, as though still wondering why he didn't risk disappointing his father. His father, the powerful ILWU area arbitrator. His father, who hung out with Harry Bridges. His father, whose picture hangs at the front of the restaurant where we're eating. Waterfront jobs went from father to son like a valuable inheritance. That was the tradition in San Pedro, and no matter how seductively some other vocation called, you listened to your father first.

He tried taking accountant classes at night school, but that fizzled, and he became a full-time clerk whose main ambition was to stay alive, always an issue for a clerk standing amid the swinging cargo loads and rushing jitneys. He also had to wonder whether this was such a great deal: back then, clerks barely worked during the slow winter times, and he had to collect unemployment occasionally to pay the bills. It helped that he was single and could live simply.

Just the same, the job had a basic honesty about it he liked. The hold man might have been the foundation on which moving cargo rested, but so much of shipping's operation pivoted around the clerk. It was one thing to haul a box out of a hold—they were all pretty much the same to a hold man. That box, however, had a destination, and a clerk had to make sure that once it hit the skin of the dock, it went to the right place. Every day was a little different. Sometimes, the clerk had to work with the ship's mate to figure out how to load metal coils destined for, say, North Africa or Italy, devising an arrangement that would distribute the weight evenly on the ship—or perhaps the task would be more basic, something as simple as determining if the coils would even fit through the hatches. It was much more mental than physical. Another kind of accounting, in a way.

Love describes how clerks went about their jobs before computerization. From the 1950s through the early part of the twenty-first century, each ship came with a book, sorted A to Z, listing all the cargo coming off that ship in that port. Clerks relied on that paperwork to tell them in which hatch each box was stowed and where the cargo needed to go after being discharged. In the pre-container days, once a loaded lift board swung over the side of the ship and the winch driver landed it on the dock, six longshoremen—the dock gang—would unload the cargo, described as "setting up the floor." The boxes were "custom stowed" back to back, labels facing out so that Customs could easily inspect imported cargo.

Every shipper had a mark. For instance, everyone knew that "SRC" stamped inside a diamond meant Sears, Roebuck, Company. But there might be a hundred boxes marked SRC going to various destinations, so it wasn't always as simple as just stacking the boxes and counting them. The boxes also had be sorted in such a way that the delivery clerk would know where they were headed. So the clerks would then chalk-mark the first box in a row of sorted cargo with the number of boxes, the shipper, the bill of lading, and the destination. In their books, the clerks recorded the spot in the warehouse where the boxes would be kept until they were picked up and sent out. Once all the ship's cargo had been discharged, the books went to the chief clerk, who needed to know where the boxes were located in the warehouse.

For cargo that was about to be loaded on a ship, all the boxes had to be measured so the shipper could be charged for the space the cargo occupied in the hold. The clerks used a yard stick with a metal hook on the end and quickly sized up each box. They might mark in the paperwork, "2 × 2 × 4 times 15 boxes." Then workers in the office would calculate how much space that translated into. Finally, the clerks were responsible for seeing that nothing was stolen during the sometimes weeklong process of unloading and loading a ship. Pilfering was easy in the old days, with so much cargo just sitting out there on the dock.

Today, only remnants of the old routine still hang on; technology, both the machines and the computers, has changed everything. Preferring to work at nights, Love first goes to the Local 63 dispatch hall in San Pedro, a large multipurpose room in a two-story office building five blocks from the waterfront, where a handful of clerks gather in mid-

A clerk measures boxes before the cargo is loaded onto a ship. Courtesy of ILWU Library, San Francisco.

afternoon to sign in with the dispatcher and wait for job assignments that could be anywhere in the Los Angeles/Long Beach port complex. They do have the option of calling in, but they face two disadvantages by doing so.

First, if they decide to flop on a job (turn it down) over the phone, a four-hour penalty is added to their hours worked, which makes them less likely to get work next time around; the penalty isn't assessed if they flop at the hall. Second, only clerks who sign in at the dispatch hall (rather than calling in) are eligible for the Clerk Work Opportunity Guarantee (CWOG), which requires the employers to pay them even if no job is available that night. The CWOG, paid from a fund financed through cargo fees, was originally instituted in 2002 for the benefit of clerks in smaller ports, where work was sometimes scarce; at the time the employers agreed to it because business was booming elsewhere.

Once he's assigned a job, Love reports to work at 4:30 P.M., even though the start time is 4:00. No one minds; the paperwork isn't ready, so he can't start on time anyway (however, his paid hours start at 4:00). When he finally gets the paperwork—assuming he's working as super-cargo that night—he studies the ship's bay plan, which indicates where each container is stowed and what needs to happen once a can leaves the ship. On the bay plan, a container might be marked with the designation "R" for reefer, which means it goes on a chassis and is taken to a spot in the yard where it'll be picked up later by a truck driver. That spot is assigned by the clerk, who marks it on the paperwork. Or the container may be taken to a stack, where a transtainer puts it away until it's picked up by a trucker. And because so much cargo goes east by rail, the plan may show that the container has to go to another part of the yard where it'll eventually be loaded on a train.

All of this is color-coded by Love with colored pens, "like kindergarten," he says. And to keep things even simpler, a utility tractor rig driver might be told that he or she will be taking cans to only one location all night, say, to transtainer number nine. No one gets lost or confused that way. Love may tell the hatch clerks, in preparation for an upcoming container, to have a particular UTR driver bring back a 20-foot chassis. It's communicated the old-fashioned way, by yelling.

Containers that are stacked, sometimes as many as five high, go in long rows managed by transtainers. Trouble is, if a trucker comes in and needs a container that's located on the bottom of the stack, the other cans have to be lifted off first and relocated. An appointment system would be so much better, Love says, so the containers would be ready for pick-up, eliminating the inefficiency and the long lines of trucks polluting the air with diesel exhaust. "But it will cost [the employers] a lot of money," Love notes. "It's not cheap. The labor is expensive."

Love figures he has perhaps two more years before he retires. "I've enjoyed it," he says. "I've seen everything change. I've been fortunate." Still, he worries. His wife, Sandy, has myasthenia gravis, a muscle disorder, and their plans for traveling when he retired "went in the toilet." Even though union retirees are supposed to receive health coverage—

something his wife will need more and more, even if Love himself does not—he isn't sure the employers won't dilute the benefit as the years go on. Perhaps that won't happen, but clerks and longshoremen see the jobs lost to computerization as proof that it's all about business at the docks. In their mistrust, they believe bottom lines don't include the workers' best interests.

Just the same, the accountant in Love counsels the remaining clerks that numbers go down and they go back up. "I've got it made," he says of his upcoming retirement. "I do. But there was a time when our local was down to three hundred fifty members, something like that. In the seventies ... I tell these guys, in the seventies and eighties, we had recessions. Our hours were cut. When work picks up, it'll come back. But everyone panics if they haven't been through it."

FOURTEEN

Security

PATROLLING THE WATER
Coasties

I've just met bo'sun's mate second class Christopher Hurley, and already he's whipping out his gun. Outside the Coast Guard's Los Angeles/ Long Beach office, he pulls his weapon, a black .40-caliber Sig Sauer P229 that he wears halfway down his right thigh, and bends over a large metal tube slanted toward the ground and lined with a rubbery material. He could be tying his shoe, his actions are so automatic. He sticks the gun barrel a few inches inside the tube and crisply, casually snaps back the slide. With that, he straightens, secures the gun, and lopes down the sidewalk as if eager to get away from me.

"What was that all about?" I ask from behind him.

He tells me, as if reading off a page of regulations, that he was checking to make sure a bullet wasn't loaded in the chamber. Clearing a weapon is required just after leaving the office or just before entering it.

I follow him across a parking lot and then watch him plunge-step down a steep metal-grated ramp to the narrow dock where he keeps his vessel, a white 41-foot utility boat, one of about 172 in the Coast Guard fleet. Hurley boards the boat by lightly jumping over the two feet of water between the stern and the dock and doesn't turn around to see if I follow. In fact, he hasn't yet asked who I am. His officer told him I'm going for a ride, and in the military world, that's all he needs to know.

As coxswain in charge, Hurley has three men in his crew preparing for their morning patrol, a ninety-minute cruise through both ports. They all wear standard navy blue operational-dress uniforms, including crewneck t-shirts under long-sleeve shirts, with the sleeves rolled up and secured with large, dark blue buttons. Their loose trousers make them look a little like auto mechanics. They're also wearing long-billed caps, so-called super boots (black, with 8-inch-high tops), and gun belts carrying standard-issue .40-caliber guns with twelve-bullet clips. Each man sports a different brand of sunglasses, all of them black framed. Each has the demeanor of a traffic cop about to write a ticket.

One mate is down in the engine room, a cramped space below the deck near the stern. Although this boat was built in 1976 and is old enough that the Coast Guard would like to replace it with something sleeker and faster, its engine, in contrast to the greasy, oily contraptions on some vessels, is spotless and purring, with only a few diesel fumes blowing out the small hatch above it.

Another mate takes out a small, long, wooden box, opens it, and casually pulls out one end of a hundred-round gun belt, which he loads in the holding chamber on a .60-caliber M240 machine gun mounted on a metal post next to the boat's portside railing. The arrangement looks added on, and indeed these boats weren't designed to carry the kind of weaponry reserved for pitched battle. He grabs a ragged white bungee cord—about the only thing on the boat that looks worn—and wraps it twice around the barrel, using it to strap the gun to the railing so that it points forward and won't swivel during the trip. When I ask him what kind of gun it is, he doesn't know. He steps into the cabin a few feet away, talks to Hurley, and comes back out to tell me. This reinforces the image I have of the Coast Guard being centered more on rescuing hapless boaters than on their primary mission here, which is to repel any nefarious types hell-bent on blowing up parts of the port, among other possible evil deeds.

Among those deeds, a deliberate explosion seems to be the most common scenario feared by the imaginative people who work in disaster speculation, or what might be called preparing for all possibilities. A 2006 Rand Corporation study describes a lamentably viable means of smuggling weapons into the country via a container—and then turns up the heat, hypothesizing a situation in which "terrorists conceal a 10-kiloton bomb in a shipping container and ship it to the Port of Long Beach. Unloaded onto a pier, it explodes shortly thereafter." This wouldn't completely destroy the two ports, they argue, but might allow terrorists to use them as a conduit to devastate the country's second-largest city and, by extension, throw the nation's economy down on the mat. (Not to be dismissive toward such a bomb, but for comparison, modern U.S. nuclear weapons range from 100 to 550 kilotons.)

Indeed, the Rand authors write, sixty thousand people could die instantly or shortly thereafter from radiation poisoning. Six million more would flee the city, and regional gasoline supplies would run low because the blast would also take out Long Beach area refineries, which produce one-third of the gas west of the Rockies. Last, the "early costs" would top $1 trillion. "In general, consequences would far outstrip the resources available to cope with them," the report dryly notes.

Obviously, atomic blasts and lesser terrorism have been considered by those in charge of security at the port. "If something happened to one part of the port," Captain Paul Wiedenhoeft, Coast Guard captain of the port, tells me, "it may cause me to consider taking security measures that would affect the entire port complex." In other words, blow up even a few pilings, and the whole place gets shut down, disrupting the national economy for days or even weeks.

Wiedenhoeft has that kind of broad authority, even more so since the Coast Guard became part of the Department of Homeland Security in 2003 and the original mandate of the "Coasties," to watch over U.S. coastal maritime interests (venturing into international waters on occa-

The Coast Guard patrol boat makes its unscheduled run through the port.

sion), turned into the nation's first line of defense for all the open and very vulnerable ports. In many ways, this was always the Coast Guard's job; it's just that after the 9/11 terrorist attacks, the emphasis shifted from concentrating on marine safety and environmental issues to terrorism prevention. (According to some in the port, they've ignored nearly everything else in deference to security.)

Although there hasn't been an attack on a domestic port since 9/11, Los Angeles and Long Beach are thought to rate high on any terrorist's target wish list. In 2003, when California's attorney general compiled a list of possible locations that terrorists could be eyeballing in the state, Long Beach ranked third among 624 potential targets; Los Angeles was sixth on the same list. Clearly, the 150 active-duty Coasties who work on the sliver of land jutting out from Terminal Island, where their base is located, have a lot to worry about. It should be noted, however, that Wiedenhoeft downplays the nuclear-bomb-in-a-container scenario posited by so many disaster prognosticators as a "low probability" event. The current emphasis is on less spectacular, but almost as disruptive, small explosions that might kill a few people and close the port.

Our unnamed vessel (it needs another 20 feet in length before the military considers it worthy of a name) is ready to leave for its morning cruise. One of the crew unwraps the mooring line from a cleat, and the boat slowly moves out of the enclosed dock area—about half the size of an Olympic pool—and into the Port of Los Angeles's Main Channel, where we start the patrol at an easygoing 5 knots.

Clearly, no one on board expects to see terrorist hordes storming the port. Just the same, from the cabin, the crew carefully watches what they call "critical infrastructure" and the spotty marine traffic— it's a slow day, I'm told—for anything suspicious. When I press for an idea of what the patrol is looking for, I get a lightweight example of a mysterious package hanging from the dock. Any other explanation is veiled or truncated by claims of this or that being classified. And, as Wiedenhoeft puts it, he doesn't want terrorists learning too much and gaining a tactical advantage. What he considers worthy of attention is on a need-to-know basis, and as far as he's concerned, guys like me don't need to know.

In some ways, the patrol's purpose is a little more subtle than actually trying to spot bombs or even people who might be placing them on a pier or other structure. The Coast Guard cruises through the ports all day, passing any particular spot at random times so the "bad guys" (a popular term that seems to have been resurrected from old Roy Rogers movies) never know when the good guys might show up. This theoretically prevents those mysterious packages from ever appearing.

"When you look at how we've improved since 9/11," Wiedenhoeft says, "that's clearly one of the things we've done. The presence has come up. We're out there, and that presence has a good deterrent effect, I think."

Naturally, many people want more security than a few lightly armed Coasties touring the ports in thirty-year-old boats, and there's no shortage of jawing on the subject. Perhaps one of the more impressive studies on that topic came in 2006 from the Public Policy Institute of California, which in 296 pages manages to convincingly show there's only so much anyone can do to keep the ports safe. As the study puts it, "There is no way to completely inspect all of the millions of containers entering the United States.... Inspecting each thoroughly would bring commerce to a halt, exactly the kind of reaction that terrorists hope to generate."

Wiedenhoeft, for his part, knows there's only so much he can do and relies on other deterrents besides the patrol boats, while always trying to balance security interests with commerce. It's a tricky equation that, again, he explains only in broad generalities.

It all starts ninety-six hours before a ship arrives in port. The carrier is required to send an advance notice of the cargo stowed in each container and the name of the port where the container was loaded on the ship. While Wiedenhoeft is cagey about what his staff specifically scrutinizes when they receive the manifests, he does say, "That gives me time to look at who's coming here, where they're coming from, what they're carrying, who's on board, a number of other issues. And those are all hit against a number of different intelligence sources and databases, and that allows me to make a risk-based decision on who I'm going to board."

In effect, according to other sources, each of those items is given a point value, and if a particular ship racks up a high score, it might be told to anchor far outside the port in open water and wait for a Coast Guard boarding party. In other cases, when the security risk isn't seen as quite so high, the boarding can wait until the ship is docked.

The boarding option, which sounds dramatic, is really another way to show a presence because, after all, a boarding team can't actually inspect the thousands of containers most ships carry. Instead, the members of the boarding party, which might number six or more, clamber up the Jacob's ladder the ship's crew sends down for them. They first verify that the crew roster matches the personnel on the ship and that the cargo manifest is consistent with what the boarding team sees. Beyond that, however, the one to two hours they spend on board come down to looking for anything suspicious based on first impressions, such as noticing a crew member who is acting fearful or doesn't appear to know what he's doing. It should be noted that the Coast Guard also boards recreational craft from time to time, spending about fifteen or twenty minutes on an inspection.

The boarding crew may decide that a ship is poorly maintained, an environmental hazard, and shouldn't be allowed in the port at all, where it might leak oil or simply sink. Not all ships that come here are spiffy examples of modern nautical design; some are simply rusty, break bulk— carrying tubs, limping about the seas like the maritime version of junk-yard trucks.

On the day of our interview, Wiedenhoeft tells me that just one ship is being boarded. He allows, however, that it's possible (though he implies that it's improbable) that they would check out each of the 20 or so ships that enter the port every day. In fact, the Coast Guard boards 50 to 60 ships in the port complex each month; nationally, an average of 122 ships each day get a visit from the Coasties.

The patrol boat—this crew doesn't routinely board ships—slides along the East Basin Marina, where Hurley spots a man in a skiff talking on a cell phone and obviously adrift. As the patrol boat slows, Hurley leaves the cabin and carefully scoots along the narrow deck beside the cabin to the bow.

"My engine died," the man says as he sees Hurley scrutinizing him.

"Can we help you?" Hurley asks.

Without pausing, the man says, "Could you tow me in? My slip is near here."

The man tosses Hurley a line, which he secures to a cleat. As the patrol boat slowly starts up again, another man in an even smaller boat approaches, apparently a friend of the first boater. The two men talk for a minute, and the Coast Guard tow service ends as the two tie their boats together and the friend tows the other away. As Hurley returns to the cabin, he gives his crew a half-smile, incredulous the guy would ask them for a tow. "Got to give him credit," Hurley says.

Given that the patrol's broader purpose is to advertise the Coast Guard's constant presence in the port, this might be as exciting as it gets. However, touring the waterways to discourage any attacks may seem a tad passive for those concerned about the chance of a spectacular, region-destroying megabomb hidden on some monster ship. Those in port security see it differently. They openly worry about the more mundane scenario of somebody casually entering the port's main channel in a small boat, slipping alongside an oil tanker or pier where a ship is unloading, and setting off a boatload of explosives. So simple, so devastating, without all the bother of smuggling a nuke inside a container.

There are forty-five hundred recreational boats spread throughout the port's sixteen marinas, and many more visit from elsewhere, none of them licensed, none of them required—as a cargo ship is—to declare their intentions or what they're carrying. "We track the heck out of these big ships, but yet these small boats come and go around the ports as they please," John Holmes, the port's deputy executive director, says.

Holmes, who had Wiedenhoeft's job during the 9/11 attacks, has done what he can to limit boaters' access to the port's working areas, once open to anyone floating by. In 2007, the port enacted controlled navigation areas that are restricted to commercial activity only.

"If somebody goes there, you get an alarm and you send a boat, and you say, 'What are you doing in there?'" Holmes explains. "I came to find from my post-9/11 days that people do find out about things that are being done, and they feel better if you have sort of a plan and they feel like you're doing something. It's important to people to have confidence in what you're doing."

The Coast Guard patrol boat passes a small channel, and one of the crew points to a small ship that looks vaguely new and ancient at the same time. "That's the *Black Pearl*," he tells me, meaning the centerpiece ship in the *Pirates of the Caribbean* movies. "Just came in last night." He's also pointing out, in a roundabout way, how the Coast Guard keeps tabs on anything larger than the usual flotsam entering the port. They have a lot of eyes out there. Much of their information comes from the patrols, who have seen the harbor's waterways so consistently and so often that they immediately know if anything looks out of place. But the Coast Guard also depends on a loose network of junior G-men who happily drop a dime on anything or anyone they deem suspicious.

Longshoremen, in particular, have enthusiastically taken on this job. Union leadership touts the rank and file as "the first line of defense for our ports," which is perhaps a little overstated. "I would submit that they are a line of defense," Wiedenhoeft says. "[But] we want the *first line* to be way out there somewhere, okay? I don't want to discover bombs here." Typically, the Coast Guard gets calls from union business agents on nearly a daily basis alerting Wiedenhoeft's staff to suspicious activity, which normally turns out to be someone trespassing or tourists taking pictures from a public sidewalk. (While everyone I talked to is convinced that photography suggests behavior that warrants closer inspection, according to security expert Bruce Schneier, the idea that terrorists first photograph their intended target is "nonsense." Of all the recent major attacks, as well as the less publicized ones, he writes, "Real terrorists . . . don't seem to photograph anything." As Wiedenhoeft concedes, terrorists can go to Google Earth to get all the views they need.)

The Coast Guard also relies on its auxiliary, a nationwide volunteer band of thirty-one thousand civilians who, for the price of a tank of gas for their boats, work with the Coast Guard in nonmilitary and non–law enforcement activities such as search and rescue operations and, of course, patrolling the waters for "suspicious activity."

In addition to roving human eyes, the port has also installed 350 cameras throughout the facility, some of which feature military-grade night vision and heat detection and are powerful enough to make out details on Catalina Island, more than 20 miles away. When I see the bank of monitors connected to these cameras, I wonder how anyone can pay attention to every view. They can't. Instead, a computer is programmed to watch for any movement in a specific view during a specific period, say, the night, when a facility is closed. The software compares each recorded frame with the previous one—thirty times a second—and if one frame includes something substantially different (it ignores birds flying through, for example), an alarm goes off and police are sent to the location.

Nathan Ewert, who is with the port's infrastructure protection division of the port police, figures that little nefarious behavior can get past the cameras. "Now that we have three hundred and fifty extra eyes and analytics on those eyes, we expect our call volume to increase. Not a great deal, but still we'll have three hundred and fifty more citizens throughout the port, the way we look at it, able to indicate and identify areas of crime."

About 11:15 A.M., the patrol boat reaches the Port of Long Beach's entrance. By this point, the crew is relaxed, gossiping in the cabin, while the smooth, open water has only three ships anchored for various reasons—nothing they don't already know about. "Coming up!" Hurley yells from the cabin, and the boat's engine roars as it powers up to 15 knots. We circle from Long Beach back to San Pedro Harbor and the Port of Los Angeles, and before 11:30 we return to the Coast Guard dock on Terminal Island. If there were any bad guys out there, they surely saw us.

Port Police

I spend another morning on one of the four boats run by the marine unit of the port police, which was added to the port's police department in 2007. Like the Coasties, the three men aboard first project a professional, we-don't-take-crap-from-anyone demeanor. That's helped by the fact that they're all wearing Glock 21 handguns (a .45-caliber weapon with a thirteen-bullet clip), Kevlar vests underneath their black uniform shirts, black pants over black high-top boots, and the kind of black shades that make them look imposing.

This pose lasts about twenty minutes after we leave the police dock. Soon they loosen up a little, periodically reattaching their scowls whenever they search the waters and piers for the ever-vague "unusual

Los Angeles port police officers Kiyohiko Amano and Mark Pagliuca watch the docks for suspicious activity while on patrol.

activity." Still, a kind of vulnerability leaks through when I ask Officer Mark Pagliuca about the black tape on their badges. "Is that for the four Oakland officers killed a few days ago?" He nods, and even behind the slick 5.11 Tactical Falcon sunglasses, I can tell he hurts.

Unlike the 41-foot utility boats still used by the Coast Guard, the port police patrol the harbor in 31-foot SAFE boats (built by SAFE Boats International in Port Orchard, Washington). Although a SAFE boat looks like an ungainly, large rubber boat with a cabin on it, the hull is actually solid polyethylene foam, able to resist a number of indignities, including small arms fire, that would otherwise cripple a craft. "Even if you cut this in half, it won't sink," Pagliuca says proudly. And as for the ungainly part, the boats can hit a maximum speed of 50 miles per hour. (The Coasties have also recognized the boat's utility and are replacing their old craft with SAFE boats, including a bruising, two-engine model that can easily reach freeway speeds.)

At least two of these boats are in the water all day and night, randomly buzzing through the port to keep the bad guys off balance, working twelve-hour shifts three days a week. According to Pagliuca, they have a pretty varied list of responsibilities:

- Look for safety violations such as speeding (the wake can make boats in the marina bob and bump against the pier, causing damage)
- Clear recreational boaters from the controlled navigation areas
- Look for people on the highline—the edge of the pier—who aren't employees
- Deal with assorted craziness, such as the guy at the fishing dock who inexplicably jumped into the water and swam under the pier, facing death from hypothermia (they fished him out before he died)
- Assist the Coast Guard when requested
- Act on alerts from the Joint Terrorism Task Force regarding intelligence on smuggling, drug activity, or other illegal or suspicious occurrences

While Pagliuca stands at the stern looking from side to side, Officer Kiyohiko "Kiyo" Amano sits in the cabin with a trainee, Al Garcia, who's piloting the boat. Using binoculars, Amano peers out the window at the cruise terminal, currently occupied by a Royal Caribbean ship. If there's one place port officials and the Coast Guard fret about the most, it's the cruise terminal (I'm sure they wouldn't call it fretting, but they sound worried to me). With 1.2 million passengers coming and going on their Mexico vacations, the facility is seen as a top target for terrorists.

"Look at what you typically think of as a terrorist mindset," Wiedenhoeft argued during our interview. "What would you want to do? You want to create some fear. You want to injure as many people as possible.

So where does that start? Well, one would think that starts with something that has a lot of passengers. Start with the cruise terminals."

Or, as Holmes put it, "We try to focus on the things we think are high probability."

To that end, before each cruise ship, some capable of carrying fifty-four hundred passengers, comes into the port, port police divers plunge into the dark water to inspect the pier's underwater portion for explosives. Before the vessel enters the Main Channel, a sea marshal—part of the port police department—boards the ship along with the port pilot and secures the engine room and the bridge. Then two port police SAFE boats pull alongside and escort the ship to the dock. At the terminal, dogs sniff incoming luggage and supplies for explosives. All passengers are checked by U.S. Customs and Border Protection (CBP) to ensure they don't have arrest warrants. On average, they find at least one person per cruise who is wanted for something.

This is an example of a security calculation some refer to as "high probability–low consequence events versus low probability–high consequence events." In other words, they're looking for the most likely places an attack might take place. The physical damage might be small, but shutting down the port even for a couple of days would cost the entire country's economy billions of dollars and would crank up the paranoia to such a level that security would trump commerce, with efficient cargo movement hampered by overly careful inspections.

The reason such an equation exists is that security funds are limited and officials would rather spend their money going with the higher odds of an attack on the cruise terminal or other facility than dumping millions on something out of a suspense novel plot. Having said this, they do quickly add that they're looking at *everything*. But officials do seem to believe the bomb-in-a-container scenario, however massive the damage might be, is less likely than someone going after such a tempting target as a cruise ship loaded with people. Then again, it's a little unclear where the cruise terminal fits into this equation, given that it could be a little of both—call it high probability–high consequence.

CHECKING THE CARGO

Still, it's hard to ignore those hundreds of thousands of containers flowing through the port each month and what might be inside, ready to do us harm. Digging through the cargo, however, isn't the job of either the Coast Guard or the port. The heavy lifting in this case is performed by the CBP. As Javier Larios, CBP section chief for the ports of Los Angeles and Long Beach, puts it, "The anti-terrorism mission drives everything we do in terms of screening cargo—knowing what's coming in—and people and conveyances."

Indeed, the CBP agents are a busy bunch, enforcing more than six hundred laws and regulations for more than sixty different agencies, encompassing immigration; alcohol, tobacco, and firearms; consumer product safety; food and drugs; agriculture and agro-terrorism; and intellectual property rights (watching out for bootleg products). The fees they collect make the CBP the federal government's second-highest revenue producer—$34.5 billion in 2008. Only the IRS brings in more money.

First initiated in early 2003 through the U.S. Container Security Initiative, the CBP's cargo screening process begins twenty-hour hours before goods bound for the United States are loaded on the ship at a foreign port. At this time, carriers are required to provide the CBP with an electronic cargo manifest. An automated targeting system compares this information against a database of "anomalies," which might be something as simple as incomplete paperwork. When a problem is found, the containers have to be pulled aside and the mistakes corrected before the cargo can be loaded. In addition to the automated system, inspectors working for the CBP, the FBI, and the Coast Guard also pore over the manifest, both before loading and while the ship is on the water, looking for risk factors such as suspicious shipments (there is no clear public definition of what constitutes such a shipment); and they consult other intelligence databases for further assistance in deciding which containers will require a closer look.

According to Larios, if there's enough concern over a cargo's security threat, they will stop the ship before it even enters the harbor and board it for an at-sea cargo inspection. Otherwise, they will flag the containers they want to examine more closely, and the carrier is then required to pull those cans off to the side once they're unloaded at the port.

I first meet Larios at the Long Beach office building where the CBP occupies several floors. Some of the more than five hundred officers employed here move in and out of the lobby, all wearing dark uniforms and packing heat, many with intense demeanors that all say the same thing: don't mess with me. Larios himself, however, is a friendly, open man with a well-trimmed mustache and a helpful, public relations flair about him: he wants me to know just how important the CBP is.

Certainly one of the agency's biggest tasks is inspecting cargo containers. So he takes me to the Evergreen America terminal, where we pass the same long line of trucks I encountered with driver Anthony Branch (described in chapter 10). We stop at a spot where five green and white cranes are unloading containers from a ship. Here, CBP officers are randomly pulling loaded utility tractor rigs out of line and directing them to an area off to the side of the cranes. In addition to examining containers that are flagged ahead of time, the officers can also target a ship and without warning run its containers through a Vehicle and Cargo Inspection System (VACIS) scan, which uses gamma rays to produce an image of the contents much like an X-ray. Altogether, they scan about 6 percent of the total containers coming through the port.

Just as we arrive, four UTRs have been waved over after containers have been loaded on the chassis; they're parked in a line marked by orange cones. The longshore drivers of the rigs jump out and walk around to a row of containers parked about 20 feet to the side. They lean against the cans, showing no emotion at the impromptu break. The VACIS vehicle, about the size of a large pickup truck, edges near the first UTR. A large boom extends out the rear of the truck and hangs over the top of the first container. Three officers sit in the truck's cab; the two in the back are reviewing each container's contents on a manifest supplied by the shipper—in this case, the container holds furniture made in China. As they do this, another officer trots along the line of containers with a handheld radiation detector so sensitive it often picks up harmless readings known as NORM (naturally occurring radioactive materials) coming from such items as building materials or the phosphate in fertilizers.

After a few minutes, they tell the VACIS driver they're ready to scan the containers. He radios the four officers outside the vehicle, telling them to step aside; they have to stay at least 5 feet from the boom. As the VACIS truck slowly moves along the line, gamma rays shoot out in a narrow, vertical beam from the boom's business end, which is pointed back toward the truck. The gamma rays penetrate each container's thick metal hide, are collected by an instrument behind the cab, and produce an image on a computer in the truck. One of the officers monitors the screen, comparing the fuzzy gray images—indecipherable blobs to my eyes—to the manifest he's just reviewed.

And something doesn't look right. As the picture forms, nearly black shapes appear at the rear of one of the containers; they don't resemble furniture, which usually isn't so dense that it goes black. The operator applies different contrast levels to the picture, and while he can make out other items such as lamps and a table, the black shapes remain unidentifiable. He tells the driver to radio the officers to pull this container aside.

A longshoreman drives the rig about 50 feet away from the original line, and four officers bring over a bolt cutter and a copy of the manifest. One, Officer Weihang Huang, cautiously approaches the can's back door. Even though the CBP has yet to find any explosives in a container, the others gather behind him with the kind of edgy expectation that says "trust no one."

Huang first wraps a blue webbing around the two door handles so the contents can't spill out when he unlocks the door. He takes the bolt cutters and quickly, easily cuts through the green container seal, a small plastic device on the latch; an intact seal indicates no one has opened the container since it was filled and closed. Each seal has a number and is logged on the cargo documents. Huang slowly opens the door and pulls a relatively heavy 12 × 11 × 10 box from the top and sets it down on the chassis frame. With box cutters, he slices through the sealing tape and hands the box to the other officers, who pull out a ceramic birdhouse.

Larios examines it and asks to see another box. They conclude there's no reason to hold up the container anymore. After sealing the boxes with "Inspected by U.S. Customs" yellow tape, they place them back in the container and put on a CBP seal, which is recorded in the paperwork.

Had there been more reason for suspicion, the container would have been driven by a CBP-approved driver to one of four warehouses the agency maintains near the port. Of the containers first inspected at the dock, about 6 percent are sent to this warehouse for further examination. Larios emphasizes, however, that they would never send a container with possible radioactive material or bombs inside over public roads; they would deal with it there at the terminal. Often, the suspicious cargo turns out to be goods that have been declared as something else on the manifest, typically to avoid customs fees. That is, the shipper might list a container's contents as cheap sneakers when the real cargo is expensive electronics, in order to avoid paying the higher customs fees that come with pricier items.

Altogether, of the roughly 12,000 containers coming from foreign shippers each day to the port complex, about 720 are given the VACIS treatment, and 40 to 50 are opened for further inspection. It's estimated that even if the port's four scanners were working twenty-four hours a day, the number of inspected containers would rise only slightly, to 10 percent of the total.

Longshoremen see this from ground level and think the CBP is missing something: the thousands of empty containers coming through the port from the land side and leaving on ships for return trips to Asia. Every ILWU manifesto on port security emphasizes the danger of empty containers. In early 2006, the ILWU director of port security, Mike Mitre, testified before a Senate committee and made it clear that empties are a potential problem:

U.S. Customs and Border Protection officer Weihang Huang inspects containers with a radiation detector.

On any given day, as much as 40 percent of the containers delivered into West Coast ports consist of empty containers.... Containers marked as empty provide a golden opportunity. The good news is that unlike containers filled with cargo, the inspection of empty containers is quick and easy. It is a relatively cheap and painless way of confirming the absence of a dangerous substance or device, and the absence of persons illegally attempting to gain access. This, of course, makes the inspection of "empty" containers all the more compelling and an absolute necessity in any port security program.

Mitre then demonstrated the kind of fertile imagination so many people have when it comes to possible terrorist acts:

Once the cargo within the container has been unloaded at its eventual destination, there is no system, protocol, or requirement in place making the last shipper responsible for closing and sealing the doors. As a result, this empty container will travel over the roads of the U.S. unlocked and open. It may serve as a platform or vehicle for anything or anyone who may desire to do harm to our country. It may lie unattended on city streets or even within the port for days or even weeks until it is returned to the terminal for shipment [usually back to Asia.] Who knows what has been stored or smuggled inside? Who knows what kind of plan someone may come up with utilizing this empty container?

It's not apparent people are listening. In an otherwise comprehensive November 2006 report on port security by the California Senate Office of Research, empty containers entering the ports are never mentioned as a possible threat, and the Pacific Maritime Association has waved off the concern with little comment. Longshoremen see the PMA's reaction as simply the employers' desire to avoid hiring the extra union personnel to crack open the empty containers.

I ask Larios about this, and he replies that the Coast Guard and the CBP conducted random searches of empty containers over a two-year span. "And all the empty containers that we examined over the last few years, we haven't found anything. Nothing but dirty containers."

While most of the hand-wringing has been over container inspection, the Transportation Security Administration (part of the Department of Homeland Security) in 2006 began to turn its own efforts toward inspecting longshoremen and others who work at the docks. As of April 2009, the Transportation Worker Identification Credential, or TWIC, is required at all U.S. ports in order to enter a facility unescorted. As part of the application process, workers must submit biometric information such as fingerprints, sit for a digital photograph, and pass a TSA background check, along with paying a $132.50 fee.

The ILWU has had problems with the TWIC card. Peter Peyton, a former member of the union's legislative action committee, told a congressional hearing in 2002, "As a general matter of policy, the ILWU membership opposes background checks on any workers." He pointed out that there was not one example of a union member involved in criminal conspiracies at a West Coast port. The union's primary concern is that members could be denied a TWIC card if something in their background, such as a criminal record, raises a red flag.

Then ILWU president Jim Spinosa implied in his keynote speech at the 2006 union caucus that TWIC background checks could be used by anti-labor government types to harass the rank and file. "If the government uses the Terrorist Watch list and the TWIC background checks to come after our union," he said, "if they dare to turn this into a McCarthyite witch hunt, let me assure you, the ILWU will respond with our full fury and force and that of our many friends. We will not provoke this fight, but we will not back down." No doubt Spinosa was thinking of Harry Bridges's travails with the government, which spent years trying to deport him over his alleged connections to the Communist Party (see chapter 6).

According to the TSA, about 3.5 percent of all applicants are initially denied a TWIC card. This denial can be based either on "permanent disqualifying offenses," which include felony convictions for treason, murder, or a crime involving transportation security, or on "interim disqualifying offenses" such as smuggling, robbery, or an assault that took place within seven years of the application. An applicant can appeal if the reason for the denial is incorrect—for example, if a conviction is older than seven years. The TSA says it responds to appeals within an average of thirty-three days, but critics charge that it often takes much longer; they point out that during the appeal a TWIC-less worker is unable to enter the port and make a living.

Just the same, the ultimate issue is, has the TWIC card made the ports safer? Peyton admits it's been a successful deterrent, but he claims it's possible to get a forged card for $300. "If there's really somebody who wants to do something bad," he says, "they're going to know the system, and there's nothing that's shell-proof."

KEEPING ORDER ON LAND

Porfirio Blas, senior lead officer for the Los Angeles port police, has been on the job since 6:30 A.M. Late in the afternoon on this day in September 2006, at the APM gate, pier 302, a truck driver has scraped up alongside another truck while waiting in line to get inside the terminal, breaking the second truck's side-view mirror. This normally wouldn't have required Blas's attention, but the offending driver refused to show his identification, and the private security guards at the gate called the police to handle it.

Blas—known to other officers as Porfie—seems amused he has to deal with this. His job, like that of the Coast Guard patrol, is as much about cruising the port's streets and terminals to show a presence as it is about mediating minor traffic accidents. He drives down Terminal Way and turns off to the APM gate, where the street is clogged with trucks waiting two or three blocks from the gate. The queue has a hellish, chaotic feel to it, engines rumbling in idle and brakes whining through the din. The drivers, mostly hidden in their cabs high above the pavement, look out their windows with the grim faces of people being tortured. On this windless, warm October day, the diesel fumes invisibly hover over the metal herd. Close your eyes and you can imagine the tiny black particles raining down on your face and flying into your lungs like microscopic gnats.

The three-abreast trucks take up much of the road, and Blas has trouble maneuvering past them on the right side, where a lane is supposed to be open for emergency vehicles. He honks his horn as though this will somehow part the trucks, but the gridlock is so intense that it takes several minutes before there's space for the trucks to move out of the way. I start to wonder what would happen if this were a true emergency and we had to reach the gate quickly.

Meanwhile, Blas patiently sits in front of a sign that reads, "This facility is currently operating at MARSEC level one security level." This is the Coast Guard's three-tiered Maritime Security assessment; level one signifies that only minimum-security measures are in use. Level three means that the port is potentially under attack or has already been assaulted in some way. At the moment, security at the gate seems a tad superficial. Only truck drivers with identification and a pick-up or delivery job are allowed in; however, the clerks at the gate can't see into the lofty cabs, and it's been well established that someone could simply hide in a sleeper compartment and be smuggled inside.

Blas finally reaches a security guard who's directing traffic about 100 yards from the gate. "I heard you were here yesterday and I missed you!" she yells with delight. She leads him to the two trucks in question while explaining the situation, and Blas takes it from there. When I ask her if this congestion is typical, she grins, "Oh, it's light today." About ten minutes go by before Blas returns to the car. He says, "No injuries, no report. Ha-ha." He has a habit of ending his statements with a fidgety chuckle.

We continue to the head of the line and inside the APM terminal, where Blas gives me a quick primer on container seals. He points out an eclectic collection of small plastic and metal devices locked in place where the two doors of the container meet. Each is marked with a unique number recorded in the container's paperwork. The seals are not meant to actually lock the container; instead, they provide an indication of whether or not it's been tampered with. That is, if a seal is broken— it usually takes a bolt cutter to do so—it means someone has opened

This container seal indicates whether or not the container has been opened since cargo was placed in it.

the container. However, with drills and other equipment, thieves (or terrorists) are able to slip off the seal without anyone noticing that the container's been opened. Electronic seals are available that can transmit a message to a receiver if they've been tampered with, but they aren't yet in common use.

Blas drives about the stacks of containers in the yard, all awaiting transport to somewhere. Maybe because it's such a huge place, the activity seems spread out and light. But after a moment, I realize that trucks are constantly whizzing through the yard, most exceeding the speed limit, crisscrossing around the container stacks. Blas can't hand out speeding tickets inside the yard, so his main purpose is simply to show up at random times as a deterrent to thieves and terrorists, but he admits the chaos is unnerving. "I don't like driving here," he says. "Too scared. Ha-ha."

He adds that the work is a lot easier since the 9/11 security crackdown. "This is just a normal day, today," he says, adding that with the limited access at the gates, "it's easier for us. All I have to do is drive through. That's it."

One seedy example of how things have changed is that prostitutes no longer hang out at the terminal gates, or even inside the piers (there weren't always fences to keep people out). Blas remembers a pimp who used to frequent the docks with his ladies, who specialized, it would seem, in lonely ship crews. "In the old days—hoo!" he says.

Blas continues his rounds, working an assigned zone (among four in the port where police patrol). He often drives some eleven hours, touring three or four terminals of the five in his zone along with two oil terminals, ship services, a fish off-loading dock, and a railroad repair yard. The actual cop work isn't that strenuous, and the port is perhaps the quietest he's seen it since he joined the force in 1984 after working four years at Los Angeles International Airport.

On this afternoon, the radio is strangely quiet. Even the dispatcher sounds as though she's gone home out of boredom. Blas does allow that the evening may pick up with a few arguments, drunks, or fights. But any suspicious characters or packages to liven up the day? "Very rare," he says, without his usual chuckle. "Very rare."

FIFTEEN

The New Normal

THE TRUCK MAKER

When Balwinder Samra delivered his prototype electric truck to the Port of Los Angeles during the first week of 2008, Geraldine Knatz, the port's executive director, went to Costco and bought him a case of Cup-a-Soup. This might have been more an unintentional message than a joke. Samra had just spent more than a half million dollars of the port's and the state's money to build the truck, and considering that neither benefactor was all that flush with cash at the time, this came across—just a little—as the most Knatz could afford for a bonus. For his part, Samra had been subsisting on instant soup, working twelve-hour days, and scraping through on the $527,000 grant that was supposed to result in the ultimate solution to truck pollution at the port.

I suppose this suggests that when you're trying to build the world's most powerful electric truck, capable of pulling any load that comes off a ship, even a six-figure bank balance gets spread rather thin and you don't eat out a lot. Not that this equation for deprivation seems to matter much to Samra. "I was having more fun, to be honest, than anybody," he admits, "because engineers see their product and [see] that it's working—you've broken a technological barrier. And you feel, if you don't have money to eat, well, that can wait. It was very exciting."

And potentially profitable. Samra's publicly traded company, Balqon Corporation, has since taken a $5 million order from the port for twenty-five more trucks as a demonstration project. Longshoremen will drive these rigs and develop the kind of routine necessary with an electric vehicle (that is, drive in the morning, charge during lunch, drive in the afternoon, and so on). Other ports are at least talking about getting their slice of the green pie that electric trucks represent for the future of shipping. Balqon also has upcoming deals with companies that have committed to buy its trucks but prefer to keep their names off the record for now. And, in an initial bid to go international, the company signed a deal in June 2010 to sell its trucks in Costa Rica.

It would seem that the trucks should be an easy sell. Beyond the zero-emissions aspect, the vehicles are cheaper to operate. The port calculates that an electric truck costs 20 cents a mile, while a diesel truck is four to nine times more expensive, depending on fuel costs. In addition, electric trucks are especially suited for drayage work and the short distances involved. Balqon's latest drayage truck, the Nautilus XE30, pulls loads using a lithium ion battery and a 300-horsepower motor, has a maximum speed of 55 miles per hour, and can go 90 miles with a full load. And charging is relatively quick, usually taking only as long as a lunch break or the time between shifts (that's just to keep it running; a full charge requires eight hours).

From all appearances, this began in modern mythological fashion, that is, the standard entrepreneurial saga of starting a business from Samra's garage in 2005. Self-employed, forty-three years old, and living off savings, Samra, along with two fellow engineers who had day jobs, met every evening and worked until midnight on a device for large electric vehicles called a controller. The controller is the electronic version of a carburetor, essentially interpreting the driver's needs—more power here, less power there—and then sending that information to the engine.

This nocturnal tinkering went on for a year and a half before they were able to peddle the product to truck companies, which they assumed would buy the controller and install it in an as-yet-undeveloped electric truck. However, the manufacturers suggested that the three simply build their own trucks. Around the same time, word got out that these guys had figured out a way of powering large, heavy vehicles using standard lead acid batteries and their new controller.

By late 2006, the chairman of the port's harbor commission, David Freeman, had heard about the three engineers, and he took Samra out to lunch to learn more. With no apparent concern that doling out cash required a bureaucracy's lengthy approval process and not just his handshake, Freeman offered Samra a grant to build for the port a truck that never needed a single hydrocarbon. After four more months, checks in equal amounts came from the port and from California's South Coast Air Quality Management District, which joined in funding the project, and it appeared the moonlighting was about to pay off.

"If I was married, I don't think this would have ever happened," he says, his voice rising slightly, perhaps as he thought about his family back in India putting the screws to him for being an unemployed bachelor. "Wives don't like the idea of income not coming in. And you're running around buying machine parts for three thousand dollars, and she feels she just lost a couch or something."

"Honestly, if David Freeman didn't come in here and say, 'I've got this idea—you've got to meet this guy with this truck,' it would not have been on my radar screen," Knatz tells me. "But I like to think I'm a risk taker. . . . It could have fallen flat on its face, and I could have been on the [front page] of the *L.A. Times* for giving somebody half a million dollars to try something, and what a waste—I wasted money. But fortunately it worked."

(It should be noted that funding Balqon's first truck was not part of the port's Clean Truck program, described in chapter 10, although it certainly dovetailed with the program's philosophy of encouraging companies to drive the cleanest vehicles possible.)

Sitting at the head of a large conference table in Balqon's Harbor City offices, where the trucks are built, just down the road from the port, Samra—who is Balqon's president, chairman, and CEO—tells his tale with long detours through the engineering details, the geeky stuff that he finds so satisfying when he thinks of all the issues that he and his crew overcame to make electrons haul cargo. As his passion pours out over how they calculated the correct battery size or how many hours they spent in software development, I wonder if there's anything a little more personal he hasn't told me, something that shows this is more than just an engineer exulting over his creation. There is, and it comes out more as an aside than anything he seems interested in discussing.

In 1992, then working for Taylor-Dunn, an industrial vehicle manufacturer, Samra took a vacation in Mexico City. There, he says, "I noticed all these trucks running around downtown, and I said all these should be electric. It seems like they're not going anywhere." That is, an electric vehicle doesn't idle when stopped in a traffic jam, sending out fumes; it just sits like a brick and does nothing. He mused, just think what that might do to reduce the city's infamous air pollution.

With the engineer in him improbably joining his inner risk-taker, he went back to the office and proposed an electric van. Within a few months, he had sold four hundred to a Mexican delivery company, creating what he figures was the world's largest electric fleet. He had done something that most people don't do—he acted on inspiration. At a time when no one knew from ultrafine diesel particulates or even figured that an electric truck was practical, let alone needed, Samra took a few moments thinking shop when he should have been relaxing and quickly made himself the king of electric trucks.

He leans back in his chair, appearing pretty satisfied with the memory. "It was an ability to take today's reliable technology, finding an application where it would work and perfectly perform," he explains in a lecturing tone. And as tempting as it might have been to mass market his creation as though it were a toaster, he has started cautiously,

A Balqon Corporation assembly worker installs a battery on an electric truck.

introducing it to the niche of drayage trucking, a market segment that is being pushed to be cleaner and greener.

He's also taking a conservative approach to building the vehicles themselves, using off-the-rack truck chassis and drive systems and merely modifying them with batteries, an electric motor, and his controller. It's so simple that, as he enters the international market, he plans to plug his components into locally built trucks, saving a fortune in setting up factories.

"Early adoption has always been an issue in the U.S. markets," he says, "so that's why we're expanding to international markets where it's a lot easier to sell electric vehicles than it is in the U.S." That is, other countries have been far more aggressive in trying to solve their diesel truck pollution problems.

Samra is creating what might be called a "new normal," that nebulous point in time when we realize there's been a shift in what we see as the usual state of affairs. In his case, it's moving from trucks powered by diesel or LNG—no matter how clean they are—to ones (at least for drayage) that are pollution-free, quiet, and have no need for oil derricks (forgetting, for a moment at least, that the electricity to power the trucks often comes from fossil fuel–powered generating plants). This point, this new normal, hasn't arrived quite yet, but the port is pushing for that generational moment when some kid looks at an old diesel truck farting fumes and reacts in puzzlement, as though she's just seen an LP record.

FIGHTING BACK AGAINST THE COMPETITION

Then again, not all new normals are quite so positive. Today, the port is also facing a downward shift in revenues that Knatz tries to describe as temporary even as she frames it within a set of lower expectations, a new normal. In early 2009, shipping volume had dropped to its lowest level in twelve years. A worldwide recession was killing business. The number of containers with imported goods going through the ports of

Los Angeles and Long Beach fell by 35.3 percent over one year; exports were down 27.6 percent. Longshoremen, in particular, felt the sting. In February 2009, the average shift was made up of 660 workers, compared to as many as 1,500 three years before. The hundreds of nonunion casuals hired during the 2004 backlog (described in chapter 7) were largely unemployed because most of the remaining jobs now went to registered longshoremen.

"We're down in a slump," Knatz says without her usual ebullience. "We're going to come back up. We're going to bounce back, but we're not going to bounce back to normal. We're going to bounce back to a new normal." Even though she tells her staff this as a mild morale booster, it's really more of a fatalistic way of looking at things. It will be years, the underlying message comes through, before the massive, ever-increasing volumes return.

Well, if they ever return. Other ports—Knatz's competition—want some of the import action that made the Port of Los Angeles such a powerhouse. Places like Houston, Savannah, and Charleston are all arguing that they have the infrastructure wherewithal—or will have in the near future—to make them just as attractive as Los Angeles/Long Beach. On average, it's cheaper to send cargo by ship, so some shippers who move cargo to the Midwest or the East Coast might bypass Los Angeles to avoid the extra charges of continuing east by rail or truck, which are more expensive modes of transport. Then again, rail is faster and trucks speedier still, a factor that sometimes trumps the higher costs. That said, shippers are always looking to cut expenses, and they may decide that saving a few bucks here and there by journeying from Asia directly to Gulf Coast or East Coast ports is worth the extra time.

In addition to these competitive American ports, Mexico is planning a privately funded $4 billion project in Punta Colonet, currently a tiny seaport on the Pacific Ocean 150 miles south of San Diego. When this new port opens in 2014, it will be capable of handling two million containers a year. In mid-2006, Kansas City Southern opened a rail line from another Mexican port, Lazaro Cardenas, to Laredo, Texas. While the small port handles in one year the same number of containers that the Los Angeles/ Long Beach complex sees in one week (putting it thirty-fourth on the list of North American ports), Lazaro Cardenas is seen as an overflow option when the two behemoths are overwhelmed with cargo.

And then there's Canada. Knatz tells me, "Someone snuck us a Power-Point that shows the Canadian government—the government itself—is spending seven million dollars on a marketing campaign to Asia. It's basically, 'Serve America's Heartland through Canada.'"

In particular, the port in Prince Rupert, north of Vancouver, British Columbia, is aggressively going after her customers. The Canadian facility was helped by COSCO-CKYH Alliance's decision to locate a terminal there in July 2008, which boosted volume by 300 percent over the first half of the year, even as other ports were losing volume because of the recession. In a January 2009 press release, the Prince Rupert Port Authority let U.S. West Coast ports know just who was coming after them: "Strategically situated on the direct great circle route from Asia, Prince Rupert is more than a day's sailing time closer to Asia than Vancouver and Seattle and nearly three days closer than LA/Long Beach." And while the amount of cargo headed to the Canadian port is still tiny compared to the competition—its newest facility, the Fairview Terminal, looks like a Target parking lot compared to Los Angeles's sprawling Terminal Island—the press release adds that Prince Rupert has "extensive capacity to expand."

On top of all this, the Panama Canal, once a constricted waterway unable to handle the supersized ships built to move eight thousand containers in one trip, is being doubled in capacity, so there's no longer an excuse for simply dumping off cargo in Los Angeles instead of continuing east to, say, Houston or Norfolk, Virginia. The $5.25 billion canal project is scheduled for completion in 2014. The Virginia Port Authority already sees one-third of its business coming from Asia via the canal, and the canal expansion will only help it attract more business to its piers. As Knatz puts it, "The new normal for West Coast ports is a much more competitive environment."

During our last interview in early 2009, Knatz doesn't sound especially pessimistic—she says she thrives on challenges such as this—but the new normal isn't exactly what she expected when I first met her in late 2006. At that time, she predicted doubling business in a few years, and the discussion was all about how to make the terminals more efficient so they could handle the load. "Ultimately, I think that the port does have capacity in the way of utilizing our existing assets better," she told me. But now, she sounds a little tired at times, and when I ask about the past boomtown predictions, she admits, "It's not going to happen."

"Go back to 2005, 2006," Michael DiBernardo, the port's director of marketing, says, "[we were] saying that by the year 2030, we're going to be at 35 million TEUs [units for measuring cargo] between the two ports. And that was showing year-after-year growth of about six percent, I think. And we haven't seen that."

And although no one at the port was saying it publicly during this heyday, many suspected all along that the new normal—they didn't know what that would be—could eventually creep into the picture. According to Michael Keenan, the port's harbor planning and economic analyst, "Our average growth rate over the last ten years has been more like a ten percent growth rate. And we knew that was unsustainable. We knew—nobody could really predict the crash in the way it happened, but everyone did anticipate that we couldn't continue—we wouldn't keep growing at the pace that we were." Just the same, port documents written in 2009 still predict volume will double by 2030.

For the moment, however, the port has cut back on some capital projects, including their long-touted waterfront project. "Because of financial reasons," Knatz says, "we have to say, okay, we're not going to spend two hundred million dollars this year, we're only going to do fifty million, whatever. We're always going to keep something going. And it's always going to be in the queue for construction. And I heard from the community—'We don't think you'll ever approve anything.' They've got that perception out there. We're going to prove them wrong."

Amid all this, Samra is building his electric truck empire and waiting for customers who might be currently cutting back on new expenses. When we talk in mid-2009, he's producing one truck a week and figures he can double that output as soon as he hires more people to assemble the vehicles. The current production is all going to the port, which ordered twenty hostlers, or yard vehicles, which haul containers inside the terminal. Each vehicle costs $189,950. The port also bought five street-legal trucks (the unlicensed hostlers aren't allowed on public roads) for $208,500. Altogether, Balqon is being paid more than $5 million.

For its patronage, the port is receiving a $1,000 royalty on every truck Samra sells to a third party anywhere in the world. This wasn't part of the original deal he signed when Freeman first offered the half million dollar grant, but Samra—who tells me that he wasn't used to the idea of receiving money with no need to pay it back—suggested the royalty as a way of showing his appreciation for the port's support. "We had an obligation," he says. "We felt like we owed half a million bucks to somebody." The South Coast Air Quality Management District is also being paid the royalty. According to a port document, the money "will be dedicated to further advancements toward a 'zero-emissions port.'" That is, the new normal.

SIXTEEN

Hawse Piper

When Ed Brooks and his tugboat, the *Master,* first sidle up alongside the *Xin Chang Sha,* there's a surreal moment when the ocean is blocked so completely from his view that it seems as though the tug has been swallowed whole by the enormous Chinese shipping vessel. An ominous humming fills the background as engines, splashing water, and wind all beat together like a storm in the distance. Dreamlike, an incongruous sign painted on the monstrous hull appears—a large white arrow pointed down, with the word TUG in block letters above it.

Brooks glances out the portside window from the wheelhouse, which is two stair flights up from the *Master*'s deck. Even at that height, all he sees is a steel hull, eclipsing everything. If he were to go outside right now (which wouldn't be such a great idea, since he's about 6 inches from the *Xin Chang Sha* and there's no one else to steer), he could look behind him unimpeded to his companion tug, the *Leader,* following at the ship's stern about 860 feet away, a smeary glob of red and white looking like some brightly dressed stranger you might notice on the other side of a football stadium.

It's an odd, nearly claustrophobic sensation to be hull to hull with the *Xin Chang Sha,* a moving wall of dark steel that's just aching to crush you. Standing on the *Master*'s deck and peering up at the disinterested

Chinese crew in their orange overalls checking out the view of the port, I feel vulnerable and small. Really, really small.

Brooks steers the *Master* with a casual intensity, lightly grasping the pitch wheel's hub, twitching one direction, then another, as if he's adjusting a volume knob. Huge tires ring the tugboat and brush against the ship's hull without exerting any appreciable force. The towline, kept taut at a 45-degree angle, runs from behind the ship's bow to the *Master's* stern, which faces forward. That may seem as though the tug is technically going backward, but in the omnidirectional world of so-called water tractors, this makes perfect sense.

The *Xin Chang Sha* is a China Shipping Line vessel built in 2005, capable of carrying about two thousand 40-foot containers, many stacked seven high. Such giants are largely unable to steer through the port's Main Channel at a slow 3 knots without help from a tugboat. From a distance, it looks as if the *Master* and the *Leader* are herding the *Xin Chang Sha* through the open water near the harbor's entrance.

This may explain why Brooks is, in a sense, hardly aware of the size differential between the two vessels. He's got a lot of muscle in his tugboat—two engines totaling 4,800 horsepower—and even though he isn't technically in control (the port pilot on board the *Xin Chang Sha* is calling the shots), he drives the *Master* with such confidence that the container ship becomes a big, dumb cow waiting to be pushed or pulled in the right direction.

"Look at that thing," Brooks tells me, pointing to the ship. "A big ol' hunk of steel coming in here, and we're going to stick it in a berth." As if realizing that sounds a bit cavalier, he adds that no one can make a mistake. "You have to do this right. You don't do it right, it's huge."

An hour before coming on board the *Master,* Brooks attended a labor union meeting with management in the Crowley Maritime Services office, a spare, second-story collection of desks and small offices overlooking the Main Channel at berth 86, from which Crowley's ship assist operation is run. Crowley has been around since 1892, when Tom Crowley began his marine services in San Francisco Bay with a single

Tugboat captain Ed Brooks maneuvers the *Master* alongside a cargo ship.

Whitehall rowboat, a distinctive craft with flared sides and a straight bow that was used for, among other things, ferrying sailors from ship to shore and back again.

Legend has it that Crowley helped a bank during the 1906 earthquake by squirreling away its cash on one of his boats to protect the money from fire and looters, and the bank, forever grateful, made sure he had a ready source of loans to grow the company. In 1914, Crowley added wooden, steam-powered tugs to his services, and his direct descendants expanded into commercial shipping, vessel construction, salvage, and oil service and logistics.

Crowley's grandson, Tom Crowley Jr., is the current president and CEO of the company as well as its principal stockholder. He makes a healthy $2.8 million in salary and benefits, overseeing a small maritime empire of 4,300 employees and a 280-vessel fleet that recently brought in $1.47 billion in revenue.

And yet, for all that, Brooks maintains it's still a family-like operation. Indeed, the Crowley progeny own the majority of the company. Soon after we meet, Brooks, unprompted, talks of being with the company since 1984 and how he maintains a certain warmth for Tom Jr. himself. With Brooks's wife, Alice, serving in the navy and being deployed to Guantanamo Bay for a year, taking care of his eleven-year-old son would have been a big problem if the company had not given him more flexible hours. "It's not, like, gee, too bad, Brooks," he says, describing the company's reaction. "It was, hmm, what can we do?"

After Brooks finished his meeting, he walked to the Crowley dock, where three Voith Water Tractors sat end to end. He met up with Chad Macaulay, the *Leader*'s pilot for that shift, and they talked about the meeting. Each four-person tugboat crew works two weeks on, two weeks off, living on the boat during their time and splitting the days into six-hour shifts. Brooks and Macaulay both have the noon to 6:00 P.M. time slot, known as the mate's watch. When that shift ends, they get dinner and a rest before starting up again at midnight for another six hours. While this does allow for unusual commutes—Brooks lived in Hawaii while his wife was stationed at Pearl Harbor—it takes a couple of days to decompress from what could only be described as a fragmented sleeping pattern. Brooks has his eye on a senior position coming up (he's earned a captain endorsement on his license but doesn't refer to himself by that rank), in which the six-hour shifts are closer to normal days, that is, 6:00 A.M. to noon and 6:00 P.M. to midnight.

Brooks cut off the conversation with Macauley because the two men had just been dispatched to meet the *Xin Chang Sha* outside the harbor. He climbed over a tire and onto the *Master*. There's something unsinkable-looking about these boats: they aren't the sleekest, most elegant vessels you'll ever see, but you can depend on them floating, no matter what. The red flared hulls are lined with huge tires, recycled from a mining company's earth-moving equipment, which ring the boat to protect it from directly brushing against the hulls of the ships it pushes and pulls. The rest of the tug, from the deck up, is painted white, with the name CROWLEY in red letters midship on the cabin where the crew lives and eats. Above the cabin is perched the octagonal glass-enclosed wheelhouse, looking like a bottle cap stuck on top of the boat.

While we prepared to leave the dock, it was clear that Brooks's affection for the *Master* was largely an appreciation of its functionality. He described the twin engines with a sort of reverence, even attributing to them an extra 200 horsepower they don't really have. But most of his praise went to the Voith Schneider propulsion system, an eggbeater-like propeller that sits underneath and just forward of the wheelhouse. This so-called cycloidal propulsion uses six hydrofoil-shaped vertical blades attached to a round plate. Each blade can move independently as the plate spins and create thrust in any direction just by how they're positioned.

Even after using this latest technology for several years—the *Master* was built in 1999—Brooks is still a little giddy about how maneuverable his boat is. It's more like a helicopter, given the way it can move forward, backward, and side to side, shifting directions within seconds. When a pilot is berthing a ship or taking it away from the docks, the tugboats are frequently repositioned so they can fine-tune the operation. The previous technology, twin-screw propellers, could never swing a tugboat around as quickly into position as the cycloidal propellers can. The *Master* is also capable of pulling on the ship while running sideways, a maneuver called an indirect, which is far more stable than doing this from the stern or bow. Brooks was excited about demonstrating the indirect to me.

"When you're doing a ship assist," he said, "there's a lot of maneuvering. That's the thing about a tugboat. You're really a boat handler. There's a lot of skill. You're really finessing."

As Brooks entered the cabin area, the boat's captain, Bill Privette, was standing outside the bathroom in jeans and a shirt with a small white towel in his hand. "Welcome aboard," he said, confused about seeing a visitor in the cramped hallway. He disappeared for a moment before walking to the stern to smoke a cigarette. With twenty-nine years working in the maritime industry, mostly on tugs, Privette told me he was sticking with the job another year. "I think thirty years is a good number for retirement," he mused and then went on to exult over the *Master*'s ability to move sideways. Clearly, for these guys who've known much older systems, the thrill had not worn off the cycloidal propellers.

With his shoulders at a sideways angle, Brooks shuttled through the narrow cabin hall to a steep stairway, and then another, before entering the wheelhouse, where he seemed so comfortable you'd think he was in his living room watching television. The *Leader* pulled away from the dock, and Brooks followed it into the Main Channel. The engines are directly below but make little sound. As Brooks approached the *Xin Chang Sha,* the port pilot, Captain Doug Rill, had already radioed the Vessel Traffic Service to let them know he was on board. He then switched the radio frequency to channel 77, where he could communicate with Brooks, opening with a casual greeting, "Good afternoon, *Master.*"

Brooks grabbed a microphone hanging from the ceiling, pulled it toward him, and answered the pilot, "Good afternoon."

Brooks continued moving along the ship's starboard side to behind the bow, where the word TUG in big white letters is painted on the hull. This is where the ship's ribs inside the hull have been reinforced to stand up against the pushing from tugs in port after port. Brooks lightly scraped the hull below the ship's name and slightly in front of the TUG sign, enough that the tires flattened out, absorbing much of the pressure.

"*Master,* starboard bow. *Leader,* center aft," Captain Rill directed the two tugs.

Brooks radioed back, "Starboard bow. *Master.*"

The *Leader* moved into position behind the ship, where most of the tug-assisted steering takes place. Once the *Master* reached the bow, the

The tugboat *Leader* follows behind a cargo ship, awaiting instructions from the port pilot aboard the ship.

ship's crew tossed a heaving line with a weight on the end (so the wind can't blow it in the water) to Henry, the *Master*'s able seaman. Henry holds the tugboat apprentice position, learning the job and perhaps working his way up to Brooks's job. Henry attached a slightly bigger messenger line to the heaving line, and the two were pulled up to where the crew could hook the messenger line into a winch. This hauled up the heavier towline, with a diameter of 8 ½ inches, at the end of the messenger line. The crew then secured the towline to a fireplug-like structure called a cruciform, and the two vessels were finally connected. Henry's job was finished for the moment.

We are now joined to the *Xin Chang Sha* and are at the point where I start to realize we are essentially a Chihuahua in charge of a Great Dane. I'm unnerved; Brooks is cheerful.

He started his tugboat career from the bottom up, which makes him, in the maritime world, a "hawse piper," someone who pulled himself up the anchor chain and crawled through the hawse hole, a large grommet-like structure where the anchor chain leads through the ship's bow and to a winch. Brooks came from a long line of British merchant marines, among them his grandfather, who would take him to the New York docks to see the *Queen Elizabeth* or the *Queen Mary* filling their berths in far grander style than a container ship.

"I've always been around ships," he explains while driving through the Main Channel. "And when I'd look out on the horizon and see the ships' smoke out there, you know, back in the old days, I'd see the ships leaving the Port of New York—I knew that was my future."

He first entered the maritime job market as a shipyard runner, driving parts, before becoming an apprentice pipe fitter. On that job, he met someone whose brother worked for Crowley. The introduction that followed brought him to the union hall and sent him out to sea at twenty-five. "My first ship took me around the world," he says. "My very first ship. I knew I made the right choice." After six years on open water, he moved to tugs.

Brooks is now fifty-one years old, with close-cropped hair and a Fu Manchu mustache that makes him look a little out of place anywhere but on the boat. He wears sneakers, faded and loose jeans, a gray sweatshirt, and black Ray-Ban sunglasses; and he is a friendly, contradictory combination of blue-collar worker, iconoclast, and family man who values domestic stability.

"I have always felt uncomfortable being a nine-to-five kind of person, you know," he tells me, carefully choosing his words when I ask why he likes the job. "Going to work and having a routine. I have a routine now, but this is my office. That's what I like about it. I have a lot of things introduced that are unexpected or unknown, and I've always thrived on that. The challenges, the variations. This is not a typical job, and I don't think I've ever been a typical person. I wasn't a typical kid. I've always been, for lack of a better word, adventurous."

Now inside the port's waters, the *Leader* is told to pull the ship's stern to starboard with an indirect move while Brooks pushes it to port, so they can make a tight left-hand turn. The berthing process that follows seems to use his assistance sparingly, with Captain Rill adjusting the ship's position as much with the bow thrusters as with the tugs, which perform light-handed maneuvers called push/pulls to nudge the vessel into place. All of this requires a fine sense of timing on Rill's part to know just how much a tug should push or pull so the ship doesn't crash into the dock.

"It takes a lot of balls to do that job," Brooks says of the pilots.

The docking continues, turning into a duet of sorts between the tugs and Rill, who gives a command that the tug driver acknowledges with a toot of the peanut whistle. This reduces chatter on the radio that can interfere with the commands, which sometimes come quickly, one after the other.

"*Master*, ahead easy." (Whistle)

"*Master*, stop." (Whistle)

"*Leader*, stop." (Whistle)

"*Master*, ahead easy." (Whistle)

"*Master*, ahead easy." (Whistle)

"*Master*, 45 aft." (Whistle)

"*Leader*, stop." (Whistle)

"*Master*, a little stronger." (Whistle)

And so it goes until finally Captain Rill is satisfied and radios, "*Master*, I'm going to turn you loose. I enjoyed it. Thank you very much."

"Okay, Captain," Brooks responds, grabbing the microphone. "You're very welcome." They're so cordial, you'd think we were at a dinner party.

Henry appears on the deck to retrieve the towline, which the ship's crew releases. Brooks moves the *Master* out from the ship and over his loudspeaker calls to the Chinese crewmen, "*Shay, shay, nay*."

"I said, thank you, I think. I could have said, you look queer!" he laughs, adding that his daughter taught him the phrase. I learn later that the Mandarin word for "thank you" is *xièxiè*. The crew members walk away, with one barely waving back.

Brooks points the boat in the direction of his next job, an oil tanker

A tugboat tied into the bow of a ship. In this position, it will be used for steering the ship if necessary.

called the *Torm Sara*, and leaves his chair for a small desk behind him, where he jots down a few notes on the job. He then calls the Crowley dispatcher with the time for the *Xin Chang Sha* job—1500 to 1615—which will be billed to China Shipping. Brooks doesn't know how much Crowley makes on the job, given that each carrier is charged differently, with discounts going to those who bring in the most business. Based on published prices, however, the rate is probably in the $1,000-an-hour range.

The *Torm Sara*, a 744-foot-long, double-hulled tanker built in 2003, is docked at berth 189, a liquid bulk terminal in the East Basin run by Vopak North America. Brooks eyeballs the tanker and surmises it's about half full, judging by the waterline. Ahead of us is a break bulk ship, slowly moving to the Main Channel without tugs, something that's allowed as long as the ship has thrusters both fore and aft, which some people call built-in tugs. In that situation, it's up to the pilot to decide whether tugs are needed, Brooks allows, but at this point, mid-afternoon, winds are starting to build, and taking a ship out without assistance is questionable. A tanker, however, has no such option. Coast Guard regulations require tethered support—tugs at fore and aft—so that in case the ship loses control, it won't run aground or collide with a pier or another ship, with the attendant risk of breaking open and spilling its load.

This particular tanker, managed by a Danish company and registered in Singapore, isn't going very far at the moment—just to the anchorage area outside the Port of Long Beach, where it will sit waiting for another terminal to open up so it can unload the rest of its cargo.

"*Leader.* Good afternoon," the pilot, Captain Mark Coynes, calls over the radio.

"*Leader.* Good afternoon," Macaulay replies.

"*Master.* Good afternoon."

"Good afternoon." Brooks explains that Coynes is a Long Beach pilot assigned to this ship because he has a more complete knowledge of the anchorage area in his home port. He shows me a map of the port and the anchorage area, designated by large circles, in the center of which a ship will drop anchor. The ship can then pivot around that center point as the winds and currents dictate without hitting another ship anchored nearby.

Pulling a ship out from its berth is far simpler than putting it there, and the tanker and the two tugs quickly enter the East Channel and then the Main Channel. The ship runs at just 3 knots but seems to reach the harbor entrance quickly, where the crews release the towlines and the tugs return to the harbor by simply reversing course; they don't even turn around.

Brooks calls in the time, 1630 to 1720. His six-hour shift is nearly over. As he returns to the Main Channel and the next job at the TraPac terminal, pier 144, and a container ship called the *Mol Endurance*, Henry finishes cooking dinner. This evening, the fairly lavish spread includes scallops, shrimp, orange roughy, salad, mixed vegetables, and rice.

Before 6:00, Brooks invites me to dinner and heads down to the galley after Bill Privette takes the wheel. While we eat, Brooks and Henry watch the financial news on an overhead television that buzzes and pops from poor reception. While he flosses, Henry, a Hawaiian in his late thirties, begins a rambling dissertation on junk bonds.

At the moment, the boat isn't moving, just idling at the *Mol Endurance*'s stern. Privette and a trainee, Jim Brown, are waiting for a second tug, which hasn't shown up because the port's too busy at the moment. After about forty-five minutes, the pilot, Captain Jim Dwyer, decides he can manage with just one tug plus bow thrusters, and he orders the lines to the dock released. This is as much a financial decision as anything: the longshoremen who handle the lines are getting paid to sit around and wait, and if the pilot doesn't absolutely need another tug, it makes more sense to go now.

The longshoremen struggle with the thick white hawser rope, prying it off the dockside mooring bollards. Finally Dwyer gives Brown the command to pull away. Brown answers with a peanut whistle.

If anything, Brown is the antithesis of a hawse piper. At twenty-four, he's about to graduate from the California Maritime Academy in Vallejo, without going to sea and without climbing any anchor chains. Like Brooks, he steers the boat from the pitch wheel's hub, but without the same calm confidence. He goes through brief streaks where he seems cautious before returning to a more assured demeanor.

"Give me a little line," Dwyer radios. "I might need indirect."

Brown renders the line, meaning he lets it out while the winch holds it taut. The line runs from a drum through the staple—a massive, upside-down U-shaped device welded to the boat below the deck—and then up to the ship. Brown watches a gauge measuring how much force is on the line, and as he turns the tug into an indirect, where he's nearly parallel to the ship, the numbers go to 28 tons of force on the line, and then to 32 tons. The tug's engines, usually fairly quiet, roar, and water churns around the boat as it pulls on the ship to help it negotiate a turn into the Main Channel. The wheelhouse starts to tip to the starboard side, and Privette warns me to grab my camera, which is about to slide off the desk.

"You can come out of indirect now," Dwyer radios. Brown toots the peanut whistle.

The winds, first noticeable a short time ago, are now reaching 35 miles an hour on the boat's wind gauge. We're at the *Mol Endurance*'s stern, which pivots to one side and then the other, and it's obvious Dwyer has to continually steer from port to starboard to compensate for the winds pushing on the ship's side, so high and so huge a target. The gusts spike at 45 miles an hour. Waves crash 20 feet in the air over the boulder breakwater near the harbor's entrance.

About a quarter mile from Angels Gate, Dwyer releases the *Master* and thanks Brown for his assistance. While a radio plays "Whole Lotta Love," Brown calls in the hours, 1750 to 1900. The ship's crew members release the line and wave to Henry. The *Mol Endurance* passes through the gate, headed for Asia, and in the windswept haze, another ship is coming in.

Compared with my introduction to the Port of Los Angeles more than a decade before, when all I saw was the chaotic urgency of getting containers off a ship, this scene appears tranquil. I'm about to write some romantic twaddle in my notebook about how the ship is literally sailing into the sunset, but I see Brown's expression, which says this is as routine as it gets, and I realize that there's really nothing special about the moment. Cargo comes in. Cargo goes out.

But if it were actually that dull, I wouldn't have had any material for a book. That idyllic last glance at a ship hardly represents a place that actually turned out to be quite messy, perhaps so much so that I could be forgiven for avoiding the nearly impossible task of wrapping up the story with a neat, contrived conclusion. The port resists such a treatment.

I suppose that's what made the Port of Los Angeles interesting—no, fascinating—to me. I knew the place was huge, and I expected a certain degree of complexity to come from that; but as soon as I sat down with retired hold man Art Almeida in 2004, I discovered that conflicts both large and small ooze from the docks. It isn't just that longshoremen are in a continuous tussle with their employers, which makes for some juicy stories. Nor is it that the port's operations bang up against some community residents' ideas of what makes a good neighbor. Instead, it's about how all these confrontations are symptoms of larger issues that the rest of us should be concerned with.

On the surface, there's the port's tick-tock operation, which occasionally breaks down over, say, a dispute between longshoremen and the employers and affects someone someplace far from the docks. Perhaps the result is nothing major, just a few pairs of shoes or some CD players that hit store shelves a couple of days late because the containers carrying them are delayed. Maybe a store in Milwaukee loses a customer or two to the competitors down the street.

But there's a larger point, the union would say. ILWU members are fighting to maintain not just their jobs but the healthcare and pension benefits that they believe are their right. After all, they'll work for thirty, forty, fifty years, often in difficult conditions, helping to make gobs of money for their employers, so why shouldn't they be rewarded for their labor? White-collar workers sitting behind a desk using their noggins (and perhaps advanced college degrees) to make a living may wonder why somebody driving a utility tractor rig pulls down nearly six figures while they can't crack the $60,000 mark. But many longshoremen don't even try to justify the apparent largess they enjoy; instead, they argue, this should be the sort of compensation everyone gets.

The most visible outcome of that debate between the longshoremen and the employers is perhaps a labor slowdown or even a strike (which can affect so many beyond the port). But the union's point is indeed correct: it should also put the rest of us in the uncomfortable position of questioning the fairness of our jobs and our salaries. Personally, I got some great stories out of writing about the fight, but I couldn't help but wonder what my efforts are really worth. I certainly never expected that kind of introspection when I climbed up the Jacob's ladder to board the *Wan Hai 312* and watched a port pilot at work.

The local fight over the pollution coming from port operations has more straightforward global implications, but it doesn't make you any more comfortable. All you have to do is take a step or two back to realize that every port in the world no doubt has the same problem to one degree or another. But we can go even further: diesel trucks are everywhere, and wherever they travel, they leave behind ultrafine particles, with respiratory problems and heart disease to follow. Plus, there's the issue of trying to meld a large industrial operation with a residential area. Whose priorities are given top consideration?

We can reach out even further, to the global economy, to examine how the port connects most of us to the rest of the world and how that connection has infiltrated our lives. It's no longer some fairly trivial, albeit personal, matter of whether we pay a few cents less for that watch made in China; rather, it's about jobs—yours and theirs—and billions upon billions of dollars going somewhere. Even if you wanted to hide from it, you can't.

In my naïveté, I began this story thinking it was far simpler than it turned out to be. In the wheelhouse of that tug, even after my years of research, I was still clinging to that image of the ship peacefully leaving the port, headed west into a sunset. But then the high winds slapped the tugboat so forcefully that I had to grab a nearby desk to steady myself. I looked back at the tanker, and it was struggling just to leave the port.

REFERENCES

INTRODUCTION

American Association of Port Authorities. "Port Industry Statistics." www
.aapa-ports.org/Industry/content.cfm?ItemNumber=900&navItemNumber
=551 (accessed April 19, 2010).

Port of Long Beach. "History." www.polb.com/about/history/default.asp (accessed March 30, 2009).

Port of Los Angeles. "About the Port." www.portoflosangeles.org/idx_about
.asp (accessed April 19, 2010).

———. "An Economic Powerhouse." www.portoflosangeles.org/newsroom/
press_kit/economic.asp (accessed April 19, 2010).

———. "Facts and Figures." www.portoflosangeles.org/newsroom/press_kit/
facts.asp (accessed April 19, 2010).

———. "Jobs Portfolio." 2008. www.portoflosangeles.org/pdf/JobsPORTfolio
.pdf (accessed April 19, 2010).

———. "Port History." www.laporthistory.org/level3/port_history.html (accessed July 14, 2010).

———. "A Profile of the Port of Los Angeles." www.portoflosangeles.org/
newsroom/press_kit/profile.asp (accessed April 19, 2010).

———. "TEU Statistics (Container Counts)" and "Historical TEU Statistics,
by Calendar Year." www.portoflosangeles.org/maritime/stats.asp (accessed
June 30, 2010).

Queenan, Charles F. *The Port of Los Angeles: From Wilderness to World Port.* Government and Community Relations Division, Los Angeles Harbor Department, 1983.

Author observations at Terminal Island, pier 300. 1998.

I. VALET PARKING

Adamik, Beth. Interview by author. February 9, 2007.

Containership-Info. "*Wan Hai 312.*" www.containership-info.com/vessel_9248 693.html (accessed June 23, 2010).

IPU Group. "Why Choose Manual Diesel Engine Starting?" www.ipu.co.uk/ starting_info.asp?id=160458 (accessed January 3, 2008).

KABC-TV. "Cargo Ship Hits Bridge in San Pedro Harbor." August 27, 2006. http://abclocal.go.com/kabc/story?section=news/local&id=4501986 (accessed June 30, 2010).

Malahni, Trisha (Port of Los Angeles media relations). E-mail to author. October 1, 2009.

Marine Engineer World. "Loss of Compressed Air." www.free-marine.com/ i3lossair.htm (accessed January 3, 2008).

McPhee, John. "The Ships of Port Revel." *Atlantic Monthly,* vol. 282, no. 4, October 1998.

Morgan, Captain James. Interview by author. February 9, 2007.

National Transportation Safety Board. Letter to Crescent River Port Pilots Association, Safety recommendations re: *Bright Field.* February 6, 1998.

Pilot card for the *Wan Hai 312.* Wan Hai Lines Ltd. Undated.

Port of Los Angeles. "Maersk Sealand, APM Terminals, and the Port of Los Angeles Announce Opening of Pier 400 Container Terminal: The World's Largest." Press release. August 8, 2002.

———. "2007 Mariners Guide."

———. *Port of Los Angeles Shipping Handbook 2006/2007.*

———. "Port of Los Angeles Tariffs." June 30, 2006.

Rogers, Captain Ron. Interviews by author. February 9, 2007; August 29, 2007.

San Pedro Chamber of Commerce. "Vincent Thomas Bridge." www.sanpedro .com/sp_point/vtbrdg.htm (accessed July 14, 2010).

SembCorp Marine. "Second of a Series of Six 2,646 TEU Container Vessels to Be Delivered to Wan Hai Lines." Press release. January 11, 2006.

Author observations on *Wan Hai 312.* February 9, 2007.

2. A CARPET OF CONTAINERS

Containership-Info. *"Ludwigshafen Express."* www.containership-info.com/vessel
_8902577.html (accessed June 23, 2010).

———. *"OOCL Japan."* www.containership-info.com/vessel_9102306.html (accessed June 23, 2010).

Pacific Maritime Association. "Dispatch Summary, June 18, 2010." www.pmanet
.org/?cmd=main.content&id_content=2142617442 (accessed June 23, 2010).

Port of Long Beach. "Facts at a Glance." www.polb.com/about/facts.asp (accessed June 23, 2010).

Port of Los Angeles. "About the Port." www.portoflosangeles.org/idx_about.asp
(accessed June 23, 2010).

———. "Maersk Sealand, APM Terminals, and the Port of Los Angeles
Announce Opening of Pier 400 Container Terminal: The World's Largest."
Press release. August 8, 2002.

Author observations. June 18, 2010.

3. MOVING CANS

American Association of Port Authorities. "Port Industry Statistics." www.
aapa-ports.org/Industry/content.cfm?ItemNumber=900&navItemNumber
=551 (accessed April 14, 2009).

American Presidents Line. "APL History—Containerization." www.apl.com/
history/topics/innovate/contain.htm (accessed February 22, 2006).

Baker, Arley (Port of Los Angeles media relations). E-mail to author. April 21,
2009.

Campbell, Rachel (Port of Los Angeles media relations). E-mail to author.
January 4, 2007.

Caris, Eric. E-mail to author. January 5, 2007.

———. Interview by author. November 21, 2006.

Castanho, John. Interview by author. August 29, 2006.

Chaney, Connie. Interviews by author. June 1, 1998; June 13, 1998; February 19,
2004.

China Shipping North America. "About Us." www.chinashippingna.com
(accessed April 2, 2009).

Containership-Info. *"Xin Wei Hai."* www.containership-info.com/vessel_9312
573.html (accessed December 29, 2006).

Crouthamel, Jeff. Interview by author. April 9, 2009.

Dekker, Neil. "Aiming High." *Containerisation International,* January 2005.

Greenberg, David. "China Shipping Seeks Added Damages in Port Battle." *Los Angeles Business Journal,* May 3, 2004.

Harbor Ship Supply. "History." www.shipsupplygroup.com/index-3.html (accessed May 7, 2008).

ILWU *Dispatcher.* "Shocking Death on Oakland Docks Demands Answers and Action." September 2008.

MacDonald, Marc. E-mail to author. June 6, 2007.

————. Interview by author. June 5, 2007.

Malauulu, Vivian. "Death on the Docks." *Random Lengths,* May 2–15, 2008. www .randomlengthsnews.com/images/IssuePDFs/rl_5_01-08web.pdf (accessed June 30, 2010).

Natural Resources Defense Council. "City of Los Angeles and Community and Environmental Groups Reach Record Settlement of Challenge to China Shipping Terminal Project at Port." Press release. March 5, 2003.

Natural Resources Defense Council, Inc., et al. v. City of Los Angeles, et al. State of California Court of Appeals, Second Appellate District. Documents filed by Natural Resources Defense Council, October 30, 2002.

Pacific Maritime Association. *2008 Annual Report.* www.pmanet.org/pubs/Annual Reports/2008/PMA%202008%20Annual%20Report.pdf (accessed July 2, 2010).

Pettit, David. "China Shipping Redux." *Switchboard,* Natural Resources Defense Council Staff Blog, December 23, 2008. http://switchboard.nrdc.org/ blogs/dpettit/china_shipping_redux.html (accessed July 2, 2010).

Port of Los Angeles. "Facts and Figures." www.portoflosangeles.org/newsroom/ press_kit/facts.asp (accessed May 29, 2009).

————. *Port of Los Angeles Handbook 2009.* www.portoflosangeles.org/pdf/Shipping _Handbook_2009.pdf (accessed July 1, 2010).

————. "Port of Los Angeles Tariffs." June 30, 2006.

Price, Tom. "Local 13's Carlos Rivera Dies in Dockside Tragedy." ILWU *Dispatcher,* May 2008.

Showalter, John. "The Deadly Side of Longshore Work." ILWU *Dispatcher,* May 2008.

————. "Two Deaths at Port of Oakland Prompt Safety Actions by Union." ILWU *Dispatcher,* January 2008.

Tabor, Damon. "Swept Away by Currents." *Wired,* April 2009.

Taggart, Stewart. "The 20-Ton Packet." *Wired,* October 1999.

Wahner, Christoph M. "Daily Vessel Casualty, Piracy, and News Report." Law Offices of Countryman and McDaniel, Los Angeles. www.cargolaw.com/presentations_casualties.php (accessed July 24, 2010).

Wallstein, Peter, and Richard Simon. "GOP Allies Abandon Bush in Fight over Arab Port Deal." *Los Angeles Times,* February 23, 2006.

Weiss, Kenneth R. "Plague of Plastic Chokes the Seas." *Los Angeles Times,* August 2, 2006.

White, Ronald D. "Huge Month Says Volumes about Changes at L.A. Port." *Los Angeles Times,* November 21, 2006.

———. "Imports at U.S. Ports Hit Record High." *Los Angeles Times,* September 13, 2006.

———. "Ports' Value Underscored." *Los Angeles Times,* March 22, 2007.

———. "Shipping Industry Sees Signs of Slowing." *Los Angeles Times,* June 10, 2006.

Author observations at China Shipping terminal. November 21, 2006.

4. THE LANDLORD

Freeman, David. Interview by author. February 22, 2007.

Knatz, Geraldine. Interviews by author. November 11, 2006; December 14, 2006; January 5, 2007; February 13, 2009.

Port of Los Angeles. "About the Port." www.portoflosangeles.org/idx_about.asp (accessed April 19, 2010).

———. "An Economic Powerhouse." www.portoflosangeles.org/newsroom/press_kit/economic.asp (accessed April 19, 2010).

———. "Facts and Figures." www.portoflosangeles.org/newsroom/press_kit/facts.asp (accessed April 19, 2010).

———. "A Profile of the Port of Los Angeles." www.portoflosangeles.org/newsroom/press_kit/profile.asp (accessed April 19, 2010).

Trade Impact Study: Final Report. Prepared for the Port of Los Angeles, the Port of Long Beach, and the Alameda Corridor Transportation Authority by BST Associates. March 2007. www.portoflosangeles.org/DOC/REPORT_ACTA_Trade_Impact_Study.pdf (accessed July 3, 2010).

White, Ronald D. "Huge Month Says Volumes about Changes at L.A. Port." *Los Angeles Times,* November 21, 2006.

———. "Imports at U.S. Ports Hit Record High." *Los Angeles Times,* September 13, 2006.

5. THE DIESEL DEATH ZONE

Adams-Lopez, Theresa (Port of Los Angeles media relations). E-mail to author. January 11, 2007.

Appy, Ralph. Interview by author. March 23, 2006.

Bailey, Diane, et al. *Harboring Pollution: The Dirty Truth about U.S. Ports.* Natural Resources Defense Council and Coalition for Clean Air. March 2004. www.nrdc.org/air/pollution/ports1/ports.pdf (accessed June 26, 2010).

Baker, Arley (Port of Los Angeles media relations). E-mails to author. April 27, 2007; February 23, 2010.

————. Interview by author. January 29, 2009.

California Air Resources Board. Minutes of meeting, April 20, 2006.

California Department of Transportation. "Busiest Highway Interchanges." *Los Angeles Almanac,* www.laalmanac.com/transport/tr27.htm (accessed March 19, 2007).

Caris, Eric. Interview by author. November 21, 2006.

Davis, Erin Cline. "Dirty Air Has Toxic Components; L.A.'s Notorious Air Pollution Is Hardest on Kids." *Los Angeles Times,* December 10, 2007.

DiBernardo, Michael (Port of Los Angeles director of marketing). Interview by author. May 25, 2010.

Esparza, Christina I. "Giant Cargo Terminal Debuts." *Los Angeles Times,* August 9, 2002.

Freeman, David. Interview by author. February 22, 2007.

Genis, Sandra. *Review of Previous Environmental Documents.* Port of Los Angeles Community Advisory Committee. August 2004.

Greenberg, David. "Mayor Seeking Ouster of Port Official amid Probes." *Los Angeles Business Journal,* June 21, 2004.

Gunter, Janet. Interview by author. May 10, 2010.

Houston, Douglas, Margaret Krudysz, and Arthur Winer. "Diesel Truck Traffic in Port-Adjacent Low-Income and Minority Communities: Environmental Justice Implications of Near-Roadway Land-Use Conflicts." *Transportation Research Record: Journal of the Transportation Research Board* 2067 (December 1, 2008): 38–46.

International Longshore and Warehouse Union. "Statement by David Beeman, Health Benefits Officer, Local 13 . . . concerning the California Air Resources Board's Emissions Reduction Plan." Press release. April 20, 2006.

Jerricks, Terelle. "The Blast Zone." *Random Lengths,* December 22, 2005.

KCBS-TV. "Ships Skirt Calif. Coast to Avoid Pollution Rules." March 22,

2010. http://cbs2.com/local/cargo.ships.pollution.2.1580042.html (accessed June 26, 2010).

Kirdahy, Matt. "America's Most Dangerous Jobs." *Forbes,* August 25, 2008.

Knatz, Geraldine. Interviews by author. November 11, 2006; December 14, 2006; January 5, 2007; February 13, 2009.

Lewis, Judith. "The Greening of Ships." *LA Weekly,* December 15, 2005.

Los Angeles Times. "Council Scraps $540,000 Pact with Ex-Port Chief." November 17, 2004.

———. "Pollution Solution." Editorial. June 10, 2006.

———. "Toward Cleaner Ports." Editorial. December 18, 2005.

Martinez, Adrian. Interview by author. May 11, 2010.

Mavar, John. "What's Right with San Pedro!" *San Pedro Magazine,* April 2006.

McGreevy, Patrick, and Deborah Schoch. "L.A. Port Director Resigns." *Los Angeles Times,* September 18, 2004.

Miller, Dr. John. Interview by author. May 10, 2010.

———. Letter to Port of Los Angeles, "Comments on Draft 2010 CAAP Update from Port of Los Angeles Community Advisory Committee's EIR Subcommittee." May 5, 2010.

Natural Resources Defense Council. "City of Los Angeles and Community and Environmental Groups Reach Record Settlement of Challenge to China Shipping Terminal Project at Port." Press release. March 5, 2003.

Newton, Jim. "Once Rivals, Local Ports Clear Air in Partnership." *Los Angeles Times,* July 4, 2006.

Orton, Bill. "Unionists Examine Pollution Health Risks." ILWU *Dispatcher,* October 2005.

Park, Noel. Interviews by author. May 8, 2006; June 23, 2006.

Pomfret, John. "California Fights Filth of Its Ports." *Washington Post,* August 3, 2006.

Port of Long Beach/Port of Los Angeles. *San Pedro Bay Container Forecast Update.* Prepared by Tioga Group Inc., IHS Insight. July 2009. www.portoflosangeles .org/pdf/SPB_Container_Forecast_Update_2009.pdf (accessed July 20, 2010).

———. *San Pedro Bay Ports Clean Air Action Plan.* December 2006. www.polb .com/civica/filebank/blobdload.asp?BlobID=3452 (accessed July 30, 2010).

———. *San Pedro Bay Ports Clean Air Action Plan, Draft 2010 Update, Technical Report.* April 2010. www.cleanairactionplan.org/civica/filebank/blobdload .asp?BlobID=2441 (accessed July 20, 2010).

Port of Los Angeles. "Air Quality Monitoring Results Show Less Diesel Exhaust in Air around the Port of Los Angeles." Press release. April 6, 2010.

———. "First Ever Clean Air Conference for Pacific-Rim Ports Attended by More than 25 Different Ports." Press release. December 15, 2006.

———. "Goods Movement." www.portoflosangeles.org/maritime/good_move ments.asp (accessed May 21, 2010).

———. "Intermodal Logistics and Port of Los Angeles/Port of Long Beach Rail Infrastructure." Public rail workshop presentation, October 22, 2009.

———. "Los Angeles Harbor Commission Approves San Pedro Waterfront Project with Plans for Additional Cruise Ship Facility in Outer Harbor." Press release. September 30, 2009.

———. No Net Increase Task Force. Minutes of meeting, October 27, 2004.

———. "Rail and Intermodal Yards." www.portoflosangeles.org/facilities/rail _intermodal_yards.asp (accessed May 21, 2010).

———. "Report to Mayor Hahn and Councilwoman Hahn by the No Net Increase Task Force." June 24, 2005.

Port of Los Angeles, Board of Harbor Commissioners. Minutes of meeting, February 15, 2006.

Port of Los Angeles, Community Advisory Committee. "Health Effects of Diesel Exhaust Air Pollution." August 28, 2003.

———. Minutes of meetings, May 16, 2006; February 16, 2010.

Port of Los Angeles, Environmental Management Division. *Draft Findings of Fact and Statement of Overriding Considerations, Berth 97–109 [China Shipping] Container Terminal Project, Environmental Impact Report.* December 12, 2008. www.portof losangeles.org/EIR/ChinaShipping/FEIR/_FOF_SOC%20.pdf (accessed June 26, 2010).

Roosevelt, Margot. "Los Angeles Is Still the Nation's Smoggiest City." *Los Angeles Times,* April 28, 2010.

Rosenberg, Paul. "The Changing Face of San Pedro: Noel Park's Well Deserved Reputation." *Random Lengths,* March 4, 2004.

———. "Green Bargain: $50 Million Trust—Real Deal or Cheap Knock-Off?"/"Balancing the Risks." *Random Lengths,* April 18, 2008. www.random lengthsnews.com/images/IssuePDFs/rl_april18_08web.pdf (accessed June 30, 2010).

———. "Port Designs Draw Praise, But Downtown Connections Remain Questionable." *Random Lengths,* April 1, 2010. www.randomlengthsnews.com/ images/IssuePDFs/2010-apr/rl_04–01–10.pdf (accessed June 30, 2010).

———. "Railyard Expansion Hearing Draws Community Opposition." *Random Lengths,* May 2, 2008. www.randomlengthsnews.com/images/IssuePDFs/rl _5_01–08web.pdf (accessed June 30, 2010).

Sabin, Lisa D., et al. "Dry Deposition and Resuspension of Particle-Associated Metals near a Freeway in Los Angeles." *Atmospheric Environment* 40, no. 39 (December 2006): 7528–7538.

Sahagun, Louis. "L.A. Port Wants to Relocate Fuel Sites." *Los Angeles Times,* November 14, 2001.

Schoch, Deborah, and Jessica Garrison. "Port Chief Had Fiscal Ties to Firm." *Los Angeles Times,* October 27, 2004.

Showalter, John. "Saving Lives by Cutting Pollution." ILWU *Dispatcher,* March 16, 2006.

South Coast Air Quality Management District. *Multiple Air Toxics Exposure Study (MATES-II).* Chapter 5, "Regional Model Evaluation." March 2000. www.aqmd.gov/matesiidf/matestoc.htm (accessed June 20, 2010).

"The *S.S. Sansinena* Tank Ship Explosion." Los Angeles Fire Department Historical Archive. www.lafire.com/famous_fires/761217_SansinenaExplosion/19770200_CalFireman_Wagon48toOCD/19770200_CalFireman_Wagon48toOCD.htm (accessed April 28, 2010).

Stecker, Joshua. "Talk about the Passion: Noel Park." *San Pedro Magazine,* April 2006.

Therolf, Garrett. "Wong Guilty on 14 Counts." *Los Angeles Times,* July 25, 2008.

Weikel, Dan. "Plan May Ease Air Pollution at Ports." *Los Angeles Times,* July 6, 2006.

White, Ronald D. "A Contentious Cargo Plan." *Los Angeles Times,* January 19, 2007.

Wilson, Janet. "Study Doubles Estimate of Smog Deaths." *Los Angeles Times,* March 25, 2006.

———. "A Trade Boom's Unintended Costs." *Los Angeles Times,* April 23, 2006.

———. "Trucks Targeted in Clean-Air Drive." *Los Angeles Times,* November 12, 2006.

Winer, Arthur. "Air Pollutant Exposure." UCLA Institute of the Environment, *Southern California Environmental Report Card, 2004,* 12–21. www.ioe.ucla.edu/media/files/RC04.pdf (accessed June 26, 2010).

———. Interviews by author. December 18, 2007; March 26, 2009.

Zahniser, David. "Wong Gets 5 Years for Corruption." *Los Angeles Times,* October 11, 2008.

Author observations during Port of Los Angeles Board of Harbor Commissioners public meetings. May 17, 2006; December 28, 2006.

Author observations during Port of Los Angeles Community Advisory Committee meeting. May 10, 2006.

6. THE UNION

Alvarez, Albert. Interview by Tony Salcido. April 24, 1989. ILWU Local 13 Oral History Project, Urban Archives Center, Oviatt Library, California State University, Northridge.

Bridges, Harry. "Harry Bridges: An Oral History about Longshoring, the Origins of the ILWU, and the 1934 Strike." ILWU Oral History Collection. Edited by Harvey Schwartz. www.ilwu.org/history/oral-histories/harry-bridges.cfm (accessed October 14, 2004).

——. "Harry Bridges: Worker, Founder, Visionary." Interview by Noriko Sawada Bridges. 1978. ILWU Oral History Project, vol. 4, parts 1–3. Edited by Harvey Schwartz. www.ilwu19.com/history/founder1.htm; www.ilwu19.com/history/founder2.htm; www.ilwu19.com/history/founder3.htm (accessed October 14, 2004).

Dickson, Del. *The Supreme Court in Conference (1940–1985): The Private Discussions behind Nearly 300 Supreme Court Decisions.* New York: Oxford University Press, 2001.

Dragovich, Pete J. Interview by Hector Rojas. November 25, 1984. ILWU Local 13 Oral History Project, Urban Archives Center, Oviatt Library, California State University, Northridge.

Gaitan, Henry. Interview by Tony Salcido. June 16, 1988. ILWU Local 13 Oral History Project, Urban Archives Center, Oviatt Library, California State University, Northridge.

Grassi, Pete. Interview by Tony Salcido. March 1990; June 21, 1990. ILWU Local 13 Oral History Project, Urban Archives Center, Oviatt Library, California State University, Northridge.

ILWU Local 19. "Harry Bridges, A Biography." www.ilwu19.com/history/biography.htm (accessed October 14, 2004).

——. "History: Longshoreman's Strike of 1916." www.ilwu19.com/history/1916.htm (accessed October 14, 2004).

Immigration and Naturalization Service, U.S. Department of Justice. "Records Relating to Harry Bridges." ARC Locator 296490, www.media.nara.gov (accessed October 14, 2004).

Kagel, Sam. "Representing the Union: Sam Kagel, Harry Bridges, and the 1934 Strike." ILWU *Dispatcher,* September 2005. ILWU Oral History Collection. Edited by Harvey Schwartz. www.ilwu.org/dispatcher/2005/08/kagel_bridges_strike.cfm (accessed July 23, 2010).

Kelly, Elbert, Jr. Interview by Tony Salcido. May 7, 1996. ILWU Local 13 Oral

History Project, Urban Archives Center, Oviatt Library, California State University, Northridge.

Kuvakas, George. Interview by author. April 7, 2006.

Langley, Al. Interviews by Tony Brown and Tony Salcido. April 3, 1984; May 13, 1986. ILWU Local 13 Oral History Project, Urban Archives Center, Oviatt Library, California State University, Northridge.

Levenson, Lew. "California Casualty List." *The Nation*, vol. 139, August 29, 1934.

Los Angeles Times. "Police Praised for Port Duty." August 15, 1934.

————. "Port Police Quell Mob." June 12, 1934.

————. "Port Quiet after Riots." May 16, 1934.

————. "Terrorists Beat Eight." July 18, 1934.

Love, George. Interviews by Tony Salcido. May 16, 1989; May 19, 1989; May 30, 1989. ILWU Local 13 Oral History Project, Urban Archives Center, Oviatt Library, California State University, Northridge.

MacEvoy, John D. Interviews by Tony Salcido. October 20, 1989; October 25, 1989. ILWU Local 13 Oral History Project, Urban Archives Center, Oviatt Library, California State University, Northridge.

"The Mexican American Longshoremen of Local 13." Interviews by Daniel Beagle, David Wellman, and Harvey Schwartz. 1983–1984. www.ilwu.org/history/oral-histories/mex-am-longshore.cfm (accessed March 26, 2006).

Nelson, Bruce. *Workers on the Waterfront: Seamen, Longshoremen, and Unionism in the 1930s.* Urbana: University of Illinois Press, 1988.

Perry, Louis B., and Richard S. Perry. *A History of the Los Angeles Labor Movement, 1911–1941.* Berkeley: University of California Press, 1963.

Peyton, Peter. Interview by author. November 27, 2006.

Phelan, Arthur J. "Report to District Director, Immigration and Naturalization Service." April 8, 1938. http://media.nara.gov/media/images/37/17/37-1609a.gif (accessed October 14, 2004).

Quin, Mike. *The Big Strike.* New York. International Publishers, 1979. Originally published in 1949.

Rapport, Morris, and Harry Jackson. "Immigration and Naturalization Service Report to Department of Justice." October 2, 1934. http://media.nara.gov/media/images/37/17/37-1604a.gif (accessed October 14, 2004).

San Francisco Chronicle. "Bay Dockers Pledge Appeal Aid to Bridges." September 11, 1952.

————. "Hero in a Blue Collar." September 6, 1992.

————. "ILWU to Stop Work—Bridges Protest." September 9, 1952.

San Francisco Daily News. "3 Killed, 31 Shot in Widespread Rioting." July 5, 1934. www.sfmuseum.org/hist4/maritime17.html (accessed July 31, 2010).

San Francisco News. "Ex-Red Guard Names Bridges." April 23, 1941.

—————. "Police Battle Stevedore Mob, Arrest Many." July 3, 1934. www.sf museum.org/hist/thursday/html (accessed April 13, 2004).

Selvin, David F. *A Terrible Anger: The 1934 Waterfront and General Strikes in San Francisco.* Detroit: Wayne State University Press, 1996.

Stahl, Joe. Interview by Harvey Schwartz. December 7, 1983. ILWU Oral History Project. Edited by Harvey Schwartz.

Thayne, Edward. Interview by Richard Amesqua. October 27, 1983; December 13, 1983. ILWU Local 13 Oral History Project, Urban Archives Center, Oviatt Library, California State University, Northridge.

Walker, Robin (ILWU librarian). E-mail to author. May 11, 2010.

Wilson, Corky. Interview by Harvey Schwartz. December 7, 1983. ILWU Oral History Project. Edited by Harvey Schwartz.

7. THE EMPLOYERS

Arian, Dave. Interview by author. April 22, 2009.

Bonney, Joseph. "Spinosa: Don't Blame ILWU for Delays." *Journal of Commerce,* March 2, 2005.

McEllrath, Robert. "President's Message." ILWU *Dispatcher,* September 2008.

McKenna, Jim. Interviews by author. November 11, 2004; November 29, 2004; February 8, 2005; May 24, 2007; January 14, 2010.

Miniace, Joe. E-mail to author. September 6, 2006.

—————. "Statement of Joseph N. Miniace." U.S. House of Representatives, Committee on Transportation and Infrastructure, Subcommittee on Coast Guard and Maritime Transportation, and Subcommittee on Water Resources and Environment. Washington, D.C. May 23, 2001. www.pmanet.org/?cmd=main .content&id_content=2142587263 (accessed July 17, 2010).

Pacific Coast Longshore Contract Document, July 1, 2002–July 1, 2008. www.ilwu19 .com/edu/pclcd2008.pdf (accessed July 18, 2010).

Pacific Coast Longshore Contract Document, July 1, 2008–July 1, 2014. www.pmanet.org/ pubs/laborAgreements/2008–2014%20PCLCD.pdf (accessed July 23, 2010).

Peltz, James F., and Ronald D. White. "Rail Traffic Disruption Could Threaten Economy." *Los Angeles Times,* January 13, 2005.

Peyton, Peter. Interview by author. November 27, 2009.

Spinosa, James. Interview by author. January 3, 2007.

Stallone, Steve. Interview by author. February 8, 2005.

Tyler, Jeff. "Lining Up for the Big Job Lottery." National Public Radio, *Marketplace*, August 19, 2004. http://marketplace.publicradio.org/shows/2004/08/19_mpp.html (accessed July 23, 2010).

Veiga, Alex. "No Letup in Cargo Logjam at L.A., Long Beach Ports." Associated Press, September 28, 2004.

———. "Union, Ports Conduct Job Lottery in California." Associated Press, August 19, 2004.

Waterfront Coalition. "Clean Truck Fee." www.portmod.org/POLICY/Clean%20Truck%20Fee.htm (accessed March 23, 2009).

White, Ronald D. "Lottery Is Port of Entry for Applicants." *Los Angeles Times*, August 20, 2004.

White, Ronald D., and Leslie Earnest. "Delays Mount at Local Ports as Shipping Surges." *Los Angeles Times*, September 27, 2004.

———. "Port Complex Is Far from Being Shipshape." *Los Angeles Times*, October 21, 2004.

8. THE IMPORTER

Alcohol and Tobacco Tax and Trade Bureau. "Importing Alcohol Beverages into the U.S." www.ttb.gov/itd/importing_alcohol.shtml (accessed August 25, 2006).

South African Wine Information and Systems. "Statistics." www.sawis.co.za/info/statistics.php (accessed August 25, 2006).

U.S. Department of Agriculture. "U.S. Imports of Wine and Beer, 2001–2005." www.fas.usda.gov/scriptsw/bico/bico.asp?Entry=lout&doc=1318 (accessed August 25, 2006).

Wilkinson, Jeremy. E-mail to author. June 10, 2010.

———. Interviews by author. March 31, 2006; July 18, 2006; May 12, 2010.

Wine Institute. "U.S. Wine Exports by Year, 1986–2005." wwww.wineinstitute.org/communications/statistics/exports.htm (accessed August 25, 2006).

Author observations at UNLVino 32nd Annual Wine Tasting Event. May 6, 2006.

9. THE SHIPPER

Allen Group. "Dallas Logistics Hub." Brochure. 2007.

Associated Press. "U.S. Trade Deficit Up in April." June 10, 2006.

Dimsdale, John. "End of International Quotas on Textiles and Chinese Imports to U.S." National Public Radio, *Marketplace,* March 10, 2005.

Garrison, Trey. "Port Dallas." *Dallas CEO,* February 2007.

Jingjing, Jiang. "Wal-Mart's China Inventory to Hit U.S. $18B This Year." *China Business Weekly,* November 29, 2004.

Knatz, Geraldine. Interview by author. September 6, 2007.

Los Angeles Times. "Trade Gap Hits Record in October." December 15, 2005.

McCormack, Richard. "Wal-Mart's Imports Soar; U.S. Exports Junk." *Manufacturing and Technology News,* October 28, 2005.

Peyton, Peter. Interview by author. November 27, 2006.

"The Shipper" (name withheld by request). Interview by author. September 18, 2007.

Author observations at Dallas Logistics Hub. September 19, 2007.

Author observations along Union Pacific Sunset Route. September 16–17, 2007.

10. *LOS TROQUEROS*

American Trucking Association. "About ATA." www.truckline.com/About/Pages/default.aspx (accessed June 17, 2010).

American Trucking Association, Inc. v. The City of Los Angeles, et al. U.S. District Court, Central District of California, Western Division, order, April 28, 2009.

———. Findings of Fact and Conclusions of Law. August 26, 2010.

———. U.S. Ninth Circuit Court of Appeals opinion, March 20, 2009.

Baker, Arley (POLA media relations). E-mails to author. May 6 and 9, 2007.

Bernstein, Sharon, and Sara Lin. "Truckers Block Freeway in Protest." *Los Angeles Times,* May 1, 2004.

Boston Consulting Group. "San Pedro Bay Ports Clean Truck Program: CTP Options Analysis." Analysis for the Port of Los Angeles. March 2008. www.portoflosangeles.org/CTP/CTP_Analysis.pdf (accessed July 31, 2010).

Branch, Anthony. Interview by author. April 29, 2009.

California Department of Finance and Economic Data. "Median Family Income, California." www.dof.ca.gov/html/fs_data/LatestEconData/FS_Income.htm (accessed July 1, 2010).

Covarrubias, Jose. Testimony before the U.S. House of Representatives, Committee on Transportation and Infrastructure, Subcommittee on Highways and Transit. *Hearing on Assessing the Implementation and Impacts of the Clean Truck Programs at the Port of Los Angeles and the Port of Long Beach.* May 5, 2010.

http://transportation.house.gov/Media/file/Highways/20100505/Covarrubias
-%20Independent%20Truck%20Driver.pdf (accessed July 22, 2010).

Fox, Mike. E-mail to author. July 15, 2010.

———. Interviews by author. April 29, 2009; July 1, 2010.

Holmes, John. Testimony before the U.S. House of Representatives, Committee on Transportation and Infrastructure, Subcommittee on Highways and Transit. *Hearing on Assessing the Implementation and Impacts of the Clean Truck Programs at the Port of Los Angeles and the Port of Long Beach.* May 5, 2010. http://transportation.house.gov/Media/file/Highways/20100505/Holmes-%20Port%20of%20LA.pdf (accessed July 22, 2010).

Husing, John E., Brightbill, Thomas E., and Crosby, Peter A. "San Pedro Bay Ports Clean Air Action Plan, Economic Analysis: Proposed Clean Truck Program." September 7, 2007. www.polb.com/civica/filebank/blobdload.asp?BlobID=4397 (accessed July 31, 2010).

Lanier, Robin. Letter to Long Beach Board of Harbor Commissioners. December 12, 2007.

LaRosa, Vic. Interviews by author. March 11, 2009; March 26, 2009.

Lewis, Judith. "Off-Road Rebellion." *LA Weekly,* May 4, 2006.

———. "Ports of Exhaust." *LA Weekly,* March 2, 2006.

Mack Trucks. "Bulldog Line." Brochure, 2008.

Moore, Thomas Gale. "Trucking Deregulation." *The Concise Encyclopedia of Economics.* www.econlib.org/library/Enc1/TruckingDeregulation.html (accessed May 9, 2007).

Nevarez, Ernie. Interview by author. May 24, 2006.

Patel, Sejal. *From Clean to Clunker: The Economics of Emissions Control.* A report jointly published by Los Angeles Alliance for a New Economy (LAANE), Sierra Club, BlueGreen Alliance, and the International Brotherhood of Teamsters. April 15, 2010. www.cleanandsafeports.org/fileadmin/files_editor/FromCleantoClunker.pdf (accessed July 22, 2010).

PayScale. "Hourly Rate Snapshot for Truck Driver, Heavy/Tractor-Trailer Jobs." www.payscale.com/research/US/Job=Truck_Driver%2c_Heavy_%2f_Tractor-Trailer/Hourly_Rate (accessed July 1, 2010).

Port of Los Angeles. "Clean Truck Program, an Update." PowerPoint presentation. September 12, 2008.

———. "The Clean Truck Program Will Go Forward October 1, 2008, Despite Pending Legal Action." Press release. August 5, 2008.

———. "Court of Appeals Denies ATA Attempt to Stop Landmark Environmental Initiative to Clean Los Angeles' Air." Press release. September 24, 2008.

———. "Heart of Los Angeles' Clean Truck Program Moving Forward." Press release. April 29, 2009.

———. "Port of L.A.'s 2009 Air Emissions Inventory Continues to Show a Decreasing Trend in Port-Related Air Pollution." Press release. June 3, 2010.

———. "Port of Los Angeles to Begin Collecting Clean Trucks Fee February 18, 2009." Press release. January 22, 2009.

———. "Port of Los Angeles Offers Financial Assistance for Clean Trucks." Press release. August 7, 2008.

———. "Port of Los Angeles Posts Its Proposed Clean Truck Program Concession Agreement." Press release. May 9, 2008.

———. "Port of Los Angeles Proposes a Clean Truck Program." Press release. March 17, 2008.

———. "Ports of Los Angeles and Long Beach Defend Clean Truck Program in Court Filing." Press release. August 21, 2008.

———. "Proposed Clean Trucks Program Fact Sheet," *San Pedro Bay Ports Clean Air Action Plan,* April 2007.

———. "Response to Lawsuit Filed by the American Trucking Association." Press release. July 28, 2008.

Port of Los Angeles/Port of Long Beach. "Container Diversion and Economic Impact Study." Prepared by Moffatt & Nichol and BST Associates. September 27, 2007. www.portoflosangeles.org/CTP/CTP_Diversion_092727 .pdf (accessed July 31, 2010).

———. "San Pedro Bay Ports Allocate $6.3 Million to Continue Gateway Cities Fleet Modernization Program." Press release. March 15, 2007.

Potter, Fredrick. Testimony before the U.S. House of Representatives, Committee on Transportation and Infrastructure, Subcommittee on Highways and Transit. *Hearing on Assessing the Implementation and Impacts of the Clean Truck Programs at the Port of Los Angeles and the Port of Long Beach.* May 5, 2010. http:// transportation.house.gov/Media/file/Highways/20100505/Potter-%20Team sters.pdf (accessed July 22, 2010).

Radford, Leslie. "*Troqueros* Declare Victory!" April 27, 2007. http://la.indymedia .org/news/2007/04/197485.php (accessed July 31, 2010).

Rajkovacz, Joe. Interview by author. June 22, 2010.

Roosevelt, Margot. "State Orders Diesel Trucks to Clean Up." *Los Angeles Times,* December 13, 2008.

Total Transportation Services Inc. "Our Clients." www.tts-i.com/about_us/ client_list.htm (accessed February 17, 2009).

U.S. Department of Transportation. "General Leasing Requirements." Federal

Motor Carrier Safety Administration Regulations, www.fmcsa.dot.gov/ rules-regulations/administration/fmcsr/fmcsrruletext.aspx?chunkKey= 090163348008ef8d (accessed June 29, 2010).

U.S. House of Representatives Committee on Transportation and Infrastructure, Subcommittee on Highways and Transit. *Hearing on Assessing the Implementation and Impacts of the Clean Truck Programs at the Port of Los Angeles and the Port of Long Beach.* May 5, 2010. "Summary of Subject Matter, May 3, 2010." http://transportation.house.gov/Media/file/Highways/20100505/SSM_HT .pdf (accessed July 22, 2010).

Waterfront Coalition. "About the Waterfront Coalition." www.portmod.org (accessed March 23, 2009).

White, Ronald D. "Agency Objects to Clean Truck Program." *Los Angeles Times,* October 30, 2008.

———. "Cleanup at Ports Starts to Pay Off." *Los Angeles Times,* February 23, 2009.

———. "Immigration Rallies Fuel Resolve of Port Truckers." *Los Angeles Times,* May 4, 2006.

———. "Lottery Is Port of Entry for Applicants." *Los Angeles Times,* August 20, 2004.

———. "Port's Clean-Rig Program Is Running on Empty." *Los Angeles Times,* January 27, 2009.

———. "The Ports' Short-Haul Truckers Endure Long Hours, High Costs." *Los Angeles Times,* September 21, 2005.

White, Ronald D., and Louis Sahagun. "Risk Seen in Port Plan." *Los Angeles Times,* March 8, 2008.

Zerolnick, Jon. *The Road to Shared Prosperity: The Regional Economic Benefits of the San Pedro Bay Ports' Clean Trucks Program.* Los Angeles Alliance for a New Economy, Coalition for Clean and Safe Ports. August 2007. www.community benefits.org/downloads/Road_to_Shared_Prosperity.pdf (accessed July 22, 2010).

Author observations riding with Anthony Branch. April 29, 2009.

11. THE HOLD MEN

Almeida, Art. Interviews by author. March 15, 2004; May 6, 2004; November 2, 2004.

Arian, Dave. Interviews by author. July 11, 2006; April 22, 2009.

———. *The Right to Get in the Fight.* San Pedro: Harry Bridges Institute, 2008.

Bridges, Harry. "On the Beam." ILWU *Dispatcher,* October 21, 1960.

———. Speech before the Fiftieth Anniversary Convention of the American Association of Port Authorities. September 28, 1961.

Fairley, Lincoln. *Facing Mechanization: The West Coast Longshore Plan.* Institute of Industrial Relations, University of California, Los Angeles, 1979.

———. "The ILWU-PMA Mechanization and Modernization Agreement." Presentation at the Industrial Relations Research Association. May 5, 1961.

———. "Possible Loss of Work Resulting from Elimination of Double Handling in Los Angeles Harbor." Memo to Harry Bridges. September 18, 1960. ILWU Library.

Glazier, William. "Automation and the Longshoremen: A West Coast Solution." *Atlantic Monthly,* vol. 206, no. 6, December 1960.

Hagel, Otto, and Louis Goldblatt. *Men and Machines: A Story about Longshoring on the West Coast Waterfront.* San Francisco: ILWU-PMA, 1963.

"ILWU Coast Labor Relations Committee Report." Presented before the Longshore, Shipclerks, and Walking Bosses Caucus, October 15, 1957.

ILWU *Dispatcher.* Editorial. August 30, 1957.

ILWU Local 19. "The ILWU Story: The New Union." www.ilwu19.com/history/the_ilwu_story/the_new_union.htm (accessed January 11, 2007).

McKenna, Jim. Interview by author. May 24, 2007.

Miniace, Joe. Interview by author. August 14, 2006.

Pacific Coast Longshore Contract Document, July 1, 2002–July 1, 2008. www.ilwu19.com/edu/pclcd2008.pdf (accessed July 18, 2010).

Peyton, Peter. Interview by author. July 3, 2009.

"Shippers Beware." *Journal of Commerce,* April 5, 2004.

Spinosa, Jim. Interview by author. January 3, 2007.

———. Keynote address to the ILWU Thirty-third International Convention. July 21, 2006. www.ilwu.org/dispatcher/2006/06/spinosa_convention-keynote.cfm (accessed August 14, 2006).

"Strike of 1971." Pacific Maritime Association. www.pmanet.org/index.cfm?cmd=main.content&id_content=2142586624 (accessed January 11, 2007).

Winter, Jennifer Marie. *30 Years of Collective Bargaining: Joseph Paul St. Sure, Management Labor Negotiator, 1902–1966.* Chapter 4: "Toward Mechanization: St. Sure and the PMA, 1952–1959." Pacific Maritime Archives. www.pmanet.org/?cmd=main.content&id_content=2023238683 (accessed December 31, 2004).

12. THE WOMEN

Bates, Forest, et al. vs. Pacific Maritime Association, et al. U.S. District Court, Central District of California, case no. CV 75–1346–WMB. May 31, 1978.

Carelli, Richard. "Firemen Suit." Associated Press, December 5, 1978.

Chaney, Connie. Interviews by author. April 24, 1995; June 1, 1998; February 19, 2004.

Flores, Mark, et al. vs. Pacific Maritime Association, et al. U.S. District Court, Central District of California. Filing. February 7, 1992.

Golden, Deborah Taylor, et al. vs. Pacific Maritime Association, et al. "Consent Decree." U.S. District Court, Central District of California, case no. 80–04770–RMT. February 26, 1990.

———. "Response of Class Counsel to Objection to Proposed Modifications to Golden Consent Decree." U.S. District Court, Central District of California, case no. 80–04770–RMT. February 26, 1990.

Hunt, A. Thomas. Interview by author. May 28, 1998.

———. Resume. Undated.

Lewis, Madeline. "A. Thomas Hunt: The *Los Angeles Daily Journal* Profile." *Los Angeles Daily Journal,* November 30, 1982.

Los Angeles Times. "Disbarred Lawyer Pleads Not Guilty to Fraud Charges." May 5, 1995.

Madigan, Rick. "Lawyer's Fall Ends in Jail." *The Outlook,* April 5, 1995.

Pacific Maritime Association. *1998: The Journal Continues. Annual Report.* "A Litigious Year: Claims of Discrimination in Hiring and Promotion." Pacific Maritime Association, 1999. www.pmanet.org/ar_1998/pdf/1998_Annual_Report_page04–19.pdf (accessed July 24, 2010).

Reinglass, Michelle (second attorney for plaintiffs, Golden Consent Decree). Interview by author. May 19, 1998.

Shibley, George. Letter to Lou Loveridge and Louis Rios, June 6, 1983. Harry Bridges Institute, San Pedro.

Simon, Stephanie. "Civil Rights Lawyer Faces Felony Charges." *Los Angeles Times,* April 5, 1995.

Weikel, Dan. "Contention on the Waterfront." *Los Angeles Times,* November 30, 1998.

———. "Judge Lets Hiring Goals for Women Dockworkers Lapse." *Los Angeles Times,* June 22, 1999.

———. "Judge Stalls Dockworker Settlement." *Los Angeles Times,* January 23, 1999.

Williams, Gretchen. Interviews by author. April 30, 2007; August 1, 2008.

13. THE CLERK

Fairley, Lincoln. "The ILWU-PMA Mechanization and Modernization Agreement." *Labor Law Journal* 11 (July 1961): 664–680.

———. "Possible Loss of Work Resulting from Elimination of Double Handling in Los Angeles Harbor." Memo to Harry Bridges, September 18, 1960. ILWU Library.

ILWU Local 63. "Summary of PCCCD Technology Framework Arbitrations." www.ilwu63.net (accessed June 30, 2009).

Love, George. Interviews by author. August 4, 2005; September 6, 2006; April 22, 2009.

Pacific Maritime Association. Letter to ILWU Local 63, April 28, 2009. "Denial of CWOG for Payroll Week ending April 24, 2009."

Peyton, Peter. Interviews by author. November 27, 2006; July 3, 2009.

14. SECURITY

Blas, Porfirio. Interview by author. September 27, 2006.

"Blast Effects." www.nukefix.org/weapon.html (accessed April 10, 2007).

Christoffersen, John. "GE Developing Device for Port Security." Associated Press, September 28, 2004.

Curry, LCDR Anthony C., and Robert T. Spaulding. "Central California Area Maritime Security Committee." U.S. Coast Guard, *Proceedings,* Spring 2006.

Drogin, Bob. "Port Security Cards Draw Ridicule." *Los Angeles Times,* March 22, 2009.

Ewert, Nathan. Interview by author. May 7, 2009.

FLIR Systems. "Ranger III Thermal Imagers." www.flir.com/cvs/americas/en/security/products/rangeriiims/ (accessed May 20, 2009).

Gamez, Cristina (U.S. Coast Guard). E-mail to author. May 26, 2009.

Haveman, Jon D., and Howard J. Schatz, eds. *Protecting the Nation's Seaports: Balancing Security and Cost.* San Francisco: Public Policy Institute of California, 2006. www.ppic.org/content/pubs/report/R_606JHR.pdf (accessed July 25, 2010).

Holmes, John. Interviews by author. April 5, 2007; February 13, 2009.

Hymon, Steve. "LAX Heads State List of Terrorist Attacks." *Los Angeles Times,* February 22, 2003.

Jacquelin, Peter. E-mail to author. April 30, 2007.

Laidman, Dan. "Keeping Watch over Suspicious Cargo." Copley News Service, June 26, 2006.

Larios, Javier. Interview by author. May 8, 2009.

Marine Exchange of Southern California. "VTS User Fees." www.portoflos angeles.org/Tariff/CircularNo35B.pdf (accessed April 23, 2009).

McKenna, Richard (Marine Exchange of Southern California). Interview by author. April 23, 2009.

McLaughlin, Lindsay. "The ILWU Goes to Washington." ILWU *Dispatcher,* March 2006.

Meade, Charles, and Roger C. Molander. *Considering the Effects of a Catastrophic Terrorist Attack.* Santa Monica, Calif.: Rand Center for Terrorism Risk Management Policy, 2006. www.rand.org/pubs/technical_reports/2006/RAND _TR391.pdf (accessed July 25, 2010).

Mitre, Michael. Testimony before the U.S. Senate Commerce, Science and Transportation Committee. *Oversight Hearings on Security of Terminal Operations at U.S. Ports.* February 28, 2006.

Pagliuca, Mark. Interview by author. March 24, 2009.

Peyton, Peter. Interview by author. July 3, 2009.

———. Testimony before the U.S. House of Representatives, Transportation and Infrastructure Committee, Coast Guard and Maritime Transportation Subcommittee. *Hearing on Security Credentials for Port Personnel.* February 13, 2002. www.hsdl.org/?view&doc=7681&coll=limited (accessed July 25, 2010).

Port of Los Angeles. "Port of Los Angeles Awards Contract to Design Joint Container Inspection Facility." Press release. June 22, 2006.

SAFE Boats International. "SAFE Boats." www.safeboats.com/default/boats_ collar.php (accessed March 27, 2009).

Schneier, Bruce. "The War on Photography." *The Guardian,* June 5, 2008. www .guardian.co.uk/technology/2008/jun/05/news.terrorism (accessed March 20, 2009).

Transportation Security Administration. "Transportation Worker Identification Credential (TWIC) Program." www.tsa.gov/what_we_do/layers/twic/ index.shtm (accessed March 30, 2009).

U.S. Coast Guard. "Aircraft and Cutters." www.uscg.mil/datasheet/41utb.asp (accessed March 27, 2007).

———. "General Information on the U.S. Coast Guard." www.uscg.mil/top/ about/overview.asp (accessed March 29, 2007).

———. "The U.S. Coast Guard Auxiliary." www.auxpa.org/who-r-we.html (accessed March 29, 2007).

————. "U.S. Coast Guard Maritime Security (MARSEC) Levels." www.uscg
.mil/safetylevels/whatismarsec.asp (accessed March 27, 2007).

U.S. Customs and Border Protection. "National Workload Statistics." www.cbp
.gov/xp/cgov/about/accomplish/previous_year/national_workload_stats.xml
(accessed May 22, 2009).

U.S. Government Accountability Office. "Combating Nuclear Smuggling: Corruption, Maintenance and Coordination Problems Challenge U.S. Efforts to
Provide Radiation Detection Equipment to Other Countries." GAO *Highlights,* March 2006. www.gao.gov/highlights/do631ihigh.pdf (accessed July 25,
2010).

————. "Combating Nuclear Smuggling: DHS Has Made Progress Deploy-
ing Radiation Detection Equipment at U.S. Ports-of-Entry, but Concerns
Remain." GAO *Highlights,* March 2006. www.gao.gov/new.items/do6389.pdf
(accessed July 25, 2010).

Vanzi, Max. *Port Security: California's Exposed Container Ports, The Case for More
Post-9/11 Protection.* California Senate Office of Research, November 1, 2006.
http://sor.govoffice3.com/vertical/Sites/%7B3BDD1595–792B-4D20
–8D44–626EF05648C7%7D/uploads/%7BCAEBE661-A2ED-41DE-A50C
-BA1A07161DAB%7D.PDF (accessed July 25, 2010).

Vartabedian, Ralph. "U.S. to Install New Nuclear Detections at Ports." *Los
Angeles Times,* July 15, 2006.

Weikel, Dan. "Danger Abides at L.A.'s Ports." *Los Angeles Times,* September 11,
2006.

White, Ronald. "A System to Keep Tabs on Ships." *Los Angeles Times,* March 31,
2007.

Wiedenhoeft, Captain Paul. Interviews by author. March 14, 2007; April 20,
2009.

Author observations during Coast Guard patrol. March 23, 2007.

Author observations during Port of Los Angeles Port Police patrol. September 27, 2006.

Author observations during Port of Los Angeles Port Police, Marine Unit,
patrol. March 24, 2009.

15. THE NEW NORMAL

Balqon Corporation. "Balqon Corporation Introduces Extended Range Lithium-
Ion Powered Electric Yard Tractor for Warehousing and Port Applications."
Press release. January 19, 2010.

DiBernardo, Michael. Interview by author. February 13, 2009.

Dickerson, Marla. "It's Full Speed Ahead for Mexican Seaport." *Los Angeles Times,* August 28, 2008.

Keenan, Michael. Interview by author. February 13, 2009.

Knatz, Geraldine. "Approval of Three-Year Agreement with Balqon Corporation." Memo to Board of Harbor Commissioners, April 10, 2008.

———. E-mail to author. May 14, 2009.

———. Interview by author. February 13, 2009.

Kraul, Chris, and Ronald D. White. "Panama Is Preparing to Beef Up the Canal." *Los Angeles Times,* April 25, 2006.

Port of Los Angeles. "Electric Truck Demonstration Project Fact Sheet." Undated.

———. "Port of Los Angeles and South Coast Air Quality Management District Roll Out World's Most Powerful Heavy Duty Electric Truck." Press release. May 16, 2008.

Port of Los Angeles, Environmental Management Division. "Approval of Memorandum of Agreement." Memo to Board of Harbor Commissioners, January 4, 2007.

Prince Rupert Port Authority. "2008 Cargo Traffic Steady, Despite Global Economic Decline." Press release. January 21, 2009.

———. "First Quarter 2009 Results." *54 North* newsletter, May 2009.

Samra, Balwinder. Interviews by author. May 5, 2009; April 2, 2010.

White, Ronald D. "Changing Trade Patterns Threaten Ports' Relevance." *Los Angeles Times,* November 28, 2008.

———. "Mexican Port Gets American Connection." *Los Angeles Times,* June 20, 2006.

———. "Port Cargo Levels Are Sinking Faster." *Los Angeles Times,* March 2, 2009.

———. "Ports Reflect U.S. Slump." *Los Angeles Times,* September 2, 2008.

———. "Port Traffic Plunges Further." *Los Angeles Times,* March 19, 2009.

———. "Recession Creates a Load of Problems for Truckers." *Los Angeles Times,* January 7, 2009.

———. "Shifts Get Scarce amid a Slowdown in Cargo." *Los Angeles Times,* January 19, 2009.

Winer, Arthur. Interview by author. March 26, 2009.

16. HAWSE PIPER

Brooks, Ed. Interview by author. April 12, 2007.

Chan, Vera H-C. "Crowley Maritime: $1 Billion Business Started with a Rowboat." *San Francisco Business Times,* July 1, 2005. http://sanfrancisco.bizjournals .com/sanfrancisco/stories/2005/07/04/focus6.html (accessed July 26, 2010).

Containership-Info. "*MOL Endurance.*" www.containership-info.com/vessel _9261736.html (accessed April 13, 2009).

Containership-Info. "*Xin Chang Sha.*" www.containership-info.com/vessel _9312559.html (April 13, 2009).

Crowley Maritime Corporation. "Company Overview." www.crowley.com/ aboutus/company-overview.asp (accessed April 13, 2009).

———. "Corporate History." www.crowley.com/aboutus/history.asp (accessed April 13, 2009).

———. "Crowley Maritime Corporation Notes to Consolidated Financial Statements." December 31, 2006. U.S. Securities and Exchange Commission document. www.sec.gov/archives/edgar/data/1130194/000095012307003017/ y30961e30961e10vk.htm (accessed April 24, 2007).

———. "Fleet Description." www.crowley.com/ship-assist-escort/fleet.asp (accessed April 13, 2009).

———. "Ship Assist & Escort." Brochure. 2003.

———. "Thomas B. Crowley Jr." www.crowley.com/aboutus/Thomas-B -Crowley-JR.asp (accessed April 13, 2009).

Pacific Maritime Association. "Dispatch Summary." www.pmanet.org/?cmd =main.category&id_category=114/id_content/2142601666 (accessed April 8, 2007).

Price, Tom. "IBU Deckhand Fatally Injured in Tug Accident." ILWU *Dispatcher,* May 2007.

Privette, Bill. Interview by author. April 12, 2007.

Voith Group of Companies. "Voith Water Tractor—The Hallmark of Improved Ship Safety." Brochure. 2006.

Whitehall Rowing and Sail. "The History of the Whitehall." www.whitehallrow .com/legacy_html/history.php (accessed April 13, 2009).

Author observations on the *Master* tugboat. April 12, 2007.

INDEX

Metropolitan shipping line, 94
Miller, John, 71, 82, 89; on Geraldine
 Knatz, 91
Miniace, Joe, 129, 131; 2002 contract
 talks, 138; on union busting, 201
mitigation: defined, 64; port aesthetics
 mitigation program, 64
Mitre, Mike, 246
Mol Endurance, 275
Morgan, Captain Jim, 9
move, defined, 165
*Multiple Air Toxics Exposure Study
 (MATES-II)*, 71, 90
multiple handling of cargo, 192
Mulvey, John, 57
Murphy, Frank, 123

National Labor Relations Board, 201
National Organization for Women, 208
National Recovery Act, 97
naturally occurring radioactive mate-
 rials, 245
Natural Resources Defense Council
 (NRDC), 89; and China Shipping
 lawsuit, 34, 69; and Clean Truck
 Program, 177; port ratings, 82
Negrete, Freddy, 190, 194, 196
Nelson Line, 94
Nevarez, Ernie, 166, 168
nitrogen oxide, 73, 79
No Net Increase Task Force, 64, 79,
 80, 81
Norfolk, Virginia, 261
Northwest San Pedro Neighborhood
 Council, 86

Occupational Safety and Health
 Administration, 45
Orient Overseas Container Line, 26, 27
"owner-operator," 166; advantages of,
 170, 181; drawbacks of, 167, 170; ex-
 penses, 174; lease agreements, 167
Owner-Operator Independent Drivers
 Association (OOIDA), 168, 177

Pacific Maritime Association (PMA),
 44, 125, 193, 201, 207, 248; accident
 statistics, 44; and Harry Bridges,
 123; lock-out of 2002, 56
Paddy Hurley's, 100
Pagliuca, Mark, 240, *240*
Palos Verdes Peninsula, 3
Panama Canal, 135, 261
Pan Atlantic, 36
Pan Pacific, 94
Papadakis, John, 86
Park, Noel, 62, 76, 80, 83; background,
 65; and China Shipping lawsuit,
 69; on Clean Air Action Plan, 81;
 on low-profile cranes, 62; and
 MATES-II, 71
Parker, Dick, 106
peanut whistle, 21, 272
Perkins, Frances, 121
Peyton, Peter, 124, 139, 161; on TWIC
 cards, 249, 250; on union busting,
 202
Phelan, Arthur J., 120
pier 100, 35
pier 400, 26, 66, 87
PierPASS, 165
Plant, T. G., 107, 108
PMA. *See* Pacific Maritime Association
Port Import Export Reporting, 127
Port of Long Beach, 2; American
 Trucking Association lawsuit,
 178; Clean Air Action Plan, 58, 79;
 Queens Gate, 26
Port of Los Angeles: aesthetics miti-
 gation program, 64; American
 Trucking Association lawsuit, 178;
 Angels Gate, 26, 276; APM termi-
 nal, 26, *28,* 250; Board of Harbor
 Commissioners, 4, 57, 61, 68, 76, 81,
 91; cargo backlog of 2004, 56, 126;
 cargo volume, 2, 260; China Ship-
 ping lawsuit, 34, 64, 68; Clean Air
 Action Plan, 58, 79; Community
 Advisory Committee, 70, 72, 87, 90;

Text:	10.75/15 Janson
Display:	Janson
Compositor:	BookMatters, Berkeley
Cartographer:	Lohnes + Wright
Printer and binder:	Maple-Vail Book Manufacturing Group